# SOCIAL

## ENTREPRENEURSHIP

### *for the*

# 21ST CENTURY

*Innovation Across the Nonprofit,
Private, and Public Sectors*

## GEORGIA LEVENSON KEOHANE

New York  Chicago  San Francisco  Lisbon  London  Madrid  Mexico City
Milan  New Delhi  San Juan  Seoul  Singapore  Sydney  Toronto

Copyright © 2013 by Georgia Levenson Keohane. All rights reserved. Printed in the United States of America. Except as permitted under the United States Copyright Act of 1976, no part of this publication may be reproduced or distributed in any form or by any means, or stored in a database or retrieval system, without the prior written permission of the publisher.

1 2 3 4 5 6 7 8 9 10   DOC/DOC   1 8 7 6 5 4 3 2

ISBN 978-0-07-180167-6
MHID 0-07-180167-7

e-ISBN 978-0-07-180168-3
e-MHID 0-07-180168-5

**Library of Congress Cataloging-in-Publication Data**
Keohane, Georgia Levenson.
   Social entrepreneurship for the 21st century : innovation across the nonprofit, private, and public sectors / Georgia Levenson Keohane.
      p. cm.
   ISBN 978-0-07-180167-6 (alk. paper) — ISBN 0-07-180167-7 (alk. paper) 1. Social entrepreneurship.  I. Title.
HD60.K4823 2013
658.4'08—dc23

                                                                    2012038431

McGraw-Hill books are available at special quantity discounts to use as premiums and sales promotions or for use in corporate training programs. To contact a representative, please e-mail us at bulksales@mcgraw-hill.com.

This book is printed on acid-free paper.

*To my family*

# CONTENTS

# ACKNOWLEDGMENTS

This book owes its existence to many co-conspirators. I begin with Stephanie Frerich, the talented and patient McGraw-Hill editor who convinced me one wintry day in midtown that there was a *there* there to this project. Stephanie, I hope you still believe this is true! Thank you for all the boosts and prodding amidst my doubts and (missed) deadlines.

This work would not have been possible without the intellectual, moral, and financial support of the Roosevelt Institute, where I have found an inspiring community of colleagues and a home to think, write, and learn. Thank you to all the Fellows of the Four Freedoms Center, whose insights, camaraderie, and convictions I have drawn on in so many different ways. In particular, thanks to Ellen Chesler, for introducing me to Roosevelt and for her unflagging encouragement throughout the writing process and to Mark Schmitt, Jeff Madrick, Jonathan Soros, and Bo Cutter, who helped me to understand how social entrepreneurship fits into a larger public policy context. I owe a special debt to Bryce Covert for her editorial assistance. And I am delighted for the chance to work more closely with Roosevelt's visionary and spirited new CEO, Felicia Wong, an important twenty-first-century social entrepreneur in her own right. Finally, I am grateful to Anne Roosevelt for our conversations about the ways in which firms can and must engage as productive and responsible citizens in society—in the business of a more shared prosperity—and for her wisdom and guidance about how this work helps fulfill the living legacy of her grandparents, Franklin and Eleanor Roosevelt.

Although this book is my first, it has been a long time in coming and bears the fingerprints of professional mentors who have shown me how one can make a career of thinking and doing: thank you to Mort Abramowitz, for opening the wide world to me at the Carnegie

Endowment for International Peace; to Josh Gotbaum, for his insistence at the September 11th Fund and always that head and heart matter in (mostly) equal parts; and to Bill Meehan, who, from my first McKinsey days, has been a wonderful collaborator and mentor.

My formal study of social entrepreneurship began, in various ways, with Paul Kennedy, Allen Grossman, Jim Austin, and William Julius Wilson, and has continued under the tutelage of some of the field's finest practitioners: Muhammad Yunus, Bill Drayton, Jose Velilla, Jessica Sager, and Aaron Lieberman. I greatly value the conversations I have had with Alan Khazei, Matt Klein, Tracy Palandjian, Audrey Choi, Kristin Morse, and Veronica White, among many others, who have helped me to appreciate how social entrepreneurship works in practice, across the nonprofit, private, and public sectors, and the spaces in between. Special thanks to four colleagues and friends: Kim Starkey Jonker, Phil Buchanan, Suzanne Immerman, and Alan Jones, for their smarts and expertise, humor, and forbearance with this book and all my other schemes.

Of course good policy analysis relies on even better fundamentals, and I have been so fortunate, from a young age, for an extraordinary education. Thank you to the many brilliant and imperturbable teachers who have taught me how to consider, scrutinize, question, and listen—skills that are very much still a work in progress.

This book is dedicated to my family. I am the luckiest person in the world for mine. To Nat, my best friend since we were nineteen, for his shared passion for policy, intellectual rigor, wit, and love; to my in-laws, Nan and Bob Keohane, for all the support they have given Nat, our girls, and me in this and all our endeavors; to my parents, Isabella and Conrad Levenson—social entrepreneurs before it was named or vogue—for their deep and abiding personal and professional commitments to equity and justice, and to making the world a better place; to my mom especially, whose example of dedication and hard work is both an impossible and inspiring standard; and to Frances and Eleanor, for believing in me and for all the good they will do in the years to come.

New York City
September 2012

# INTRODUCTION

## The Social Entrepreneurship Revolution

In less than a generation, we have witnessed a tectonic shift in the way people think about and work toward social change. The reasons are myriad and stem from both disaffection—impatience with existing programs and policies—and idealism—a profound desire for meaningful work that makes a positive impact on the world.

The groundswell of new activism, or what we call *social entrepreneurship*, is manifest across society as creative change makers test new solutions to entrenched social, economic, and environmental problems. Not all these efforts are de novo; most have their roots in a rich history of innovation for the common good. What is different about this new activism is its momentum, sweep, and fundamental approach to problem solving.

This book is not about entrepreneurs. Much excellent writing, including David Bornstein's profiles of Muhammad Yunus at the Grameen Bank and Bill Drayton at Ashoka, has chronicled the work of extraordinary change makers across the globe.[1] Rather, this book is about social entrepreneurship: the systems and ecosystems that allow social entrepreneurs in the nonprofit, private, and public sectors to flourish. The case studies that follow illuminate the motifs of the new activism: a heightened emphasis on measurement and evaluation; an embrace of competition in a number of forms, including the design and implementation of "tools" like prizes and challenges; the development of "laboratories" to foster social innovations, which can then be brought to scale; and a new thinking about asset management and investment, the nature of social value and returns, and the sources of capital available to address chronic social problems. This book also addresses some of the tensions inherent in cross-sector work, including competing definitions of public goods, the debates about who best provides them and under what circumstances, and the promise and pitfalls of more-market solutions to social problems.

## The Rise of Social Entrepreneurship

The contours of the social sector have changed dramatically over the course of a generation, in the United States and around the world. The blossoming of the nonprofit sector, described by Lester Salamon in a 1994 *Foreign Affairs* essay as an *associational revolution*, has distinct and regional geneses and manifestations, among them the emergence of civil society organizations out of the shadow of failed political regimes from Eastern Europe to Latin America and the crisis of the welfare state — in dollars and politics — in a number of more developed countries.[2]

In the United States, the pronounced expansion of the nonprofit sector has resulted in part from our shift to *third-party government*: the use of private organizations, both nonprofit and commercial, to deliver services once provided directly by public sector agencies.[3] Today, the nonprofit sector accounts for approximately 10 percent of the U.S. economy; it employs 10 million people and pays them $320 billion in wages.[4] Contrary to the prevailing narrative that government is distinct from, or at odds with, the nonprofit or private sectors, this network relationship reminds us that government remains the primary funder of social services.[5]

Of course, not all of these third-party organizations are led by social entrepreneurs. The *nonprofit sector* is an umbrella term and heterogeneous amalgam of many different kinds of entities. This book's focus on social entrepreneurship follows the movement's arc from the nonprofit sphere, where it took shape and gathered steam, through the commercial and public realms.

## Social Entrepreneurship and American Capitalism

Entrepreneurship is deeply embedded in our nation's DNA; it is also closely linked with the actual workings and ideological underpinnings of a distinctly American form of capitalism. We celebrate iconic entrepreneurs—from Benjamin Franklin to Andrew Carnegie to Bill Gates—for the way they personify the American mythos: social mobility achieved through individual ingenuity and hard work. As we will see, this notion of the power of the entrepreneur as the primary proponent of change also animates our conception of competitive market capitalism. The spirit of individual entrepreneurship undergirds the national experience, whether it is immigrants fleeing Europe for the United States or pioneers settling the American West. Entrepreneurial values inform our culture and psyche.

The rise of *social* entrepreneurship occurred during a particularly entrepreneurial period in our nation's history, one characterized by individual adroitness and a general disaffection for large organizations, government or corporate. In the private sector, it meant the blossoming of a new breed of company in the form of the tech start-up and the finance boutique, many of which produced spectacular fortunes and, in turn, a new degree of and agenda for philanthropy.

Government failure, both real and perceived, also shaped the early stages of the social entrepreneurship revolution. Many social entrepreneurs, who shared the gumption and dynamo of their private sector peers, believed that the persistence of pernicious social problems despite decades of public sector efforts to alleviate them called for distinctly *non*-government solutions. The "new" philanthropy provided both financial and ideational support for their work, fueled by the ethos of the era—an unabridged faith in the power and primacy of markets—to provide for and improve social welfare.

It is neither surprising nor coincidental that the heightened embrace of entrepreneurship in the last generation in the nonprofit, private, and even public sectors has taken place in an era of ideological and political backlash against government. An increasingly conservative sway that began, arguably, with Ronald Reagan's declaration that "government is not the solution to our problem. Government is the problem,"[6] has also resulted in today's *states versus markets* philosophical standoff.

What is critical to understand is that modern social entrepreneurship in the United States took shape against this backdrop of polarization. Somewhere along the polemical line, the idea that governments had an active and vigorous role to play in promoting entrepreneurship was lost to "market triumphalism"[7] and the belief that enterprise, social and otherwise, was a phenomenon sui generis, free of the imprint of public policy.

## The Role of Government in Promoting Entrepreneurship

What this view misses, of course, is a second and equally robust tradition in our country's history and political economy: the role that government has played in promoting private sector activity, which dates to the founding of the republic. Alexander Hamilton may have been the first architect of American industrial policy, but in the intervening centuries, any number of political leaders have used government resources in the form of dollars *and* public policy to shape markets, to incent innovation, and to bring private sector capital and energy to bear on public purpose activities, from infrastructure development and scientific discovery to the provision of a host of other public goods.

Perhaps the best-known achievements along these lines are the government-sponsored inventions during and after World War II, which produced a number of breakthroughs for civilian use, including nuclear energy, jet engines, early computers, and even drugs like penicillin. Earlier, radio and aviation were unequivocally government-abetted projects, as were so many of the country's nineteenth-century infrastructure developments, which often used things like lands grants to encourage settlement in the American West, to prime transcontinental railroad construction, and to establish the nation's agriculture and mechanical colleges (A&Ms).[8]

As conceptions of *public goods* have evolved, so, too, have policies to stimulate private investment for their provision. Regulation, government insurance, and the advent of the GSE (government-sponsored enterprise), for example, would motivate commercial lending in any number of industries, from housing and higher education to venture capital and private equity. In recent years, government's expanded market-shaping toolkit encompasses a range of positive inducements, such as guarantees, tax breaks, and matching funds, among other instruments, to encourage entrepreneurial activity in areas of market failure.

## Social Entrepreneurship for the Twenty-First Century: The Role of States *and* Markets in Advancing Social Change

The next century of innovative change making needs to recognize both these strands of the American tradition: entrepreneurship in the private sphere, often with substantial public benefit, and the government's role in promoting it. Social change and a more shared prosperity depend on states and markets working at shared, rather than cross, purposes, and a worldview that acknowledges that smart public policy and competitive enterprise, social and otherwise, are not only mutually compatible but necessarily intertwined.

To that end, this book begins with an assessment of social entrepreneurship in the nonprofit arena. We explore not only the work of innovative service providers (organizations such as Teach For America and City Year) but also the emergence of a new breed of funder that has transformed the practices of the sector when it comes to measurement and evaluation, the use of technology, the design of competitive and market-shaping tools like prizes and challenges, and more experimental and adventurous uses of philanthropic assets (mission- and program-related investments in nonprofit grantees and, more recently, in for-profit companies) to further their social missions.

Section II of the book takes up this question of enterprise and the role that the private sector can play in advancing social change. Specifically, we investigate two emerging fields of study and practice: the *impact investing* movement, and the work on *blended* and *shared-value* capitalism, which enjoins firms to look beyond strict and short-term financial returns for shareholders and to incorporate social and environment benefits (and costs) into notions of "value," which, the argument goes, can also enhance a company's long-term economic performance.

Using case studies from the Bloomberg and Obama administrations, the book's third section examines social entrepreneurship in the public sector, what has come to be known as the *social innovation* school. Here, we observe many of the tenets of change making from the nonprofit and private sectors in their government incarnation: a strong emphasis on evaluation and evidence-based solutions to social change; competitive instruments like prizes and challenges to incent innovation both within government and the social sector more broadly; policy laboratories; and new initiatives intended to shape markets and enlist more private capital for public purpose.

A series of tough debates are tackled in the book's concluding chapters. For starters, we assay the backlash that has occurred in the nonprofit sector against the business bias, and subsequent refinements to the definitions of entrepreneurship (a more collective view of social change) and the ways in which its scale and impact are understood, measured, and evaluated.

We also probe how some social entrepreneurs have evolved in their view of government (more affirming, necessary for scale) and philanthropy (heightened concerns over wealth and influence) and in their belief that philanthropy can and should complement, rather than substitute for, the work of government. A related series of questions asks when and how the profit motive can be harnessed for the public good (i.e., the opportunities and risks associated with commercialization and privatization). Finally, we return to a discussion of states and markets and conclude with an eye toward social entrepreneurship for the twenty-first century: how government and private actors can collectively work toward social change.

The ambit of this book is not unambitious. By tracing the social entrepreneurship movement across three distinct spheres of society—the nonprofit, private, and public sectors—I have made a number of significant omissions. First, this book is narrowly anthropocentric. By that I mean it centers on the world of human services: policies and programs designed to fight poverty, relieve suffering, and improve the life prospects of disadvantaged people across the globe. In a number of other fields, science and technology generally and energy and environment in particular, important innovations (e.g., cap and trade schemes to curb pollution emissions) successfully demonstrate how positive and negative externalities—the true costs and benefits—can be incorporated into price and value, and how government can help shape market solutions to entrenched problems. Although the environment examples receive mention, they are mostly beyond the scope of this book, first because of the broad literature and expertise devoted to them elsewhere, and second because this project intends to show how social entrepreneurs are attempting to devise a similar approach to social problems, which often can be even more complex to measure and solve.

In typically American fashion, this book also suffers from U.S. centrism. Although I reference social entrepreneurship efforts in various countries, mostly as a point of comparison (and the notes include reference to important scholarship with different geographical emphasis), the primary lens is the evolution of the field in the United States. The aim of this work is to situate social entrepreneurship in the larger conversation about American political economy and policy and to consider ways in which change makers from across society can collectively work toward social change in the years ahead.

I

||||||||||||||||||||||||||||||||||||||||||||||||||||||||||||||||||||||||||

# SOCIAL ENTREPRENEURSHIP IN THE NONPROFIT SECTOR

# Chapter 1

||||||||||||||||||||||||||||||||||||||||||||||||||||||||||||

# WHAT IS SOCIAL ENTREPRENEURSHIP?

Just as commercial entrepreneurship has a deep tradition in American life, so too does social entrepreneurship. Although most innovators for the public good—activists working for social change—are unknown and unsung, others have made the history books, including Benjamin Franklin, who helped establish some of the country's first fire and police departments, circulation libraries, insurance associations, and modern universities; Clara Barton, founder of the American Red Cross; Jane Addams, whose Hull House would define and inspire the larger Settlement House movement; and Martin Luther King, Jr. and the movement he led for civil rights and social justice.

Defining social entrepreneurship, however—distinguishing these activities from other good works of social service or advocacy past and present—is no small task, and is the subject of lengthy debate in the field. It turns out that social entrepreneurship is a bit like pornography, at least in the way it eludes ready definition. To paraphrase Supreme Court Justice Potter Stewart's famous ruling on the latter, social entrepreneurship is hard to define, but you know it when you see it.[1]

We begin therefore by examining the work and ideas of Bill Drayton, the founder of Ashoka: Innovators for the Public and the man widely considered to be the father of modern social entrepreneurship.

## Bill Drayton and the Birth of Modern Social Entrepreneurship

Indeed, no one has done more to shape the field of social entrepreneurship than Drayton, whose own achievements as a social entrepreneur and whose efforts over the past generation to support the work of other innovators across the globe have built a movement that redefined the way we think about social change.

Born in New York City in 1943, Drayton demonstrated from childhood a mix of extraordinary intelligence, passion, and civic activism. His heroes included Ashoka, the Indian emperor in the third century B.C.E., who unified most of the subcontinent and introduced unusual social welfare projects; Mahatma Gandhi; and Martin Luther King.[2] In 1980, Drayton committed himself fully to the idea and practice of creating a professional organization to promote the work of social entrepreneurs worldwide. He called his fledging organization Ashoka: Innovators for the Public, and through it he hoped to identify individual social entrepreneurs and bring them together in a kind of global fellowship.

Drayton believed that the kind of social entrepreneurs he was seeking— passionate, resourceful, system-changing, history-making innovators who could unbalance static social, political, and economic equations—were extremely rare. In fact, Ashoka has identified approximately one per 10 million people per year according to its own definition and selection criteria. Since 1980, Ashoka has supported the work of more than 3,000 social entrepreneurs across an enormous range of fields and geographies. During this time, the organization, like Drayton himself, has embraced both micro and macro roles in social change: supporting the work of individual entrepreneurs through funding, technical assistance, and access to a broad network of social entrepreneur colleagues and, in doing so, helping to define and build the broader contemporary field of social entrepreneurship.[3]

Drayton's experience with Ashoka—as exemplar of social entrepreneur himself and as architect of the larger field—offers some useful definitional parameters.

## Just Who and What Is a Social Entrepreneur?

### Rooted in Definition of Entrepreneur

For Drayton, Ashoka Fellow selection requires evidence of distinctly entrepreneurial qualities. "Social entrepreneurs," he says, "for some reason deep in their personality, know from the time they are little that they are in this world to make it better in a fundamental way." Greg Dees, one of the first scholars of social entrepreneurship, roots this vision and the larger field within the broader theory and economic literature on the entrepreneur, which in turn has its conceptual and linguistic origins in nineteenth-century France.[4] Economist Jean Baptiste Say wrote that the entrepreneur was one who "shifts economic resources out of an area of lower and into an area of higher productivity and greater yield." Austrian economist Joseph Schumpeter provides the dynamic notion of entrepreneurial activity we most commonly refer to today: the entrepreneur as a disruptive and generative force for change in the economy, one who helps reform or revolutionizes "the pattern of production." According to Schumpeter, the entrepreneur provides the force (the *Unternehmer*, or entrepreneurial spirit) for economic progress; successful entrepreneurship sets off a kind of cycle in which other entrepreneurs iterate and improve the entrepreneur's original product or service to the point of "creative destruction."[5]

### Resourceful, Adaptive

Drayton also emphasizes the adaptive nature of the entrepreneur; he believes the passion and conviction that drive someone to become an entrepreneur are as much idealism as an assiduous determination to find practical solutions to a problem. In fact, what makes a person an entrepreneur, he suggests, is a commitment to the "how-to" through revision and adaptation. "Every day you're modifying the idea," says Drayton. "You're seeing new opportunities. You're seeing the nuances of problems. It's a continuous process."[6]

Similarly, management guru Peter Drucker conceived of the entrepreneur as an agent of opportunism. "The entrepreneur," he wrote, "always searches for change, responds to it, and exploits it as an opportunity."[7] Howard Stevenson, who specializes in entrepreneurship at Harvard Business School, suggests that entrepreneurship is "the pursuit of opportunity beyond the tangible results you can control."[8] Both Stevenson and

Drucker extend their definitions beyond the profit-seeking realm and into sphere of *social* entrepreneurship.[9]

## The Nature of the Work: System Changing, Innovative

### System Changing

According to most scholars and practitioners, the nature of social entrepreneurship—and what distinguishes it from other social change efforts—has to do with the ambition of its scale and scope. In Drayton's view, social entrepreneurs work toward "systemic" and "far-reaching" social change. "What is the social impact of the idea?" Drayton asks. "Is the idea itself sufficiently new, practical, and useful so that ordinary people will adopt it once it has been demonstrated? How many people will be affected by this idea? How importantly and how beneficially will they be affected? Will it change the field significantly? Will it trigger nationwide impact or broad regional change?"

### Innovative, Different Kinds of Newness

The term *innovation* is often used in defining social entrepreneurship, though it is enmeshed in a hearty debate about what exactly this juxtaposition means. Etymologically the word implies newness, but newness can take many forms. According to Dees, "Successful innovation is as much a matter of execution as it is of having new ideas. . . . Innovation can take many forms. It does not require inventing something wholly new; it can simply involve applying an existing idea in a new way or to a new situation. Entrepreneurs need not be inventors. They simply need to be creative in applying what others have invented. . . . This willingness to innovate is part of the modus operandi of entrepreneurs."[10] In short, Dees suggests, "Innovation involves *establishing new and better ways for accomplishing a worthwhile objective.* For social entrepreneurs, this means new and better ways of serving your social mission."[11] Dees applies a Schumpeterian lens to suggest innovation might involve creating a new or improved product, service, program, strategy, or a new method of operations or organizational structure. Innovation, he suggests, could also mean serving an unmet need.[12]

This issue has taken on renewed vigor and salience in the public sector, as we will see in the chapters on social innovation efforts in New York

City and at the federal level, where policymakers often define innovation not as an invention but rather as a new way of approaching their work. In many cases, it seems to mean putting resources behind evidence-based programs. In this view, *innovation* equals "scaling what works." We also address the innovation (and "system-changing") questions further in Chapter 18, Social Entrepreneurship Revisited, because a good number of stalwart and effective nonprofit organizations have, for decades, achieved significant social impact but are often excluded from the "entrepreneurship" discussions because their work is not perceived as "new" or because they opt for community rather than "system-changing" solutions.

## The Business Sway

### What Makes It Social?

One of the greatest debates in social entrepreneurship centers on the influence of the business paradigm. Before exploring that debate fully, however, it is first necessary to define just what distinguishes *social* entrepreneurship from *for-profit* entrepreneurship: What makes it "social"?

This question can be answered in many ways, although primarily it rests on social entrepreneurship's primacy of social benefit or "mission-related impact."[13] For companies, profits are *sine qua non* essential for long-term scale and viability;[14] they are also a reasonably good proxy for the value a firm has created. In contrast, and nearly by definition, social entrepreneurs are working in areas of market failure. According to Dees, "Markets do not do a good job of valuing social improvements, public goods and harms, and benefits for people who cannot afford to pay. These elements are often essential to social entrepreneurship. That is what makes it social entrepreneurship."[15]

### The Business Orientation of the Social Entrepreneur

Yet for many social entrepreneurs, working in areas of market failure does not mean disregarding market tools or business practices. Rather, in social entrepreneurship, the converse is often true: a distinct business orientation. Drayton believes that the social entrepreneur has "the same 'makeup' as a business entrepreneur, in attitude, vision, bias for action and skills," but the social entrepreneur seeks to change the world's "big patterns" for the good of all. Jane Wei Skillern, Jim Austin, Herman

Leonard, and Howard Stevenson, whose *Entrepreneurship in the Social Sector* (2007) is now one of the most widely used textbooks on the subject, suggest that organizations led by social entrepreneurs "often exhibit some of the virtues commonly associated with commercial entrepreneurship, such as efficiency, dynamism, innovativeness, high performance, and economic sustainability."[16]

Having a business orientation means different things to different social entrepreneurs. For some, it amounts to the adoption of business practices, from more corporate management structures to increasingly quantitative or investment-like measurement and evaluation procedures. For others, being business friendly implies a preference for private—corporate or philanthropic—funds rather than government support. And in some cases, it has meant an effort to function more like a company by generating revenues or even profits in support of the organization's social purpose.

## Social Enterprise versus Entrepreneurship

For the most part, the social entrepreneurship movement in the United States began in the nonprofit sector where it remains focused on the entrepreneurial qualities of these organizations, rather than on their actual transformation into businesses. In recent years, however, a notable shift in emphasis, which we will explore at length in Chapters 8–13, from "entrepreneurship" to "enterprise" has advanced a more literal extension of the business analogy.

In one illustration of this trend, a number of social entrepreneurs have attempted to make their nonprofit organizations function more like businesses by generating additional revenues and sometimes even profits to sustain and advance their social missions. Of course, the notion that social purpose organizations can and should engage in some kind of trade is hardly new. It has long been a feature of the European and British economic landscape, and even in the United States, compelling examples of social-enterprises-as-businesses are found throughout our history. Goodwill Industries, for example, was founded in 1902 by Reverend Edgar Helms, a Methodist minister whose Boston congregation collected used household goods and clothing discarded in wealthy areas of the city, trained and hired the unemployed to mend and repair them, and then redistributed the goods to those in need. Today Goodwill is a global network of 180 local chapter organizations that provides job training and employment placement and others services, raising most of its $3.5 billion budget through retail thrift stores.

In fact, most nonprofits in the United States, including private schools and universities, hospitals, performing arts groups, and museums, among others, use some kind of fee-for-service model to cover a portion (if not most) of their operating costs. By some estimates, earned income exceeds donations as a source of funds for public charities (excluding religious organizations).[17]

The growing emphasis on revenue generation as part of the business bias of the sector has led to some confusion, however, about the difference between enterprise and entrepreneurship. Dees reminds us that "many activities that generate earned income are not entrepreneurial at all. . . . It would be absurd to give a social entrepreneurship award, for instance, to a major hospital simply because of its extremely high percentage of earned income from patient fees and the record profits at its gift shop and parking garage. Yet, this would be a logical implication of taking earned income as the yardstick of social entrepreneurship. High levels of earned income are often not innovative and may not be correlated with high levels of social impact."[18]

## Social Entrepreneurship Across the Sectors

In this remainder of this book, we will refer to and examine social entrepreneurship as a kind of change making that can occur across the sectors. Although the approach began, for the most part, in the nonprofit sector, ample evidence now indicates its influence is found in both the private sector, where true social "enterprises," or companies, have been created with the intention of generating financial returns and social or environmental benefit, and in the public domain, where social entrepreneurs in government are looking to incent and advance innovation throughout the social sector.

# Chapter 2

||||||||||||||||||||||||||||||||||||||||||||||||||||||||||||||||||||||||||

# EARLY SOCIAL ENTREPRENEURSHIP: THE SERVICE ORGANIZATIONS

Atransformation has occurred in the nonprofit sector and stems from the emergence of a new kind of change maker: entrepreneurial leaders who tackle entrenched problems in innovative and system-changing ways, often with a business approach or orientation to their work. What makes this transformation a revolution is its sweep, the number of social entrepreneurs in the nonprofit sector and their influence beyond.

The following case studies are not meant to be exhaustive; rather, they serve to illustrate some of the characteristics of the movement. And even though the organizations and entrepreneurs profiled are not without critics, the common tenets of their work, including ferocious resourcefulness or what Drayton calls "years of relentless grappling with the how-to issues," help us to better understand the nature of modern social entrepreneurship.

## Teach For America

Wendy Kopp, founder of Teach For America (TFA), is often held up as the defining social entrepreneur of her generation.

## Entrepreneurial

The original blueprint for TFA took the form of Kopp's 1989 undergraduate thesis at Princeton. Kopp believed that top college students were eager for meaningful career opportunities and would choose to enter professions like teaching over more remunerative possibilities, were the right structure in place. Kopp proposed a program that would hire and train recent college graduates to become teachers and then place them in schools in low-income communities across the country. At the age of 21, Kopp raised $2.5 million (her first funder, Ross Perot, made a $500,000 three-to-one challenge grant, which enabled her to attract additional support) and launched a recruitment campaign with a bootstrap staff. In 1990, TFA's first official teaching year, Kopp placed 500 college graduates in schools in New York City, Los Angeles, New Orleans, southern Louisiana, and eastern North Carolina.

## Innovative

From its inception, TFA's mission has been to enlist the country's most promising future leaders in the movement to close the achievement gap, and its ability to attract and hire high-caliber teachers relies on competitive entry. In 1990, 2,500 applicants from 100 colleges applied for those 500 spots. In 2011, 48,000 college students applied for 5,200 spots. TFA corps members must have an average GPA of at least 3.5, and almost all have held significant leadership positions in college. Over time, TFA has made adaptations to its operations model to advance its core mission, such as establishing teacher training (summer institutes) and alumni programs, and moving to a regional structure to better support its teachers across the country.

## Business Friendly

Historically, most of TFA's funding came from private sources — foundations, corporations, and private individuals. In 2002, TFA entered into its first corporate partnership with Wachovia for financial support and management expertise; soon other companies followed. TFA has also been a darling of the education reform funders (which will be discussed further in the next chapter), including the Gates, Broad, Dell, and Robertson foundations. Its business model is not uncontroversial; TFA works distinctly outside of the traditional and unionized education structure.

TFA has grown significantly in recent years. In 2005, 3,500 corps members served at 22 sites. By 2008, TFA had jumped to 6,200 corps members at 29 sites. Today, with a $180 million operating budget, TFA is the largest single provider of teachers for low-income communities; in the 2011–2012 school year, 9,000 corps members (first and second year) reached more than 600,000 students. Cumulatively, nearly 33,000 TFA participants have taught more than 3 million students in schools across the United States.

As one of the country's most closely examined education organizations, TFA has for years embraced a culture of measurement and evaluation, and it tries to measure its impact in terms of numbers of teachers trained and students served, test scores produced by TFA teachers, and the influence of TFA's alumni in the education field, both within schools and as advocates for reform efforts. Although healthy debate surrounds the interpretation of these data, many across the political spectrum have pledged their support based on what they believe to be the strength of the evidence, which is particularly true of the public dollars that have truly brought TFA to scale. When President Bush reauthorized the Higher Education Act, for example, the federal government committed $45 million over two years to TFA. TFA also received a $50 million scale-up grant in 2010 from the Department of Education's Investing in Innovation (i3) Fund, which will allow TFA to increase its teacher corps by 80 percent by September 2014. The i3 awards were made on the evidence base—proof of efficacy of the innovation model.

‖‖‖‖‖‖‖‖‖‖‖‖‖‖‖‖‖‖‖‖‖‖‖‖‖‖‖‖‖‖‖‖‖‖‖‖‖‖‖‖‖‖‖‖‖‖‖‖‖‖‖‖‖‖‖

## Social Entrepreneurship and the Education Reform Debates

Much ink has been spilled over the ideological and political battles of the contemporary education reform debates. Without attempting to reproduce them here, it is worth noting that the education reform movement largely follows the trajectory of this book: new ideas tested in the nonprofit sector by idealistic and pragmatic social entrepreneurs, which are then embraced by both private and public sector innovators.

The reform agenda, much of which was fashioned in the nonprofit sector, focuses broadly on the perceived inefficiency of the public school system. The argument suggests that, as a government monopoly, traditional public schools are not subject to external competition or accountability. Within that general framework, the reform platform has many planks: some call explicitly for greater competition and choice (through things like vouchers), while others want greater autonomy for schools, allowing principals and teachers to experiment in ways that large public bureaucracies do not typically permit. In the nonprofit sector, reformers have included, among others, charter school operators and their allies and advocates of smaller schools or experimental curricula. Reformers who insist that teacher and principal performance are at the crux of school improvement focus on training and supports for teachers and administrators; some emphasize the evaluation and standards that need to be in place to measure performance; others try to link compensation, or merit pay, to performance.

A large number of reform-minded social entrepreneurship educational nonprofits have appeared in recent years, among them: The New Teacher Project (TNTP), founded in 1997 and led for 10 years by TFA alum Michelle Rhee (who would go on to be the reform-champion—and controversial—chancellor of the D.C. public schools), which focused initially on helping urban districts improve the way they recruited, trained, and hired new teachers; New Leaders for New Schools (NLNS), launched in 2000 by Jon Schnur, an education advisor to Bill Clinton and Al Gore, which is focused on recruiting and training leaders for schools for poor and minority students; New Visions for Public Schools, founded in 1989 and led since 2000 by Robert Hughes, which has worked on developing small schools in New York City, teacher residencies, and leadership training; Citizen Schools, launched in 1995 in Boston by City Year alumnus Eric Schwarz, which now partners with middle schools across the United States to expand the learning day for low-income children by using volunteer (Citizen Teacher) run apprenticeship and other programs; and a broad array of charter schools and their CMOs (charter management organizations), including KIPP, Achievement First, Uncommon Schools, Harlem Academies, Aspire, Green Dot, and Rocketship. A host of other education social entrepreneurs, not necessarily in lockstep with the reform platform, have also emerged over the last generation. Education is arguably the largest "sector" within the field of social entrepreneurship.

IIIIIIIIIIIIIIIIIIIIIIIIIIIIIIIIIIIIIIIIIIIIIIIIIIIIIIIIIIIIIIIIIIIIIIIII

# City Year

Another of the prominent social entrepreneurship organizations that has helped to launch and shape the movement is City Year, best known as an architect and advocate of national service in the United States.

## Entrepreneurial

In 1988, Harvard Law School roommates Michael Brown and Alan Khazei envisioned a program to engage young people in service as a way to address pressing social problems in the United States. City Year began as an eight-week pilot program in Boston with 50 corps members and five initial sponsors. In 1990, City Year launched its first full-year corps in Boston and in 1993 expanded to Rhode Island. Over time, like Teach For America, City Year spread to more U.S. cities and focused more on the preparation and supports necessary for its corps members and alumni.

## Innovative

City Year's mission is "to build democracy through citizen service, civic leadership, and social entrepreneurship. It is through service that we can demonstrate the power and idealism of young people, engage citizens to benefit the common good, and develop young leaders of the next generation."

Since 1990, City Year has graduated more than 15,000 alumni, served more than 1 million children, and completed more than 26 million hours of service. City Year is currently serving in 24 cities across the United States and in two international affiliate sites located in Johannesburg, South Africa, and London, England.

## Business Friendly

From its inception, City Year has been committed to engaging the private sector in its work. Khazei and Brown believed that national service could not be strictly the purview of government, and they launched the organization with a combination of private grants and corporate sponsorship.[1] In the mid-1990s, City Year began with sponsorship from companies based in cities where City Year teams operated. In addition to funds, companies also took a hands-on approach, supplying business skills and expertise as part of the larger "service" model. Today, City Year has a large number of corporate partners that provide in-kind and financial support. Its eight National Leadership Sponsors include Aramark, Bank of America, Cisco, Comcast/NBC Universal, CSX, Deloitte, PepsiCo, and Walmart.

In 1990, when City Year was first awarded federal funds under the first Bush Administration's National and Community Service Act, City Year's leaders aimed to keep approximately a 50/50 balance between public and private (foundation and corporate) funding. This self-imposed cap on government funds was meant to ensure that government remained an investor, alongside the private sector investors, and that City Year did not become a government program.

Early on, City Year also experimented with developing sources of earned income to offset its reliance on public or private funds, an increasingly common practice of nonprofits in the 1990s. The organization's first foray into revenue-generating businesses came in 1994 with City Year Enterprise, which launched City Year Gear, a line of clothing and accessories produced in partnership with Timberland. City Year subsequently launched Care Force, a program that advised companies on their volunteer events.[2]

In recent years, City Year has significantly refocused its efforts based on research about its own core strengths and areas of social need where it could make the most difference. Accordingly, City Year is now wholly dedicated to fighting the national dropout crisis, with corps members serving as tutors, mentors, and role models in schools to help students get back or stay on track to graduate. Corps members focus specifically on three early warning indicators: attendance, behavior, and course performance in math and English. City Year's In School & On Track initiative is designed to bring City Year corps members to 50 percent of all students falling off track in City Year's 24 U.S. locations. Meeting this goal will require expanding the number of corps members to 6,000 and engaging school districts, the private sector, and the federal government through AmeriCorps as partners. This new focus has allowed City Year to better assess the impact of its efforts and, not surprisingly, with more evidence of impact, attract new funding.[3]

City Year's new focus led to the creation of a school-turnaround program, Diplomas Now, to aid the lowest-performing schools. Through Diplomas Now, City Year volunteers work with Johns Hopkins Talent Development Schools (focused on helping school district leaders) and Communities in Schools (supporting social workers in connecting with students who face significant problems, such as homelessness or abuse, and need assistance) to focus on dropout prevention. Like Teach For America, Diplomas Now won a $30 million grant from the Department of Education's Investing in Innovation (i3) Fund, an award based on evidence of impact.

# Jumpstart

Founded in 1993 by social entrepreneurs Aaron Lieberman, David Carmel, and Jordan Meranus, Jumpstart for Young Children is now a national early education organization that helps children from low-income neighborhoods develop the language and literacy skills they need to be successful in school by pairing them with college students and community volunteers.

## Entrepreneurial

Like TFA and City Year, Jumpstart began as an idea in a college dorm room. As a senior at Yale, Lieberman worked in a Head Start program and recognized that early intervention, in the form of tutoring and one-on-one attention, could make a difference in the lives of low-income preschoolers who showed signs of struggling to keep up with their peers. Lieberman, Carmel, and Meranus focused on Head Start programs as an entry point for preschoolers and on universities as a way to attract, manage, and fund classroom tutors.

## Innovative

In 1994, the social entrepreneurs formally launched Jumpstart in Boston. By 1996, Jumpstart had enlisted 100 student tutors to work with 100 pre-schoolers with a goal of improving the literacy and social skills the children would need to succeed in school. That same year, Jumpstart received its first AmeriCorps grant and opened programs in New York City and then Washington, D.C., the following year. Jumpstart developed its own curriculum and training program and created a University Affiliate Program (UAP) with universities across the country that allowed students to access financial aid work-study funds for work with community-based nonprofits. In this way, the universities, not Jumpstart, covered the bulk of the tutors' compensation. In addition, the university partners created and administered the tutoring programs for their students under the Jumpstart banner, thereby assuming responsibility for the bulk of program operations and financing. In return, Jumpstart provided an array of supports, including training, leadership conferences, and help with measurement and evaluation. Since 1993, Jumpstart has trained nearly 25,000 college students and community volunteers to deliver its program to more than 100,000 preschool children nationwide.

## Business Friendly

Jumpstart also aggressively pursued private funds and in-kind support from the new wave of social entrepreneurship funders (including New Profit and Echoing Green, described in the next chapter) and corporate partners such American Eagle and Starbucks. Like City Year, Jumpstart also flirted with revenue-generating activities and in 1999 launched a for-profit Internet company called SchoolSuccess.net, which sold early childhood education materials and expertise over the Web. SchoolSuccess raised nearly $2 million in venture capital and was eventually sold to Pearson Learning.

From its earliest days, Jumpstart also embraced a culture of performance measurement and management. The program is the subject of a Harvard Business School case study on its approach to tracking outcomes and performance management.[4] Although it has embraced business-friendly fundraising and management practices, Jumpstart's national growth strategy, like that of TFA and City Year, has relied on federal funding like AmeriCorps and work-study dollars.

## Working Today—Freelancers Union

Founded in 1995 by labor attorney and union organizer Sara Horowitz, Working Today was created to represent the needs of the growing independent workforce.

### Entrepreneurial

Horowitz came from a family steeped in the labor movement. Her grandfather was vice president of the International Ladies Garment Workers Union, and her father was a union lawyer. At age 32, Horowitz had become a labor attorney herself and an organizer with the Service Employees International Union (SEIU) 1199. However, as she observed the changing nature of the modern workforce—particularly the significant rise of the independent labor force—Horowitz believed that neither labor policies nor the social safety net had kept pace. After graduating from the Kennedy School of Government in 1994, she founded Working Today to address this mismatch.

### Innovative

Throughout the late 1990s, Working Today was chiefly concerned with connecting freelancers—approximately 35,000 of them—to benefits. In 2001, Working Today launched the Portable Benefits Network (PBN), which connected Working Today members in New York City to benefits, including health, life, and eventually disability coverage, which they could take with them to new jobs. In 2003, Working Today officially incorporated the Freelancers Union as a nonprofit organization. For the most part, union membership meant participation in the PBN, and in 2005, membership went national. Working Today remained the organization's research and policy arm. Horowitz also became increasingly visible as a social entrepreneur, earning funding early on from New Profit Inc., a Schwab Foundation for Social Entrepreneurship Award, an Ashoka Fellowship, and a MacArthur grant.

## Business Friendly

From Working Today's beginning, Horowitz hoped to infuse the New Deal–era worker protections she deeply believed in with "the spirit of modernity."[5] She felt this goal required a new kind of social system that served independent workers, themselves "a community of people with shared interests" who could form their own cooperative model to meet their needs. Horowitz called this the "new mutualism," which she believed represented a "new form of capitalism." New mutualism draws explicitly on mutual or cooperative business models: firms that reinvest profits for the shared benefits of their members (insurance companies like Principal and Metlife began life as mutuals). Agricultural cooperatives and credit unions have a similar member-as-stakeholder structure, and cooperative business models (worker-owned firms) have century-long histories in Germany and other European countries. "The for-profit community sells solutions to your problems," Horowitz said. "New mutualism is the alternative: bring people together and leverage the power of the group to create its own solutions."[6]

In 2009, Horowitz officially launched Freelancers Insurance Company (FIC), a social purpose insurance company that promised affordable and portable health insurance to New York State members. By bringing independent workers together as a group—essentially certifying them as an insurance class—FIC allows its members to access lower-cost health insurance, minimize collective risk, and mutually subsidize one another's health cost. The nonprofit Freelancers Union is the sole shareholder, and profits are reinvested in community building and advocacy for the national membership base.

||||||||||||||||||||||||||||||||||||||||||||||||||||||||||||||||||||||||||||

## Social Entrepreneurship Beyond the United States

Although we focus on these domestic examples, social entrepreneurship is hardly an American phenomenon, and its characteristics in different countries and regions reflect distinct and local political, economic, and social histories.

For decades, the social welfare states of Europe and the United Kingdom, for example, have provided directly an array of social services that in the United States are increasingly delivered via nonprofit or private (commercial) entities. Although this arrangement has begun to change in recent years, particularly in the United Kingdom, it also has meant a smaller nonprofit or citizen sector and a less prominent role for private philanthropy than we observe in the United States.

In 1997, Charles Leadbeater's "The Rise of the Social Entrepreneur" explored the growing number of social entrepreneurs in the United Kingdom who were using new approaches to address social problems such as homelessness, drug addiction, and unemployment that were once the purview of the state but under public sector reform were increasingly outsourced to private organizations. Leadbeater's influential work both reflected and stoked a growing interest in the field. That same year, Michael Young—a kind of British Bill Drayton—launched the School for Social Entrepreneurs. The Skoll Centre for Social Entrepreneurship at Oxford University's Saïd Business School, which was created in 2003, has also helped to advance the movement globally, particularly through its annual World Forum. And, as we will see in Chapter 17, the British government has also played a critical role in promoting social entrepreneurship through its Office of the Third Sector, which it created in 2006.

Many countries also have a different and more robust tradition of social enterprise than in the United States. In Europe, for example, a variety of corporate forms have for years (or, in some cases, centuries) allowed for-profit companies and firms to pursue social objectives in different ways. Social enterprises in Europe and the United Kingdom tend to be rooted in these alternative corporate forms; in other words, they are legally businesses—cooperatives, development trusts, social firms, mutuals, employee-owned enterprises, and, now, community interest companies (CICs)—with social mission and governance legally embedded in their corporate structure.

# Chapter 3

||||||||||||||||||||||||||||||||||||||||||||||||||||||||||||||||||||||||||||||

# EARLY SOCIAL
# ENTREPRENEURSHIP:
# THE FUNDERS

It is not accidental that the growing prominence of the venture capital (VC) industry of the 1990s and the spectacular wealth it produced also led to a new breed of social entrepreneurship foundation. This venture philanthropy attempted, to varying degrees, to fashion the VC model to the nonprofit sector. Even traditional foundations have been transformed in the way they approach grant making by the influences of the so-called venture model. The next chapters will examine the rise of this new cadre of funders, their business orientation and more activist and sometimes experimental approach to grant making, and the extent of their sway in the nonprofit, private, and public sectors.

## The Scientific Charity of the Nineteenth Century

In many ways, the "new" philanthropy of the late twentieth century closely echoes what historians call the *scientific charity* of the late nineteenth century, which sought more systematic, strategic, and enduring solutions to social problems, rather than simply giving alms away to the poor.[1] In the 1890s, for example, John D. Rockefeller argued that "the best philanthropy is constantly in search for finalities—a search for cause, an attempt to cure the evils at their source." This outlook provided the vision for the foundation he established in 1913, committed to attacking the root causes of poverty.

The term *venture philanthropy* was first coined by Rockefeller's grandson, John D. Rockefeller III, in 1969, when he testified before Congress about the value of tax advantaging charitable giving. According to Rockefeller III, philanthropy played an important risk-taking role in social policy: "the imaginative pursuit of less conventional charitable purposes than those normally undertaken by established public charitable organizations." However, the practice of venture philanthropy would not come into vogue until the 1990s when it became synonymous with a kind of new philanthropy that reflected the business values and methodologies of the newly rich, typically those entrepreneurs who had achieved enormous success in finance and technology and were keen to apply their business acumen to philanthropic pursuits.

Some of the first venture philanthropies were poverty-fighting organizations forged from the 1980s financial boom. In New York City, this included Paul Tudor Jones's Robin Hood Foundation (1988) and Julian Robertson's Tiger Foundation (1990). On the West Coast, the Roberts Enterprise Development Fund (1990) initially focused on the problem of homelessness in San Francisco, where its founder, George Roberts, recalls, "I could see how the power and proven practices of the business world could be applied to this problem and bring real solutions."

## Virtuous Capital: What Foundations Can Learn from Venture Capitalists

The term and concepts related to *venture philanthropy* gained wider currency following the 1997 publication of "Virtuous Capital: What Foundations Can Learn from Venture Capitalists," a *Harvard Business Review* article in which Christine Letts, William Ryan, and Allen Grossman made the case that foundations should function more like venture capital firms. Specifically, the authors argued that foundation officers should support nonprofit grantees in the same way VCs built businesses, by considering overall organizational strength and performance and not simply the merits of a particular program or project. This approach marked a divergence from the 1960s and 1970s R&D model of philanthropy, based on "tacit division of labor between foundations and the public sector," which assumed, as Rockefeller III had suggested, that philanthropies should fund and test many new ideas, and government agencies would implement and scale the successful ones. (Many of the hallmark programs of the War on Poverty, for example, including Head Start, had begun life as foundation-sponsored pilot projects.)

According to Letts and colleagues, the major flaw of this R&D model was that it gave foundations little incentive to invest in the long-term organizational capacity of their grantees: funding was relatively short lived and made in small amounts, often without an explicit link to performance. Instead, through the new venture model, foundations would provide funding over long time frames, in larger amounts, and to fewer organizations. Like their VC counterparts, foundation officers would also work closely with their grantees to develop strategy and provide technical assistance for capacity building, particularly in the area of performance measures. Finally, the authors advocated for an exit strategy to ensure that the organization remained viable even after financial support from that foundation ceased.[2]

Though the "Virtuous Capital" authors did not invent the theory, their writing reflected the zeitgeist fascination with venture capital and crystallized the analogy that would become a kind of blueprint for a wave of new funders, many of whom were already well versed in the ways of venture capital. Venture philanthropy quickly acquired its own lingo: grants became "investments," program areas became "portfolios," and program officers "portfolio managers." Nonprofits themselves no longer applied for funds or matching grants but instead "leveraged resources," not through a grant proposal but via a business plan. And performance was increasingly described in return on investment (ROI) terms.

## New Profit: The Venture Philanthropy Prototype

Venture philanthropies of all shapes and sizes soon appeared on the charitable landscape, and New Profit Inc., served as a kind of prototype of the VC analogy in action. Launched in 1997 by Vanessa Kirsch, New Profit was designed from the venture playbook. Kirsch was a successful social entrepreneur in her own right as founder of Public Allies, an organization that matched young people who wanted careers in public service with government agencies or nonprofit organizations. Although Public Allies had achieved a national presence, Kirsch knew firsthand how challenging it was to raise money from foundations interested in new ideas (per the R&D analogy) rather than expanding the work of proven programs. Kirsch became consumed with this question of scale: "What prevents social entrepreneurs from scaling their innovation at the same pace and quality as Coca-Cola?" she asked.

Accordingly, New Profit devised a three-pronged investment strategy: it would fund *scalable organizations* led by social entrepreneurs with proven track records in need of mezzanine financing; use *performance-based design*, meaning mutually agreed upon benchmarks for continued funding; and it would make *active life cycle investments*: three-to-five-year commitments of cash grants and technical assistance, often provided by consultants from Monitor, one of New Profit's strategic partners. Once the organization had scaled and reached some kind of self-sufficiency, New Profit planned to exit the investment. New Profit's first investments included Teach For America, Jumpstart, and Working Today.

## Proliferation of Other New and Social Entrepreneurship Philanthropies

By the early 2000s, the field had exploded with regional and organizational variations on the venture theme. Some of these philanthropies focus on early stage rather than mezzanine funding. Others, like Echoing Green or the Skoll Foundation, provide Ashoka-type fellowships to social entrepreneurs, and, like Ashoka, help promote the field by creating a community for social entrepreneurs. Some of these new philanthropies come in local or boutique varieties, like the Blue Ridge Foundation, founded by hedge funder John A. Griffin and led by social entrepreneur Matt Klein, which seeks to incubate start-up nonprofits in New York City with supports like office space, funding, back-office support, and other management assistance. Others, like the Tiger Foundation, have the dual purpose of supporting grantees and educating investors and donors about best-practice philanthropy.[3]

In recent years, this kind of high engagement model has taken the form of giving circles, first pioneered by Social Venture Partners (SVP) in Seattle in 1997, which requires a relatively small donation but active participation on the part of its members. Laura Arrillaga-Andreessen, founder of Silicon Valley Social Venture Fund (SV2) and author of *Giving 2.0*, says that this approach succeeds in "giving not only funds, but also leveraging the intellectual, human and network capital of our donors to support our grantees."[4] Today, SVP International represents 26 organizations and 2,000 partners across the United States, Canada, and Japan. By some estimates, 400 giving circles currently operate in the United States.[5]

## Venture Philanthropy's Influence on the Establishment

The transformations taking place in the philanthropic sector along the venture lines have not been limited to new or start-up funders. This new thinking is also evident in a number of large, established philanthropies where staff and board members are reassessing their approach to charitable giving.

One of the first to fundamentally alter its philanthropic course was the Edna McConnell Clark Foundation (EMCF), one of the nation's largest foundations. Established in the 1970s by the Clark family, heirs to the Avon company fortune, EMCF funded work in the areas of poverty, children, the elderly, and the developing world when Michael Balin took over as president in 1997. Balin, like Kirsch and others, was chiefly concerned with the question of scale and skeptical of the philanthropy as R&D model. He explained:

> Our goal is not only to help create better services and systems, but to bring their benefits to more people. Excellence begs for scale. Small may be beautiful, but it usually isn't enough. To complete our mission, it is no longer sufficient, if it ever was, to restrict ourselves to devising new strategies, confident that the public sector will adopt and replicate the ones that work best. In recent years we have invested more in the development of new ideas than their production, scale, and sustainability. That is an honorable imbalance, but an imbalance nonetheless.[6]

Balin had come to believe that foundations needed to build strong and sustainable nonprofit organizations, and in 2000, he helped radically restructure EMCF to emphasize institution building that included unrestricted grants, performance milestones, technical assistance often provided by a consulting firm partner (Bridgespan, the nonprofit arm of Bain), and a smaller portfolio of grantees focused exclusively on disadvantaged youth. Per the venture schematic, EMCF also believed that, after a multiyear commitment, it could exit the investment.[7]

As part of its institution-building strategy, EMCF launched a $120 million Growth Capital Aggregation Pilot (GCAP) to help some of its more successful grantees with proven track records (Nurse Family Partnership, Youth Villages, and Citizen Schools) scale their efforts. The idea, working with a syndicate of 19 co-investors, was to aggregate large sums of up-front growth capital for capacity building over the long term, rather than short-term project funding. In its role as lead investor, EMCF also provided technical support to the grantees.

Some call this kind of growth capital *philanthropic equity*. Here again, the idea is analogous to for-profit investing, delineating the difference between equity (episodic finance used to *build* companies) and revenue, which is more similar to fee-for-product or fee-for-service and represents a kind of *buy* approach. In 2006, the Nonprofit Finance Fund (founded in 1980) launched NFF Capital Partners under the direction of George Overholser, a former VC, to help nonprofits in their campaigns for philanthropic equity and has since assisted 18 social entrepreneurship organizations raise $325 million in growth capital.[8]

Perhaps the most high-profile metamorphosis in established philanthropy came at Rockefeller, where Judith Rodin, who arrived in 2005 from the University of Pennsylvania, recalibrated the foundation for the twenty-first century. Under Rodin, grants became *investments* that collectively made up a portfolio across which managing directors would balance and spread risk. The foundation *leveraged* strategic partnerships for greater impact. And measurement and evaluation became more central to Rockefeller's work.

In 2006, the *Economist* dubbed Rodin the "Rockefeller Revolutionary" for the foundation's shake-up.[9] Not everyone within the organization or in the field more broadly embraced the reforms, though Rodin countered that she was returning the foundation to its scientific philanthropy roots. And while Rodin became a kind of lightning rod in the debates about the new philanthropy, she was hardly alone in her efforts. Today, nearly all leaders of storied philanthropic institutions have begun to substantially reexamine their approach, including Luis Ubiñas, the McKinsey executive who took over the presidency of the Ford Foundation in 2008; Bob Galluci, who joined MacArthur in 2009; and Paul Brest, the president of the William and Flora Hewlett Foundation and author of *Money Well Spent: A Strategic Plan for Smart Philanthropy.*[10]

## Education Venture Philanthropies

The great wave of education reform social entrepreneurship organizations (including Teach For America, The New Teacher Project, New Leaders for New Schools, and others referenced in the preceding chapter) has been buoyed by the new philanthropy.

In some cases, entire venture philanthropy firms devoted exclusively to education have emerged. The NewSchools Venture Fund (NSVF), for example, was created in 1998 by social entrepreneur Kim Smith and venture capitalists John Doerr and Brook Byers to supply early-stage capital and technical support to education entrepreneurs. Since then, NSVF has raised and invested hundreds of millions of dollars across funds in education ventures (primarily, but no longer exclusively, in the nonprofit sector). NSVF's influence goes well beyond philanthropy; its alumni include people such as Jim Shelton, who now runs the Office of Innovation and Improvement under Arne Duncan in the U.S. Department of Education. NSVF is also staffed by a number of education social entrepreneurs, including Jordan Meranus, one of the original Jumpstart founders.

In other cases, new philanthropists have taken an interest in education reform alongside other policy interests. These organizations include, but are not limited to, the Gates, Walton, Wallace, and Broad foundations. The education reform movement—and certain planks of it, especially charter schools—has also received significant financial support from the hedge fund community and others with a strong business bias (what Diane Ravitch has called the Billionaire Boys Club).[11] These debates are fierce and beyond the scope of this book.

# Efficient Social Capital Markets

In 2004, Bill Meehan and his McKinsey colleagues expanded the venture paradigm further by introducing an even broader market metaphor to the philanthropic sector. "All those who give to charity, along with the nonprofits they fund, make up a vast web that we call the 'social capital market,'" they wrote. "We use the market analogy because it's a useful intellectual and communications construct and metaphor. Comparing the social capital market to markets for goods and services, including financial markets for corporate and individual capital, we can see that where the latter runs mostly efficiently, the former is woefully inefficient."[12] The authors of "Investing in Society" went on to argue that even though well-functioning capital markets are characterized by cost-efficient processes, relatively low transaction costs, robust information flow, value-driven allocation, and flexibility and responsiveness in the face of market information, the social capital markets often lack these characteristics. In recent years, the "efficient social capital markets" theory has enjoyed even greater circulation with the belief, articulated by Robert Kaplan, Allen Grossman, and others that "market mechanisms from the private sector could energize the nonprofit world."[13]

Even by way of analogy, the use of the *venture* and *capital market* lenses in philanthropy casts a powerful refraction, and one that resulted in a number of profound intellectual and practical consequences. Challenges to this view and debates about the limitations of the business metaphor and applications to the social sector have been percolating for years. In the wake of the financial crisis, however, they have gained greater attention and urgency, and are addressed more fully in section IV of this book.

One undeniable legacy of the business-bias philanthropic paradigm is its heightened emphasis on measurement and evaluation, because the only way to make social capital markets more efficient is to improve the quality of information about organizations and impact available to potential funders.[14] Like any theory, this one is built on assumptions, and the not-so tacit assumption here is that, given the right informational signals, resources (financial and otherwise) *will* flow from lower- to higher-performing organizations. These signals can only come in the form of improved proof of impact. Those measures of proof, found in the collection of evidence, are the subject of the next chapter.

# Chapter 4

||||||||||||||||||||||||||||||||||||||||||||||||||||||||||||||||||||

# NEW PHILANTHROPY AND THE VALUE OF EVALUATION

I n the chapters that follow, we will evaluate some of the important ways new philanthropy—venture and otherwise—has shaped the social sector. In particular, we focus on four areas of influence: the increased emphasis on measurement and evaluation; the use of market-shaping tools such as prizes and challenges; important experiments in technology as a force for social good; and an increased emphasis on enterprise as a means of social change.

## The Value of Evaluation

If we look beyond the inelegance of the business jargon, we find what might be the most pronounced contribution of the social entrepreneurship movement: a heightened emphasis on measurement and evaluation. In particular, the new funders have made important advances through the use of assessment tools to try to measure progress against social problems. This is especially true when it comes to applying the business analogy to social impact, with the view that grants are investments that yield some kind of "returns." Broadly speaking, however, social entrepreneur change makers are pursuing three kinds of measurements, focused respectively on:

1. demonstrating "returns," in quasi-financial or social terms.
2. improving performance of an organization's internal management or operations.
3. proving impact, emulating a kind of scientific approach.

## How Do We Know?

In the world of social entrepreneurship, the measurement and evaluation challenge is fundamentally epistemological. How do we know an organization is achieving an impact? What are the social benefits produced? How can we be sure this nonprofit is performing well?

These questions are easier to answer in the private sector. Companies are performing "well" when they produce a good or service that consumers are willing to pay for. Profits are a reasonably accurate indicator of the value of that good or service, and capital resource allocation occurs with relative efficiency, as investment dollars chase profits.

Life is more complex in the social sector.

## Early Impact Assessment

Much of the early work in impact assessment in the social sector comes to philanthropy from government-led initiatives that assessed the impact of publicly funded programs. As part of its War on Poverty, for example, the Johnson Administration created the Office of Economic Opportunity (OEO), which included a central research and evaluation arm. In the late 1960s, impact assessment was broadly adopted in the environmental field to measure the ecological effects of policies and legislation on the human environment. And in the 1970s, the Ford Foundation, in conjunction with a handful of federal agencies, created the Manpower Demonstration Research Corporation (MDRC) to improve the efficacy of a number of social policies and programs. By the 1980s, most federal agencies in the U.S. government had environmental social impact assessment procedures in place, and the World Bank and other multilateral organizations began to employ social and environmental impact assessment in project evaluation procedures. Increasingly, foundations developed their own individual assessment protocols, often based in part on these public sector models.

## Basic Methodologies

Broadly speaking, the first measurement and evaluation methodologies attempting to quantify impact were of two kinds: *cost-effectiveness analysis*, a kind of bang-for-the-buck or dollar per measure (i.e., cost per high school graduate) used when it is hard to monetize the benefits of a program, and *cost-benefit analysis*, which attempts to monetize and compare the benefits and costs associated with a given intervention.

The levels of sophistication of cost-benefit vary from simple net benefits (benefits-costs) to a ratio of benefits to costs or to measures that try to account for the value of time by discounting future benefits in a kind of net present value (NPV) way. Despite these basic categorizations, organizations differ substantially in how they account for benefits, costs, and uncertainty about future benefits.

## The Sway of New Philanthropy, SROI, and the Emphasis on Returns

Not surprisingly, the business and capital market analogies many new funders apply to their social sector investments often result in measurement and evaluation expressed in *returns* terms.

### Roberts Enterprise Development Fund: Social Return on Investment (SROI)

Founded in 1990, the Roberts Enterprise Development Fund (REDF) was one of the first philanthropies, venture or otherwise, to formally define impact assessment as a set of "returns." In 1996, under the direction of its then executive director, Jed Emerson, REDF published its first social return on investment analysis, which quantified in dollars the social value of its economic development programs. In the private sector, return on investment (ROI) is the ratio of the money gained (or lost) on an investment relative to its cost (the amount of money invested). Similarly, REDF's SROI metric aimed to measure value and return as a blend of enterprise (or financial) and social aspects.

Generally speaking, REDF's SROI analysis examines a social service activity over a given time frame (usually 5 to 10 years); calculates the dollar investment required to support that activity; identifies the various cost savings, including reduced public spending and related benefits, such as increased tax revenue; monetizes the savings and benefits in real dollar terms; discounts back to time zero of the investment; and then calculates a final socioeconomic value in terms of NPV and SROI rates and ratios. This kind of measure works well for programs such as job training and placement for the disabled or homeless, individuals on the receiving end of public benefits who can be employed in private markets.

Although REDF did not refine this model substantially after 2000, the SROI thinking and methodology has been widely adopted and modified by a range of social entrepreneurs and the organizations that fund them. However, this approach does face some significant limitations (discussed in Chapter 18). Emerson has since gone on to develop and advocate for a different version of blended value, which is discussed at length in Chapter 8.

## Robin Hood: Benefit-Cost Ratio (BC)

The Robin Hood Foundation uses a different, though related, approach. Each grantee in Robin Hood's portfolio must measure its work in a relatively standard and numerical way, whether it is meals served, students graduating high school, preschoolers entering kindergarten, or unemployed workers placed into jobs. Robin Hood then converts these data into a benefit-cost (BC) ratio, which allows it to understand the impact of each organization in absolute and relative terms. The BC measure is calculated as follows:

**BC = The poverty-fighting benefits of a program / Cost to Robin Hood × "Robin Hood factor"**

The poverty-fighting benefits of a program include the lifetime benefits that accrue to an individual as a result of the grant, and the Robin Hood factor is Robin Hood's estimate of the portion of the benefit that can be attributed to its investment. Robin Hood does not use the BC ratios to make allocation decisions among portfolios. However, Michael Weinstein, the economist who oversees programs at Robin Hood, believes that "relentless monetization" of benefits forces foundation officers to think in terms of trade-offs and marginal benefits and costs.[1] Although it differs from REDF's SROI, Robin Hood's BC ratio also attempts to measure, in comparable terms, a kind of social value produced per dollar invested. A number of other funders have adopted Robin Hood–like metrics to evaluate their investments.

## Measurement and Evaluation for Internal Management Purposes

### New Profit Inc.

Although much of the venture lingo in philanthropy focuses on returns, some new funders also emphasize the value of evaluation for internal management purposes. New Profit's *balanced scorecard* aims to do both.

The balanced scorecard was first developed by Robert Kaplan and David Norton as a kind of measurement system for companies to incorporate nonfinancial data—factors such as customer satisfaction and product quality—into their performance assessments. Specifically, the balanced scorecard tracks measures from four perspectives: financial, customer, internal business processes, and learning and growth. Vanessa Kirsch, the head of New Profit, worked closely with Kaplan and Norton to design a balanced scorecard for the nonprofits in her organization's portfolio. In addition, New Profit tied its own balanced scorecard directly to those of its portfolio organizations, linking the organization's overall performance to the performance of the individual investments. The New Profit balanced scorecard has been widely adopted by social entrepreneurs across the field for internal management purposes *and* to provide performance data to their donors.

## Proof of Impact, Evidence-Based Levels of Funding

### EMCF: Evidence-Based Levels of Funding

After testing a number of different evaluation techniques, the Edna McConnell Clark Foundation settled on an evidence-based approach to grant making that explicitly correlates levels of funding to levels of proof of a program's efficacy. In the EMCF taxonomy, early-stage organizations are those that have internal evaluations showing program effectiveness but not necessarily external verification of these findings; growth-ready organizations offer demonstrated effectiveness as determined by an external evaluator but not necessarily scientific proof; and the work of organizations poised for sustainable growth has been proven through scientifically validated evaluation—randomized control trials—to have a positive impact on participants.

According to Nancy Roob, the president of EMCF, this continuum allows the foundation to develop its own pipeline of "evidence-based, sustainable, and scalable grantees across the various stages of organizational development."[2] EMCF has been a proponent of the scientific rigor school of evaluation and an advocate of randomized control trials (RCTs) as the evidentiary gold standard.

||||||||||||||||||||||||||||||||||||||||||||||||||||||||||||||||||||||||||||||

## The Use of Randomized Control Trials in Social Policy

Randomized control trials (RCTs) are relatively new, even in the fields of medicine and science. In 1954, the developers of the Salk polio vaccine used one of the first major RCTs, involving nearly 2 million school children, to test the vaccine's efficacy. In the 1970s, only about 100 active and large-scale RCTs were under way each year in medicine; today it is closer to 10,000.

The first formal use of an RCT in social policy is widely considered to be the OEO's 1968 evaluation of a New Jersey pilot negative income tax, one of the initiatives of Johnson's War on Poverty. RCTs became more common in the 1970s when the Manpower Demonstration Research Corporation (MDRC) used them to evaluate other War on Poverty programs. In the years since, a handful of large foundations such as Ford and Robert Wood Johnson have used RCTs as part of their evaluation toolbox. However, these kind of large-scale evaluations are expensive, time consuming, and challenging to implement. In addition, critics argue that RCTs often fail to account for context or to explain *why* a particular intervention worked. The broad application of RCTs to evaluating social programs by either the government or philanthropy has therefore been slow.

In recent years, however, enthusiasm for RCTs has grown significantly in the social sector, and some funders such as EMCF have championed them as the gold standard of evidentiary proof. Much of the momentum has been generated by a new generation of social scientists who have imported methodologies like RCTs from the natural sciences into their own work. For example, in 2011, Esther Duflo and Abhijit Banerjee, the highly regarded MIT economists who run the Abdul Latif Jameel Poverty Action Lab (J-PAL), published *Poor Economics: A Radical Rethinking of the Way to Fight Global Poverty*, in which they draw on their field research that includes hundreds of RCTs to examine which kind of interventions (and under what conditions) successfully reduce poverty and which do not. Duflo and Banerjee's research is widely credited with transforming the field of international development, and the economics discipline more broadly, by powerfully demonstrating the parsing power of the RCT.[3]

Though more widespread in international development,[4] the RCT approach is gaining traction in domestic program evaluation. For example, economist Roland Fryer, who founded the Education Innovation Laboratory (EdLabs) at Harvard, has done pioneering work on race, inequality, and the achievement gap. His research, particularly on the effects of financial incentives for students and teachers on performance, has been highly influential, in part because of his use of RCTs. In 2011, Fryer won a MacArthur Award for the scope and innovation of his research, bringing even greater attention to the RCT approach.

‖‖‖‖‖‖‖‖‖‖‖‖‖‖‖‖‖‖‖‖‖‖‖‖‖‖‖‖‖‖‖‖‖‖‖‖‖‖‖‖‖‖‖‖‖‖‖‖

# Broad Sweep of Measurement and Evaluation in the Field

An increased emphasis on measurement and evaluation is now clearly manifest across the nonprofit sector. Recent studies suggest that many foundations, including the majority of large philanthropies, are engaged in some kind of formal evaluation of the impact of their grants; however, wide variation remains in just how foundations measure this impact, even among those that self-identify as venture.[5] As our examples have shown, in some cases, this highly quantitative approach is modeled on a kind of returns analogy; in other cases, the approach is more qualitative, focused on anecdotal data collection and often geared toward internal management. The point here is a significant cultural shift has occurred toward more goal setting and accountability and toward capturing the value of evaluation for internal (management) and external (fundraising) purposes. This change is evident not only at foundations, but, as we saw in the case of service providers like Teach For America, Jumpstart, and City Year, in the organizations they support.

As the social entrepreneurship fields matures, so, too, has the number and variety of organizations dedicated in some way to questions of measurement and evaluation. These "information intermediaries" (what Matthew Bishop and Michael Green call "virtue's middlemen")[6] include, among others, consultancies, boutique investors, research journals and graduate school programs, and all work to improve our answers to the basic "how do we know" questions of social change.

# The Role of Technology in Measurement and Evaluation

Not surprisingly, the Internet has radically changed how measurement and evaluation works in the nonprofit sector. In the early days of Internet technologies, nonprofits, just like their for-profit counterparts, scurried to understand how best to harness the web. The first and obvious impulse was for fundraising purposes; an e-donation was the nonprofit equivalent of e-commerce, with the hoped-for benefit of vastly increasing donations. Today, while most nonprofits have some kind of online fundraising strategy, many are enjoying and exploring the many broader ways the Internet has changed how the sector works. Nowhere is this more evident than in measurement and evaluation.

## Greater Transparency

In some cases, the Internet has simply allowed for greater and more transparent access to raw data about organizations. Guidestar, for example, aggregates information for nearly 2 million nonprofit organizations in the

United States, based primarily on IRS 990 forms but also on a variety of other sources (i.e., the nonprofits themselves and funders). Increasingly, Guidestar is also developing tools and services that allow users themselves to analyze the numbers. Similarly, the Better Business Bureau Wise Giving Alliance offers more in-depth evaluations and reports on some charitable nonprofits and their effectiveness with assessments of governance, finances, solicitations, website content, and donor privacy. Charity Navigator offers evaluations of approximately 6,000 large nonprofits with particular focus on financial health, accountability, and transparency of the organization, providing a four-star rating system on these measures.

## Facilitate Giving

A number of websites have emerged to facilitate giving, such as GlobalGiving, Give Well, Great Nonprofits, Philanthropy In/Sight, Just Give, Network for Good, iGive, and Donors Choose, among others. These organizations vary significantly in just how much vetting and due diligence they provide prospective donors. Philanthropedia, for example, aims to give expert opinion and analysis of particular organizations, a rating system, and expert mutual funds that allow donors to give to a group of preselected nonprofits. It claims to rely on verification from purported experts who have evaluated a much smaller number of nonprofits. In contrast, Great Nonprofits relies on a *crowdsource* approach, allowing anyone to post a review of or an experience with a particular nonprofit organization. By design, these testimonies are meant to be personal, anecdotal, and unfiltered.

## Expert versus Democratic Measurement and Evaluation

The crowdsource approach raises interesting questions about impact assessment. Unlike, say, a small group of PhD experts performing RCTs in the field or overseeing programs within a foundation (or even their online equivalent at a place like Philanthropedia), crowdsourcing represents a highly democratic approach to evaluation. It encourages participation, which some regard as civic engagement, but what about accuracy or rigor of analysis? What does crowdsource, or open-source more generally, tell us about the role of technology in the social sector? This question is pursued in the next chapter.

# Chapter 5

||||||||||||||||||||||||||||||||||||||||||||||||||||||||||||||||||||||||||||

# TECHNOLOGY AS A
# FORCE FOR GOOD

A number of funders have been exploring the broad intersection of technology and social change in ways that have had a profound impact on the social sector. In particular, they are harnessing the power of *crowdsource* as a kind of market model, not in the classical neoliberal economic definition but in a wisdom-of-crowds sense.[1]

## Open Innovation and Social Change

For social entrepreneurship, the first of two notable features of this *crowdsource* market has to do with "collective intelligence" and the notion that large numbers of people express opinions that, in aggregate, represent a kind of preference for a good or service that can be more meaningful or "smarter" than the opinion of any one individual. The second has to do with breadth. Because Internet technologies allow for unprecedented reach, they have the potential to unearth innovative ideas from participants in a way that resembles *design thinking* in the private sector. Not surprisingly, many of these early crowdsource experiments have come from social entrepreneurs with previous lives in the tech sector.

## Case's Giving Challenges

The Case Foundation, created in 1997 by AOL founder Steve Case and his wife, Jean, has led the way in testing how technology in general and the Internet in particular can be used to promote social change.

In 2007, Case launched the first major social media–driven philanthropic contests, two Giving Challenges. Case partnered with *Parade* magazine and Facebook's *Causes* to encourage participants to champion a cause and spread the word about it through their social networks. The idea was to incent giving and civic engagement. Over a six-week period, *Causes* Giving Challenge awarded $1,000 daily to the cause that attracted the most unique donations in a single day. America's Giving Challenge awarded four national and four global charities $50,000 each for encouraging the most people to donate to their cause. Overall, these first online challenges raised nearly $2 million from 80,000 donors.

That same year, Case also introduced the Make It Your Own Awards in which individuals or small groups of people working on community projects submitted applications, reviewed first by judges and then voted on by the online community. The winners received grants of up to $35,000 each.

The Case competitions spurred others. In 2009, when Case launched a second round of America's Giving Challenges, similar online contests underway included the Chase Community Giving Contest, the Pepsi Refresh Project, and American Express's Members Project, each of which, in different ways, invited participants to sponsor ideas to address a given problem and to vote for cash-prize winners. These early contests were important "laboratories of giving behavior,"[2] experiments with social media and Web 2.0 tools for a new kind of engagement and participant philanthropy, which would also pave the way for today's peer-to-peer lending and crowdfunding entities such as DonorsChoose, Kiva, Microventures, Kickstarter, and SoFi. More broadly, these contests provided an early demonstration of the power of crowdsource to identify problems and direct resources to them.

|||||||||||||||||||||||||||||||||||||||||||||||||||||||||||||||||

## Crowdfunding

Some of today's innovative crowdfunding exchanges and companies have their roots in these original open source experiments.

DonorsChoose.org allows public school teachers from across the United States to post classroom requests (ranging from pencils to violins to microscope slides and everything in between), and citizen philanthropist donors give money in support of those projects. In return, donors receive photos of the project in action, thank-you notes, and cost reports from the teachers.

SoFi ("where social meets finance") harnesses the power of online communities to address some of the problems of the U.S. student loan market. SoFi connects students and alumni of the same university through dedicated lending pools. The idea is that alumni earn "a compelling double bottom line return," students receive loans at a lower rate than they could via commercial or federal options, and both sides benefit from the longer-term connection.

Kiva is an online nonprofit that allows donors to lend to poor people in developing countries via Kiva's field partner microfinance institutions (and is therefore not literally peer-to-peer); loans are repaid, but any interest on these loans is returned to a donors' account, where it can be used for further lending or to support Kiva's operations. Microplace is similar to Kiva, but as a for-profit, Microplace returns the amount loaned plus interest to investors.

Kickstarter is a funding platform for a broad spectrum of creative projects across the visual and performing arts, as well as journalism, food, fashion, film, video games, and a range of other endeavors. Kickstarter is for-profit; it does not charge to list but collects a fee of 5 percent of the amount raised for all successfully funded projects. As of 2012, Kickstarter had raised $20 million for 20,000 projects.

|||||||||||||||||||||||||||||||||||||||||||||||||||||||||||||||||

## InnoCentive and Open Innovation

Case was not the only philanthropy working in this space. In 2006, as part of its new Advancing Innovation initiative, the Rockefeller Foundation partnered with a company called InnoCentive, which hosted an online global scientific community "to achieve innovative solutions to complex challenges." Firms posted scientific problems, confidentially, on the InnoCentive website, and InnoCentive would invite its community of 85,000 scientists and scientific organizations to come together to try to solve them for financial awards of $100,000 or more. Although most of the first organizations InnoCentive worked with were companies such as Boeing, Dow Chemical, Eli Lilly, and Proctor & Gamble, it soon became clear that this crowdsourcing approach could lend itself to solving a broad array of complex social problems beyond science and medicine.

In 2006, Rockefeller supported 10 challenges on the InnoCentive platform and achieved an 80 percent success rate in finding solutions. One of the most successful was posted by SunNight Solar, which looked to improve the design of a solar flashlight so that it could light an entire room. (For light at nighttime, nearly 2 billion people in poor countries rely on kerosene, lanterns, candles, or single-use battery flashlights, light sources that are often expensive, dangerous, and harmful to the environment.) The challenge was ultimately solved by an engineer in New Zealand, and today the flashlight is being used widely across the developing world.

In 2009, Rockefeller partnered a second time with InnoCentive and GlobalGiving for the Global Giveback Innovation Challenge. In this challenge, GlobalGiving used crowdsourcing to reach out to their 800 project leaders in 80 countries to generate ideas about potential challenges. After careful evaluation, GlobalGiving selected five water-related challenges, which it then presented to the InnoCentive network, where the challenges were posted for three months and where hundreds of thousands of experts could crowdsource solutions. Rockefeller provided $40,000 in cash prizes for each winning solution: an easy-to-use method to make water from Lake Victoria in Africa potable; an indicator to tell users when water exposed to UV light had been disinfected; a low-cost rainwater storage tank for Indian wetlands; a small-scale river turbine to electrify schools and medical clinics in the Peruvian jungle; and a water tank that would more efficiently use titanium oxide nanoparticles to sterilize drinking water.

Today, InnoCentive has a community of millions of problem solvers and lists and solves challenges ranging from vaccine production to oil spill recovery. In a study of hundreds of these challenges, Harvard Business

School Professor Karim Lakhani and his colleagues found that 30 percent of these problems that had evaded solution by the traditional R&D approaches of the companies prior to their InnoCentive post were solved by the InnoCentive network.[3]

Among InnoCentive's early backers was eBay founder Pierre Omidyar, whose Omidyar Network, a mission-based investment group, is premised on the belief that "every individual has the power to make a difference" and on the kind of marketplace model of economic democracy and self-empowerment that Omidyar believes eBay promotes. As we will see in the chapters that follow, Omidyar's Network supports many social entrepreneurship activities along these lines, among them open source and open innovation platforms.

## Ashoka Change Makers

Omidyar was also an early and ardent supporter of Ashoka. In the late 1990s, as the field of social entrepreneurship began to take hold in the United States and Ashoka pondered its role in promoting the field further, Omidyar encouraged Bill Drayton and Ashoka's then president Sushmita Ghosh to consider basic and existential questions about the organization: What really drives Ashoka? What was it trying to achieve? Ashoka had begun to think more broadly about change making and about a world in which everyone, not just one in 10 million exceptional social entrepreneurs, could make a difference. Omidyar's faith in individual empowerment was profoundly influential.

For Ghosh, Omidyar's eBay offered an important analogy for Ashoka. If Ashoka hoped to build a world in which everyone was a change maker, could technology be harnessed to build a more competitive citizen sector to advance social change? To this end, Ghosh believed that Changemakers, which began life as Ashoka's print magazine for social entrepreneurship before migrating in the 1990s to the web, offered a natural portal for a more open source approach to social entrepreneurship. The idea for the new Changemakers, similar to InnoCentive, was to create online competitions to generate solutions to social problems.

Ashoka soon found that people were eager to participate, and funders, both philanthropic and commercial, were increasingly interested in underwriting these kinds of challenges. Between 2004 and 2011, Ashoka hosted more than 50 online competitions, with more than $600 million passing to social innovations and hundreds of thousands of participants: 11,000 entries from 125 countries. Among the many sponsors, eBay supported competitions on jobs and employment, the Robert Wood Johnson Foundation on health, and Google on citizen journalism. According to Ghosh, the drama of the time-bound competition is critical for mobilizing innovators and a wide range of participants, which has grown to include major corporations, individual business executives, foundations, teams of scientists, school children, the U.S. army, major universities, local municipalities, and just about everyone in between. Ghosh notes that the competitions have "crazy unintended connections and consequences" and new idea generation occurs by "connecting these synapses."

## Design Thinking Applied to the Social Sector

Social entrepreneurs working on open innovation apply a kind of *design thinking* to problems of poverty. Design thinking does not necessarily require technology; it is a business practice that relies on insights from consumer behavior to inform product or service design. However, technology can enhance the way companies or nonprofits collect or combine consumer and user-generated information to advance their work.

The concept of design thinking originated in the private sector, where it means different things at different companies. In 2007, Toyota famously employed design thinking to launch the Tundra truck, extending the principle of *genchi genbutsu* — the idea that engineers should "walk around" the shop floor — into the field, where they spent time with farmers, construction workers, contractors, and loggers across the United States to better understand the diverse needs of American truck drivers. The result: the Tundra was offered in 31 design variations, with differences in features ranging from capacity and fuel efficiency to gearshift location and size of radio knobs (bigger for pickup owners who wear gloves).[4]

Similarly, eBay's Previz, an internal design thinking consulting unit within the company, shows how technology can be used to better understand and serve customers. Previz relies on consumer research to develop early product prototypes, which users then help refine. For example, eBay Local, a site that allows users to search for goods based on price and proximity, was developed via a Previz prototype.[5]

IDEO is a design firm that applies principles of design thinking to problems of poverty. According to Tim Brown, IDEO's CEO, "Design thinking is accessible as an approach to innovation in a way that technical R&D is not. . . . Design thinking is centered on innovating through the eyes of the end user and as such encourages in-the-field research that builds empathy for people, which results in deeper insights about their unmet needs."[6]

Although much design thinking in social entrepreneurship remains relatively low tech (e.g., the development of a syringe that breaks automatically after one shot to avoid unsterile reuse), open innovation technology can often enhance the process. That original SunNight solar flashlight, for example, was popular in Africa, but field researchers from the World Bank and the Department of Energy noted that it had failed to replace kerosene lamps because it could not light up an entire room. The innovator posted the challenge on InnoCentive, where it was ultimately solved by an engineer in New Zealand, with parts manufactured by a company in China. Today, the BoGo Light is distributed across Africa, Gaza, Haiti, and elsewhere.

# Chapter 6

||||||||||||||||||||||||||||||||||||||||||||||||||||||||||||||||||||||||

# THE PULL OF PRIZES

In the face of market failure, a number of philanthropists have begun to experiment with a range of new tools that help mitigate risk for innovators working to solve entrenched social problems.

## Prizes

In this sense, the Ashoka and InnoCentive–style challenges described in the previous chapter are part of a more sweeping trend toward the use of prizes in the social sector. Although the public and private sectors have long used prizes to incent innovation, particularly in the areas of science and technology, the past decade has seen an enormous growth in private philanthropy prizes for other areas of human activity, including social services and poverty alleviation. This change should not be surprising; prizes naturally lend themselves to the new philanthropic wealth and its size, appetite for risk, and faith in the market notion that competition incents innovation.[1]

Jonathan Bays of McKinsey & Company has documented the growth in the number, size, and objectives of the philanthropic *prize industry*,[2] tracing its history back centuries to the first prizes used by monarchies, universities, and commercial associations to generate solutions for a broad range of social problems. Perhaps the most cited example is the Longitudinal Prize of 1714, which led to the development of the marine chronometer, an instrument invented by clockmaker John Harrison to determine longitude at sea. Prizes in Revolutionary and then Napoleonic France to address army food shortages produced preservation techniques similar to modern canning. The Royal Agriculture Society of England regularly used prizes in the nineteenth and early twentieth centuries, and Charles Lindbergh's successful nonstop flight between New York and Paris earned him the Orteig Prize.

According to Bays, the growth of patents and grants in the second half of the twentieth century diminished the relative importance of prizes, but in the last 30 years, they have enjoyed a renaissance. In the most recent decade in particular, philanthropic prize capital has burgeoned beyond $375 million for 200 current prizes; more than 60 prizes with a value totaling $250 million have emerged since 2000. Bays notes that nearly 80 percent of the new prize money has been dedicated to inducement-style prizes that focus on achieving a specific future goal rather than on recognition of past accomplishments (e.g., prizes such as the Pulitzer and Nobel).

Yet even this simple categorization no longer holds, as philanthropists use prizes today to achieve any number of objectives. Bays offers a useful taxonomy of prizes: point solution (to solve a well-defined problem, such as InnoCentive's solar flashlight); participation (to educate, change behavior, or simply encourage engagement, as in the Case challenges); network (to celebrate and strengthen a particular community); exposition (to highlight a range of best practices, ideas, or opportunities within a field); exemplar (to set standards or influence perception); and market stimulation (to build a market by driving costs down through competition, exposing latent demand).

## Market Stimulation: Helping to Build Markets

Many prizes, of course, combine elements of each of these categories, and some are particularly focused on shaping markets where none exist. Consider the X-Prizes. Founded in 1995 by Dr. Peter Diamandis, the X-Prize Foundation aims to stimulate "radical breakthroughs for the benefit of humanity" by designing and administering prizes that are underwritten by nonprofit or commercial sponsors for at least $10 million. The Ansari

X Prize, for example, helped create an entirely new personal spaceflight industry by stimulating the market for commercial space travel. Since the prize closed in 2004 (with SpaceShipOne's winning flights), more than $1 billion has been invested in the industry.

Other X prizes are equally audacious. The Progressive Automotive X Prize, focused on climate change, awarded prizes in three competitions to design, build, and race extremely energy-efficient vehicles that could be manufactured for the mass market. The Google Lunar X Prize (commonly known as Moon 2.0) will award $30 million to the first team that successfully lands a robot, and has it travel 500 meters, on the moon; the Archon Genomics X Prize seeks a less expensive, more efficient human genome matching technique. The idea is that over the long term, these prizes will help foster markets for socially useful products, services, and industries.

## Pay for Success

Prizes also exemplify another principle of the social entrepreneurship movement: pay for success. By design, prizes shift risk from sponsors to competitors by paying awards only for successful achievement of a defined goal, which has long been the appeal of prizes to the private sector. Increasingly, as philanthropists and government entities look to improve return on investment, a contingent payout can be a more attractive than a conventional grant or contract that guarantees payment regardless of performance.

The prize landscape is still evolving. While many prizes remain focused on technical solutions to social challenges, others try to address more complex problems of social change, such as the Mo Ibrahim Foundation Prize for Achievement in African Leadership, founded in 2007 and awarded to a former African head of state who has demonstrated excellence in leadership and governance. In addition, while many prizes are still large and prodigiously ambitious in scope, InnoCentive founders Alpheus Bingham and Dwayne Spradlin note that "prize philanthropy is rapidly moving 'down-scale' to seek modular, turnkey solutions that are *part* of a bigger ecology in global problem solving."[3] Along these lines, in May 2012, the X Prize and Robin Hood foundations announced plans to jointly sponsor a $1 million prize to fight poverty in New York City, likely to focus on homelessness, access to education, or health care.

# Advanced Market Commitments

Like prizes and challenges, advanced market commitments (AMCs) offer another way large philanthropies (and governments, as we will see further on) can influence or shape markets to create social change.

## Market Failure in Public Health

Today, only 10 percent of global health research and development is devoted to diseases that affect 90 percent of the world's population. For example, AIDS and malaria together cause the deaths of millions of people each year, yet no effective vaccines exist for them nor for many other diseases that disproportionately affect the poor, even when we know that vaccines represent highly cost-effective public health interventions. Pharmaceutical companies have little financial incentive to invest in their development and production, because total market size for all vaccines in developing countries is estimated to be $500 million a year.[4]

In response to this market failure, some foundations support the development of new drugs, traditionally employing a *push* approach, often public-private partnerships in which the philanthropic investor underwrites some of the R&D costs directly to vaccine researchers or subsidizes the production cost. Recently, however, the GAVI Alliance has pioneered a *pull* model in which it harnesses market forces by focusing on demand rather than supply.

## GAVI's Innovative Pull Model

The GAVI Alliance (formerly the Global Alliance for Vaccines and Immunisation) offers a compelling example of market shaping in the face of traditional market failure: a public-private global health partnership designed to save children's lives by increasing access to immunization in poor countries.

GAVI was launched in 2000 at a time when the distribution of vaccines to children in the poorest parts of the world had begun to falter. Created with a $750 million commitment from the Gates Foundation, GAVI brings together a consortium of NGOs and funders, multilateral institutions like the World Health Organization (WHO), the World Bank, UNICEF, the vaccine industry, and governments from developed and developing countries to expand mass vaccination programs. Countries eligible for GAVI support determine their immunization needs, apply for funding, co-finance the cost of the vaccine, and implement the vaccine program. Since its founding, GAVI has helped to immunize 288 million children against life-threatening diseases, including diphtheria, tetanus, pertussis (whooping cough), hepatitis B, HIV, and yellow fever. According to WHO estimates, GAVI has helped prevent more than 5 million deaths.

GAVI has pioneered a number of new financing mechanisms for public health programs. For example, it helped launch the International Finance Facility for Immunisation (IFFIm) to accelerate the availability and predictability of funds for immunization. The IFFIm raises funds by issuing bonds in the capital markets and uses long-term government pledges as a financial guarantee and to repay interest.

In 2007, GAVI created the first advanced market commitment (AMC), an innovative funding instrument to incent vaccine development. The concept is relatively simple: purchase commitments from donor governments mitigate investment risk for pharmaceutical companies. Wealthy governments contractually agree to buy a certain number of treatments at a specified price, low-income countries also commit to a kind of copayment, and in exchange for the guarantee pharmaceutical companies are legally bound to provide the vaccines, tailored to the needs of developing countries, at a fraction of the price charged in the industrialized world.[5]

In 2009, the development of a pneumococcal vaccine—a vaccine against the most common cause of pneumonia, which claims the lives of 1 million people annually—presented GAVI with an opportunity to test the AMC concept and create a legally binding forward commitment of $1.5 billion from GAVI, donor governments, and governments receiving the vaccine. The intent of Pneumo AMC pilot is to reduce morbidity and mortality from pneumococcal diseases; estimates suggest it could save 7 million lives by 2030. To date 14 countries have introduced pneumococcal vaccines into their national immunization programs through the AMC, with an additional 39 countries expected to follow suit before the end of 2013.

The GAVI pilot is also crucially important as a model of risk mitigation. Unlike traditional push funding models, this one is distinctly pull—cash on delivery, pay-for-performance—and therefore offers a kind of market-shaping solution to a market failure, with potential application to fields such as clean energy, agriculture, or other areas of human service provision traditionally ignored by private capital markets.

# Chapter 7

||||||||||||||||||||||||||||||||||||||||||||||||||||||||||||||||||||||||||||

# ACTIVIST ASSETS

In addition to market-shaping tools such as prizes and AMCs, many funders now pursue innovation through more activist use of their financial resources, particularly at endowed foundations. Executives and trustees have begun to think about how they, as shareholders and investors, can better use their philanthropic assets to advance the mission of their organizations.

## Active Ownership: Screening and Shareholder Activism

### Screening

For years, many foundations have engaged in the kind of socially responsible investing (SRI) that applies a filter—a positive or negative screen on environmental, social, and governance factors—to the companies in which they invest their endowments. Screening can occur in various ways, from passive indexes to actively managed portfolios structured around a particular theme or issue. Negative screening is the most common form of SRI; avoiding investments in companies engaged in undesirable activities is perhaps the easiest way to align asset ownership with philanthropic mission. In 2002, for example, when the Rockefeller

Foundation initiated a grantmaking program to combat smoking in Asia, it also stopped investing in tobacco companies. Similarly, in 2007, the Boston Foundation divested in companies that engaged in business with the government in Sudan, which had been helping to finance the military conflict in Darfur.

The SRI field has grown dramatically in recent years. In 1990, Amy Domini broke ground with the creation of her Domini Social Equity Fund, which screened investments according to a basic set of environmental and social standards. Today, the Domini 400 Social Index, a market cap-weighted stock index of 400 publicly traded companies that have met certain environmental, social, and governance (ESG) standards, is one of many indices and funds that screens companies for their positive records on issues such as employee and human relations, product safety, environmental stewardship, and corporate governance, as well as for negative activities or locus of operations. Companies engaged in the business of alcohol, tobacco, firearms, gambling, nuclear power, or military weapons are almost always excluded. By some estimates, SRI assets in the United States rose 325 percent from $639 billion in 1995 to $3 trillion in 2012.

## Shareholder Activism

Some foundations use shareholder activism to exercise their voice on a range of corporate governance issues when they hold a significant stake in a company. In recent years, this kind of activism has taken various forms, such as proxy voting, filing shareholder resolutions, or direct engagement with companies and their directors on a number of corporate practices.

The Educational Foundation of America (EFA), for example, was highly successful in its efforts to help shape product content at Coca-Cola. Soon after EFA filed a resolution asking the company to use 2.5 percent recycled content in its plastic bottles, Coke introduced 2.5 percent— and subsequently 10 percent—recycled content into three-quarters of its plastic beverage containers. This change encouraged competitors to follow suit, and eventually Pepsi matched this commitment to recycled content use.

Although much shareholder activism from foundations focuses on these kinds of environmental matters, many philanthropies take on other policy issues as well. In 2008, the New York–based Jesse Smith Noyes

Foundation engaged in proxy voting for shareholder resolutions at more than 300 companies, voting for boards of directors or withholding votes when the number of women on the slate was insufficient, and supporting shareholder resolutions on executive compensation (known as say-on-pay) and the adoption of global human rights standards, among others. The $400 million Nathan Cummings Foundation has been particularly influential on corporate policy on climate change, health care, and political contributions. Cummings has also filed successful say-on-pay resolutions at Apple, Walmart, United Health Care Group, Wells Fargo, Chesapeake Energy, and at others firms, perhaps most notably at Goldman Sachs, where it led a coalition of investors, including several orders of nuns, on the issue of executive compensation. Cummings has also successfully pressed companies such as eBay to declassify its board of directors and News Corp. to release more information about its political spending. Cummings's landmark report on its experience changing corporate behavior through shareholder activism has become a kind of how-to guide for other philanthropies.[1]

Some foundations have also begun to work in concert to amplify their shareholder sway. In recent years, a number of intermediaries have emerged to help channel, encourage, and coordinate philanthropic activism, including organizations like As You Sow that "use shareholder advocacy and the financial markets to catalyze positive change within publicly held companies."

## Proactive Investment: Mission- and Program-Related Investments, a Precursor to Impact Investing

Beyond screening and shareholder activism, a number of foundations that include traditional philanthropies as well as their newer "venture" brethren have become more proactive investors in their use of endowment assets to advance their charitable objectives. Broadly speaking, mission investing can take two forms: program-related investments (PRIs), which typically come out of the 5 percent required payout foundations must make to their grantees, and the larger class of mission-related investments (MRI), which refers to investments made with the corpus of the organization's endowment (the remaining 95 percent of the institution's assets).

Traditionally, PRIs have taken the form of below-market investments in nonprofits for charitable purposes, typically loans, loan guarantees, or linked deposits for grantees to build things such as affordable housing or other community development work.

When it comes to the larger corpus, however, most foundations have been reluctant to make investments that yield concessionary returns, because the opportunity cost of these investments and forgoing market rate returns in more conventional investments today mean fewer assets available for philanthropic grants in the future. Critics of mission-related investing therefore argue that prudent, conventional investments are a better and more reliable route to funding social impact, since protecting the endowment helps preserve or grow assets for future philanthropic work.

## Increased Use of PRIs

Although PRIs are not new, more foundations are using them more frequently. This increase marks an important step in how philanthropy finances the work of the social sector and how government agencies and commercial investors approach social impact. PRIs first formally appeared on the philanthropic scene in 1968, when the Ford Foundation began making direct, low-interest charitable loans to some of its grantees. The following year, the Tax Reform Act of 1969 legally defined these kinds of investments as PRIs, paving the way for foundations like MacArthur, Packard, Rockefeller, and others to deploy them more broadly.

The initial growth in the use of PRIs, not surprisingly, coincided with the growth of the field of community development in the 1970s and 1980s, which required capital, often at below-market rates, to finance enterprise and construction in underserved areas. The evolution of the community field, and the Community Development Financial Institutions (CDFIs) that channeled PRIs to low-income communities, is explored at length in Chapter 12.

## The Heron Foundation

In the past decade, the number of foundations engaged in mission investing has doubled, and the dollars invested this way have tripled. Most of the growth in both mission-related investing (MRI) and program-related investing (PRI) has occurred at small and medium-sized philanthropies, such as the $250 million Heron Foundation in New York City. Founded in 1992, Heron has played a prominent role in advancing the MRI and PRI fields. In 1996, Heron's board of directors examined how to use the corpus of its endowment to further its charitable objectives. In the fifteen years following, Heron managed to preserve the value of its endowment by making "core support" grants within the 5 percent payout IRS requirement *and* by directing nearly 50 percent of its endowment to finance projects that might not otherwise find affordable capital in the commercial markets. In 2012, Heron moved boldly again, committing the full 100 percent of its endowment to mission investing.

Heron's leadership, track record, and its road map for mission investing have provided a model for the field (see Figure 7.1).[2]

Heron contends that this integrated approach of grants, PRIs, and MRIs enhances its philanthropic impact and belies the notion that effective philanthropy requires a Chinese wall to separate endowment and charitable investing. Heron's PRI returns are hardly anomalous. A report from FSG Social Impact Advisors (2007) shows that, over a 40-year period, 96 percent of loans made to nonprofits by foundations have been repaid. These findings went a long way toward reassuring foundation officers concerned about the risks of PRIs. Even in a strong market, low beta investments in the social sector can offer smaller but consistent yields.[3]

**Figure 7.1** F. B. Heron Foundation Mission-Related Investing Continuum

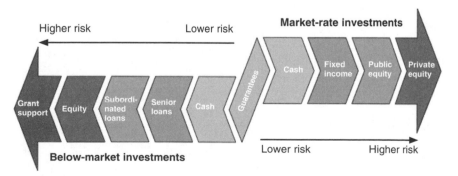

Source: Used with the permission of the F. B. Heron Foundation.

It is not only perceived risk, however, that has discouraged foundation executives from making MRIs and PRIs. Many, often rightly, believe they lack the financial expertise to evaluate program-related investments. In response, a number of organizations have emerged to help foundations overcome this obstacle. The PRI Makers Network, for example, is an association of 90 PRI grant makers that provides tools, professional development, and other resources to foundations engaged in program-related investing. More for Mission is a campaign organized by the Annie E. Casey and Heron foundations and the Meyer Memorial Trust to advance mission investing and to encourage foundations to spend an additional 2 percent of assets—or an industry total of $10 billion—on PRIs. Consultancies also offer expertise in mission investing. And collaborations between foundations have created social investment vehicles such as Living Cities Catalyst Fund ($20 million in debt capital) for community-based organizations around the country that work on urban development. For foundations new to mission investing, Living Cities allows them to "leverage the experience of the pioneers of the PRI field" without having to hire their own specialized staff.[4]

## More Sophisticated Use of PRIs: How Blended Capital Can Shape Markets

Collaboration between PRI makers has also taken the form of co-investing. The emergence of syndicates of philanthropic investors has served as a kind of market-shaping function when foundations take a first-loss position as a lender, reducing risk for commercial investors to join social purpose projects. Increasingly, these *blended* or *stacked* investments that fuse capital sources include foundations that use guarantees or deposits, not just conventional loans. The following examples also show how innovators in the nonprofit, private, and public sectors are using PRIs as part of a large capital blend to advance social change.

### Freelancers Union

In 2009, to provide its members with better health insurance coverage and more competitive rates, the nonprofit Freelancers Union (profiled in Chapter 2) created Freelancers Insurance Company (FIC), a wholly owned for-profit health insurance subsidiary incorporated in, and therefore regulated by, New York State. To fund FIC, founder Sara Horowitz brought together the Ford Foundation, Prudential Social Investments, and the newly formed New York State Health Foundation to make PRI loans to the new company. She combined their senior debt investments (which also included a loan from the New York City Investment Fund, "a private fund with a civic mission"[5]) with grants from the Rockefeller Foundation and the Robert Wood Johnson Foundation and some of the organization's own cash, and then reinvested, or downstreamed, the entire amount as equity in FIC. The FIC subsidiary provides affordable, comprehensive health insurance to more than 20,000 freelancers, their spouses, and dependents in New York State. The insurer pays dividends to the Freelancers Union, which uses the cash to repay its low-interest PRIs. Beyond covering its thousands of direct beneficiaries, the Freelancers Union uses the proceeds to help its more than 130,000 members outside of New York State find affordable health care insurance.

## New York City Acquisition Fund

The New York City Acquisition Fund, formed in 2006 by then New York City Housing Commissioner Shaun Donovan, offers another innovative example of PRI use. To create the fund, Donovan assembled a number of philanthropies (Ford, Robin Hood, Heron, Rockefeller, Starr Foundation, New York Community Trust, Gimbel Foundation, Open Society Institute, and MacArthur, among others) and commercial investors (Bank of American, J.P.Morgan, HSBC) to finance affordable housing. The fund was designed to use public and philanthropic dollars to remove risk for private investors, eventually securing $230 million to help nonprofit housing groups and small developers compete for private land sales, and to produce or preserve 30,000 low-cost apartments over the decade. The fund (explored in more detail in Chapter 14) works because the city guarantees permanent financing, if necessary, for projects that would be unable to secure construction funding from mainstream financial capital markets. Donovan was able to do this in part because of the PRI commitments of various foundations, often in the form of subordinated, low-interest loans and loan guarantees.[6]

||||||||||||||||||||||||||||||||||||||||||||||||||||||||||||||||||||||||

## Environmental PRIs

Many social entrepreneurs in the environmental community are considering ways in which program-related investments can advance their work. The David and Lucile Packard Foundation, for example, has been a leader in making environmental PRIs. These PRIs have included, among others, a $1 million investment in Ecotrust Forest Management, a fund set up by Ecotrust, an Oregon-based nonprofit conservation organization, which acquires forest land in the western United States and Canada and earns revenue using ecologically sound management of those properties, and $5 million in the form of a low-interest loan to help the Nature Conservancy purchase and conserve 2,325 acres of land surrounding Independence Lake, protecting its native fishery resources and watershed. That PRI served a critical bridge capital function, because the initial philanthropic grants from other sources were contingent upon California state bond sales, which were delayed by the 2010 budget crisis.

||||||||||||||||||||||||||||||||||||||||||||||||||||||||||||||||||||||||

# The Gates Foundation: PRIs Go from Debt to Equity

In September 2010, the PRI landscape morphed again when the Gates Foundation announced it was allocating $400 million in nongranting financial instruments to advance its antipoverty work. Like many Gates initiatives, this foray into PRIs was not the first in the field, but its scale and high profile set an important precedent for other philanthropic investors.

Gates indicated that its PRIs would be used for low-interest loans, guarantees for nonprofits, and in some cases equity investments in companies or investment funds that advanced the foundation's charitable objectives in global public health and development and American public education. From the outset, Gates committed to returning any profits to the foundation for further grant or PRI investment. The foundation also recognized that, not unlike a large prize, these equity investments could demonstrate the commercial viability of a particular firm or industry, in turn attracting other mainstream investors, thereby playing a market-shaping role.

The bulk of the first Gates PRIs were mostly conventional, like the guarantees it made for the bond offerings for KIPP and Aspire Public Schools, two of the country's leading charter school management corporations, to help build new schools. However, Gates also made a small number of equity investments in for-profit companies, such as Liquida Technologies, which develops particle-based vaccines and therapeutics, and Inigral, an education technology company.

Gates also invested in two African funds: $7 million in one targeting health businesses, and $10 million in the African Agricultural Capital Fund. The latter is another prime example of a blended investment structure with two different tranches, each earning different rates of return consistent with the risk taken or instrument issued: $8 million from J.P.Morgan invested as senior unsecured debt, 50 percent guaranteed by U.S. AID, and $17 million in equity from foundations ($10 million from Gates, $5 million from Gatsby, and $2 million from Rockefeller).

In 2012, Gates announced it was increasing its PRI pool to $1 billion, approximately 25 percent of which will be used to finance debt instruments or make equity investments in profit-making entities.

# Chapter 8

||||||||||||||||||||||||||||||||||||||||||||||||||||||||||||||||||||||||||||||

# FROM ENTREPRENEURSHIP TO ENTERPRISE

The entry of the Gates Foundation and others into the PRI field, and in particular the use of these tools as equity investments, has brought significant attention to the role of charitable investments in social purpose business. However, the Gates move, while high profile, reflects a larger and subtle but important shift in emphasis from social *entrepreneurship* to social *enterprise*, and the belief that businesses can go further toward achieving social impact than their nonprofit counterparts.

## Self-Sustaining Revenues, Scale, Organizational and Individual Self-Sufficiency

In some ways, this shift toward social enterprise represents a natural extension of efficient social capital markets theory. Recall the venture philanthropy lament about the "woeful" inefficiency of nonprofit financing and how expensive and time consuming it is to raise money in the nonprofit sector where performance metrics are sorely lacking. (By some estimates, it costs $22 to $43 for a nonprofit to raise $100 in the United States, versus $2 to $4 for companies.)[1] Of course, no one understands this better than nonprofit executives themselves, who often spend 80 percent of their time fundraising. It is not surprising that in the 1990s, we saw a number of entrepreneurial nonprofits hunt for more self-sustaining sources of revenue; think City Year Enterprise's forays into retail clothing, one of many examples of nonprofits entering the enterprise fray.

Concerns about organizational self-sufficiency are also a kind of extrapolation of age-old thinking about individual self-sufficiency. Little new can be found in the credo that "teaching a man to fish" is both morally and economically superior to enabling lifelong dependence on charity. ("Give a man a fish and you feed him for a day; teach a man to fish and you feed him for a lifetime.") This belief spans the political spectrum and is an essential aspect of American faith in individual ingenuity and enterprise. Thanks to the success of microenterprise lending, it also has become a central tenet of the international development paradigm.

In recent years, a number of hybrid structures and charitable investment funds supporting social purpose businesses have attempted to get at this independence issue at both the individual and organizational levels. By investing in the self-sustaining livelihoods of poor people in a way that virtuously recycles the capital for reinvestment and scale, this new approach to philanthropy has planted the seeds for a new kind of social impact capitalism.

# The Hybrids: Omidyar and Google

## The Omidyar Network

Before the Gates Foundation made headlines with its PRI investments, Pierre Omidyar had been using these and other charitable investment tools to demonstrate the financial viability of particular firms and industries traditionally ignored by commercial investors. The Omidyar school of social entrepreneurship and its distinct enterprise orientation have profoundly shaped the field.

In 1998, following eBay's IPO, Omidyar and his then fiancée (now wife), Pam, established a private family foundation. Over time, as Omidyar became a more serious and full-time philanthropist he began to make a clear distinction between *charity* (giving to relieve immediate suffering) and *philanthropy* (from the Latin "love of humanity," aimed at solving the root cause of problems). Furthermore, Omidyar hoped to tackle the problems of poverty with the scale and social impact of eBay.

In 2004, the Omidyars created the Omidyar Network, a limited liability corporation, which would allow them to invest in for-profit entities while using the foundation to make grants. This hybrid model was the first of its kind. "We were breaking new ground here," notes Omidyar. "Our attorneys had never seen a structure like this."[2] In 2007, Omidyar moved more formally to a venture capital–style firm while still relying on "the levers of for-profit when necessary and the levers of nonprofit when necessary." As such, the Omidyar Network describes itself as "a philanthropic investment firm dedicated to harnessing the power of markets to create opportunity for people to improve their lives. We invest in and help scale innovative organizations to catalyze economic and social change."[3] In addition to grants and for-profit investments, the Network can also engage in political lobbying, something legally outside the purview of a traditional foundation. To date, the Omidyar Network has committed a total of $442 million: $239 in nonprofit grants and $203 million in for-profit investments.

As we have seen, Omidyar has supported a number of open innovation efforts and platforms. He has also played a particularly influential role in the field of microlending, where the Network has made more than $20 million in PRIs (including a limited partnership stake in Unitus Equity Fund, the private equity arm of the nonprofit Unitus), helping to demonstrate the commercial viability of microfinance and, in the process, attracting a number of more mainstream venture capitalist and private equity investors to the field.

## Google.org

Though Omidyar was one of the first to pioneer the hybrid approach, others quickly followed. In 2006, Google created Google.org, a hybrid that would allow Google to invest in both nonprofits and for-profits. Google initially committed $1 billion to Google.org, which, like the Omidyar Network, would be able to back start-up companies, lobby legislatures, and engage in a number of activities beyond the purview of a traditional foundation. Like Omidyar, Larry Brilliant—the doctor, civil rights activist, and "global health warrior"[4] turned tech entrepreneur who was tapped to head Google.org—believed the hybrid structure would allow him to "play with every key on the keyboard."[5]

As a for-profit entity, Google.org, like the Omidyar Network, could enter into equity and debt transactions with company resources (in addition to the $1 billion, Google's founders pledged "approximately 1 percent of [Google's] equity and profits in some form"[6]) and write checks to nonprofits from the Google foundation, which was encompassed within Google.org. Google's initial plans for the new entity were grand. The organization intended to focus on "the poorest and the weakest of the world" but in a way consistent with "the Google DNA," said Brilliant, meaning any potential initiative had to be "a big enough idea."[7] Brilliant and his team chose international development, global public health, and climate change (including $45 million in renewable energy research and emerging technologies) for their initial hybrid investments.

Even though scale for each investment area was a paramount concern, Google.org was also eager to ensure that "Google had a particular expertise for each potential project," given that no wall separated Google and Google.org; in addition to capital, engineers, project managers, and other resources could flow from company to philanthropy (and back again).[8] In recent years, Google.org aligned its work even more closely with the company's core capabilities, focusing on data-centric initiatives—mapping, tracking trends, and devising alerts—in areas of public health and safety.

## Rise of the Nonprofit Investment Fund: Focus on Businesses

### Acumen Fund

Perhaps no one better articulates the link between social enterprise as business and sustainability and scale than Jacqueline Novogratz, the founder of the Acumen Fund. Novogratz, a former Chase Manhattan banker with a self-professed market orientation, launched Acumen in 2001 with seed funding from the Rockefeller and Cisco foundations to demonstrate that "small amounts of philanthropic capital combined with large doses of business acumen can build thriving enterprises that serve vast numbers of the poor."[9] According to Novogratz, "Market-based approaches have the potential to grow when charitable dollars run out, and they must be part of the solution to the big problem of poverty." Acumen's mission is "to create a world beyond poverty by investing in social enterprises, emerging leaders, and breakthrough ideas."[10]

From its inception, Acumen was designed to be a nonprofit venture capital fund. Like the venture philanthropies described earlier (e.g., Robin Hood, Tiger, EMCF, New Profit), Novogratz borrowed from the venture capital playbook, making bigger bets (an average financial commitment of $300,000 to $2.5 million) over longer periods of time (5–7 years versus 1–3 years at a typical grant maker) alongside significant investments in "human and knowledge capital" through technical assistance, particularly in business and strategic planning and performance management.[11] Novogratz, however, pushes the VC analogy further: businesses, she believes, are more effective than traditional charity in addressing poverty. With rare exception, Acumen's investments take the form of loans and equity stakes in for-profit companies serving poor people at the bottom of the economic pyramid.

In articulating Acumen's mission, Novogratz explicitly adopts the language and theory of the late C. K. Prahalad, the economist who popularized the bottom of the pyramid (BoP) approach to poverty-fighting. According to Prahalad, the billions of people in the world who live on less than two dollars a day represent a prodigious market opportunity as consumers. By selling products and services to this segment, firms can earn profits *and* serve the needs of the poor.[12]

## Patient Capital

Novogratz recognizes that the BoP markets she seeks to invest in are where commercial investors typically have shied away. Therefore, she believes that addressing the market failure requires innovative, imaginative, and new models of business that provide basic services like clean water, health care, housing, and energy at affordable prices. Novogratz also understands that these new models may need to be funded with capital *patient* enough for long time horizons—certainly longer than those required by conventional and commercial private equity and venture capitalists—and often below market rates of return. The goal of patient capital, according to Novogratz, is to maximize social, rather than financial, returns. In addition to the technical assistance already described, Acumen's investment strategy also often includes co-investing with governments and other companies, using Acumen's lower yield requirements to subsidize and attract commercial investors—the kind of blended or stacked investment we saw in the last chapter—when doing so is beneficial to low-income customers.

## Jed Emerson's Blended Value

In international development terms, the kind of below-market rates Novogratz characterizes as patient is often described as concessionary. Implicit in this definition is a trade-off of financial returns for some broader social objectives. The social enterprise take on this concept is a bit different in its attempt to move away from the *concessionary* or *giving up* mind-set by trying to identify and quantify the gains made. As Novogratz describes it, Acumen "uses philanthropic capital to make disciplined investments—loans or equity,[13] not grants—that yield both financial *and* social returns."

Some describe these multiple returns as a kind of double (or even triple, when it comes to environmental benefit) bottom line; others argue it is a false distinction. In 2000, Jed Emerson, the former head of REDF who had developed its SROI methodology, began to explore further the concept of blended value as a kind of amalgam of these different kinds of returns. According to Emerson, all organizations, non- and for-profit, and all investors produce value "that consists of economic, social, and environmental components." Blended value, he suggests, is a "nondivisible combination of these three elements, not just something we can achieve by adding up its component parts, because it is more than the sum of the parts of a triple bottom line analysis."[14]

As always, measuring and expressing blended value is challenging at best. For its part, Acumen has developed its own methodology for assessing its investments, but one that does not allow for blended value or apples-to-oranges comparisons across sectors (e.g., the value of malaria protection versus the value of water purification). Instead, the Acumen BACO (best available charitable option) asks: for each dollar invested, how much social output will be generated over the life of the investment *relative* to the best available charitable option? In other words, for an investment to be worthwhile, even if it makes a loss, it must be more cost-effective than traditional charity at achieving a set of social goals. The BACO expresses financial and nonfinancial value: it involves a cost analysis, which includes an anticipated financial return and social impact projections (e.g., the number of people protected by a bed net, or total person years of malaria protection), for a net cost per unit of social impact. Acumen also attempts to understand the potential of the business's financial sustainability and the potential to achieve scale. (For Acumen, scale means reaching approximately 1 million end users within 5–7 years with the benefits of the product or service.)

## Root Capital

Like Acumen, Root Capital is a nonprofit social investment fund. Founded in 1999 by Bill Foote, an investment banker turned journalist turned social entrepreneur, Root Capital aims to address what it calls the "capital markets gap" that exists in rural markets for small businesses on account of their size, geographic isolation, lack of collateral, and perceived risk. Root Capital invests in small and growing businesses (SGBs) that build sustainable livelihoods and transform rural communities in poor, environmentally vulnerable places, primarily in Africa and Latin America. Root Capital succeeds because it combines both grants for infrastructure building (e.g., providing business training and skills to farmers) and loans for things like working capital.

Root Capital's early investors were religious institutions, socially responsible investment funds, and foundations that made PRIs. In 2004, Starbucks provided a $2.5 million note; since then, Starbucks's investment has grown to $9 million and Root Capital's investors now comprise other corporations and government entities (including the U.S. development finance agency, OPIC). Root Capital has also forged important business-strengthening partnerships with some of these corporations. In 2010, for example, Nestlé's Nespresso funded the first of a number of projects to offer business supports to farmers in Guatemala that supplied the company with coffee beans. Root Capital provided the training (advice and assistance with managing credit systems, accounting, and general business practices) to more than 300 farmers from six farmer associations and cooperatives. As of 2012, Root Capital has reached 500,000 small-scale producers with this kind of training and more than $310 million in loans.[15]

# E+Co

Although this book's primary focus is human services, we would be remiss not to note the emergence of organizations that do the kind of work of Acumen and Root Capital at the nexus of environment and economic development.

E+Co, for example, is a nonprofit investor that makes clean energy investments—debt and equity—in businesses in developing countries, what it calls "lasting solutions to climate change and poverty" or "energy through enterprise."

The invested capital goes to small and growing clean energy businesses in poor, often off-the-government-grid communities. The idea is to satisfy the demand for clean and affordable energy through local entrepreneurs. Like Root Capital, E+Co also provides training, technology, and other technical supports to these entrepreneurs, who are working on businesses in solar photovoltaics, improved cookstoves, small hydro, biomass, biogas, liquefied petroleum gas (LPG), and solar water heaters, among others. Today, E+Co has portfolio companies in Cambodia, China, Costa Rica, El Salvador, Ghana, Guatemala, Honduras, India, Mali, Morocco, Nepal, Nicaragua, Philippines, Senegal, South Africa, Tanzania, Thailand, The Gambia, Uganda, Vietnam, and Zambia.

E+Co uses a kind of triple bottom line approach: companies it invests in must demonstrate financial returns along with positive social and environmental impact. For example, Zara Solar, one of E+Co's portfolio companies, sells solar photovoltaic systems to off-grid households. These systems dramatically reduce a family's reliance on polluting energies such as wood, kerosene, or diesel generators, which in turn translates into reductions in deforestation, air pollution, and carbon emissions. At the same time, these systems also reduce fuel costs and improve indoor air and light quality, which have any number of positive health, work, and general economic welfare benefits.

Funds of this variety—nonprofits investing in social purpose businesses—are emerging across the world and often work in concert with each other. For example, the $200 million Soros Economic Development Fund (SEDF), a private foundation created in 1997, supports economic development in post-conflict countries and in nations transitioning to democracy by investing in sustainable businesses or initiatives that strive to alleviate poverty by creating jobs or revitalizing communities. In 2008, SEDF, Omidyar, and Google.org created SONG, a $17 million investment fund in India focused on building small and medium-sized companies.

The Aga Khan Development Network (AKDN) offers another interesting example of private funds for public purpose. Founded and run by the Aga Khan, the forty-ninth hereditary imam and spiritual leader of the Shia Ismaili Muslims, AKDN focuses on health, education, culture, rural development, and overall economic development and works in more than 30 countries around the world, primarily in the poorest parts of Africa and Asia. The AKDN's annual budget for nonprofit development activities in 2010 was approximately $625 million, and the project companies of the Aga Khan Fund for Economic Development generated revenues of $2.3 billion. All profits are reinvested for other development purposes.

## Looking to the Future

Despite the market language and business orientation, organizations like SEDF, AKDN, E+Co, Root Capital, and Acumen remain decidedly nonprofit. Acumen, by its own patient capital criterion, expects that its financial returns are likely to be below market. In addition, returns are not given over to its investors; they are recycled back into Acumen's own fund for future investments. (As of 2011, Acumen Fund's total assets were $95 million.) For Novogratz, Acumen's work comes back to the link between business and scale: "Patient capital is a third way to bridge the gap between the efficiency and scale of market–based approaches and the social impact of pure philanthropy."[16]

Recently, however, some of the funds have begun to experiment with more for-profit versions of themselves, pushing further the boundaries of pure business solutions to social and environmental challenges. Acumen has launched Acumen Capital Markets, which promises returns to investors, even if they must wait 10 years to recoup. Root Capital's founders hope and anticipate that within a few years they could break even and perhaps ultimately become self-sustaining. E+Co has a number of for-profit affiliates, including E+Co Capital Latin America, founded in 2005, the fund manager for the Central American Renewable Energy and Cleaner Production Facility (CAREC), and E+Carbon, a wholly owned subsidiary founded in 2007 that commercializes carbon assets by selling the offsets from technologies that abate large quantities of greenhouse gas emissions.

Of course, the most high profile of the business-to-fight-poverty stories is that of microfinance, where Fazle Abed, Muhammad Yunus, and other pioneers of microlending showed the world what happens when you teach millions of poor women to fish. In 1970s, those working in microcredit demonstrated that lending money to poor people to start businesses could be profitable—under the right circumstances, they could reliably repay their loans—and could transform their lives by raising them out of poverty. Microcredit seemed to exemplify the virtuous power of enterprise and markets, lending to people to start businesses so that they could become self-sufficient and charging interest so that loans, when repaid, could be recycled and loaned to new borrowers. As we will see in the next chapters, the elegance of this theory and its application spread like wildfire, attracting the attention of commercial investors the world over. Today, $65 billion in microcredit loans are made to 100 million borrowers worldwide.

In the section that follows, we will discuss exactly this kind of for-profit enterprise and the ways in which social entrepreneurs in the private sector are attempting to harness market forces for public purpose. However, before we proceed, it is worth recalling how firmly rooted this kind of social purpose enterprise is in the nonprofit sector, where social entrepreneurs—people such as Bill Drayton, Wendy Kopp, Sara Horowitz, and countless others—have tested innovative approaches to social change. In addition, we have observed how so much of the capital that sustains social entrepreneurship has been supplied by a new breed of funder. The legacy of this philanthropy and its heightened emphasis on measurement and evaluation, numerous experiments with technology, open source innovation and market-shaping tools, and a much more activist approach to charitable investing have unequivocally transformed the workings of the nonprofit sector and the ways we think about achieving social change.

Yet not all of these trends are universally applauded. Although we defer many of the critiques (i.e., the sometimes belligerent tone of the new philanthropy and its ambitions, oversights and oversimplifications, the limitations of the business analogy to nonprofit work which, by definition, occurs in areas of market failure) to "Room for Debate," the final section of the book, they are essential to a more nuanced and ecumenical understanding of social entrepreneurship in the twenty-first century and of the appropriate roles of the nonprofit, private, and public sectors in advancing social change.

# II

||||||||||||||||||||||||||||||||||||||||||||||||||||||||||||||||||||||||||

# SOCIAL IMPACT IN THE PRIVATE SECTOR

## Social Impact Capitalism

In the previous section of this book, we followed the march of the social entrepreneurship revolution through the nonprofit sector, where, often with a business bias, it infused the practices of social service organizations and philanthropic funders with a new set of tools, methodologies, and expectations about how best to achieve social change. In recent years, as we have seen, many nonprofit funders have begun to push the boundaries of their investment approaches, using philanthropic assets more assertively to shape markets, in some cases using debt and equity to support social purpose businesses. We use that transition from entrepreneurship to enterprise as a starting point here, to consider ways in which the private sector, which includes for-profit, commercial companies and their investors, can advance social change. Furthermore, in the chapters that follow, we take both investor and enterprise perspectives as we trace how social entrepreneurship in the private sector reflects the growing influence of social sector values on profit-maximizing actors and activities.

The attempt to incorporate nonfinancial value and values into the private sector is not new. In the last generation, numerous efforts that fall under the evolving rubric of both corporate social responsibility (CSR) and socially responsible investing (SRI) have looked to steer the behavior and practices of firms toward the realm of socially and environmentally friendly behavior. The idea, if not to create social benefit outright, was at least to temper the more pernicious consequences of some profit-seeking activities. While this work continues, the phenomenon we describe in these chapters, a sweeping enthusiasm for *social impact* on both the enterprise and capital sides of the equation, also known as *impact investing*, or *shared value capitalism* more broadly, asks a fundamentally different set of questions about the role of business in society and whether corporations can be a, or in some cases *the*, central force for social good.

Not surprisingly, this work has gained greater urgency and wider currency in the years since the financial crisis as many across the political spectrum have questioned the stability and long-term sustainability of a fragile economic system that plunged itself into free fall and a deeply corrosive recession. These chapters are not meant to be a postmortem of the financial crisis. Indeed, an entire industry of talented economists and policy analysts are committed to that project and to helping us understand the causes and consequences of *market triumphalism*.

Instead, we examine a number of initiatives underway that try to refashion profit-seeking firms as agents of value creation and as deliberate forces for good in society. We end this discussion with a reconsideration of the role of government as market shaper and as an important catalyst in enlisting firms in the work, not only of economic recovery, but of more broad-based and long-term prosperity.

# Chapter 9

||||||||||||||||||||||||||||||||||||||||||||||||||||||||||||||||||||

# THE INVESTOR
# PERSPECTIVE:
# IMPACT INVESTING

L ike social entrepreneurship, *impact investing* is an umbrella term encompassing a broad range of activities. Much of it begins with the work we saw in the previous chapters on mission and program-related investments many foundations make in nonprofits and gradually but increasingly, in social purpose businesses. Yet advocates of impact investing suggest that its potential lies in harnessing capital beyond the philanthropic realm. The magnitude and complexity of today's global challenges, the argument goes, exceed the resources and capacity of both the nonprofit and public sectors alone; private, commercial capital is necessary to address these deeply rooted problems at scale.

Just what is impact investing anyway? Beyond some of the definitional ambiguities, three broad questions pertain: First, is there interest in impact investing beyond the philanthropic realm? Second, what are the risks associated with inviting commercial investors into the world of social impact? And third, how do we best harness private capital to bear fruitfully, productively, and responsibly on social and environmental problems?

# Just What Is Impact Investing?

## A Field Is Born: The Rockefeller Foundation Lays the Definitional Ground

In 2007 and 2008, the Rockefeller Foundation, largely under the leadership of its then managing director, Antony Bugg-Levine (now head of the Nonprofit Finance Fund), hosted a series of meetings with a range of investors from green tech to microfinance to community development who together devised the term *impact investing* to describe the common characteristics of their work, namely, for-profit, social purpose investment. They also discussed shared challenges, ranging from deal flow to measurement and evaluation, and considered how defining their collective efforts as a *field* and building a kind of industry infrastructure could strengthen the marketplace for impact investing and enhance and expand their efforts. Rockefeller went on to fund much of this infrastructure development, which helped lay the groundwork for the field.

## Defining Impact Investments: Intentionality and Blended Returns

Some important definition work has been done to try to distinguish *impact investing* both from traditional philanthropy and from strictly profit-maximizing commercial investing.

### Intentionality

The first criterion seems to focus on intentionality. According to a seminal report from Monitor, impact investors "*actively* seek to place capital in businesses and funds that can provide solutions at a scale that purely philanthropic interventions cannot usually reach." Unlike traditional socially responsible investing (SRI), which, as we have seen, seeks to screen or exclude harmful activity from a portfolio, impact investing "refers only to the social investing that actively seeks to have a positive impact." In other words, firms must have "the *explicit intention* of having a positive social or environmental impact."[1]

## Impact: Impact First, Financial First, and Blended Value

The second criterion has to do with the nature of these returns. For starters, impact investments are not grants; they are unequivocally investments in social purpose businesses that yield some kind of financial return while creating social or environmental benefit.

However, the nature of these returns, how they are defined and measured, and how they satisfy the objectives of different investors, is where things get tricky. In *Impact Investing*, Emerson and Bugg-Levine employ Emerson's blended value lens and write that impact investments are about "the integrated pursuit of financial, social, and environmental performance" and use private "capital to maximize total, combined value."[2]

Monitor defines *blend* in a different way. In the Monitor framework, the field consists of *impact first* and *financial first* investors (see Figure 9.1). It is possible to combine different capital types from the different kinds of investors to create *yin-yang* deals—along the stacked or blended capital lines we have seen (e.g., the African Agricultural Capital Fund, the New York City Acquisition Fund)—that bring together "two elements that are different and yet complementary when put together."[3]

**Figure 9.1** Segments of Impact Investors

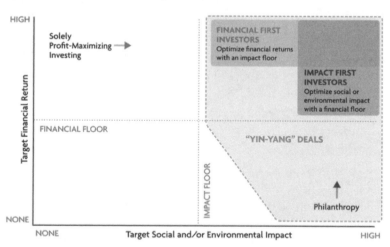

Source: Used with the permission of the Monitor Institute.

Recent research from J.P.Morgan confirms that even among those who self-identify as "impact" investors, a range of investment philosophies and expectations can be found. Some investors are unwilling to sacrifice financial returns for impact, while others are ready to cede some dollar yield for social or environmental benefit. Many investors try to balance these objectives in the belief that, for some investments, a trade-off between impact and financial first returns does not need to be made.[4]

These definitions of *intentionality* and *blended value* both apply nicely to the kind of PRI and MRI investments we saw earlier, those made by activist social entrepreneurship philanthropy, either in new or more established foundations, or even nonprofit investment funds such as Acumen that use a kind of patient capital to pursue social impact objectives. The question is whether appetite for this kind of investment can be found in mainstream, commercial investors. The initial and unapologetically massive market estimates suggest that many in the field believe—and certainly hope—that the answer is yes.

## Definitions: Where Are Impact Investment Opportunities?

Monitor's preliminary market sizing suggests that impact investing has the potential to grow to approximately 1 percent of total managed assets: roughly $500 billion in capital channeled toward social and environmental impact over the next 5 to 10 years.[5] J.P.Morgan's estimates are even more sanguine: a $400 billion to $1 trillion market opportunity with potential profits of $183 to $667 billion.[6]

Monitor's research cites investment opportunities in clean technology, microfinance, and, on the U.S. domestic front, growth in the well-established community investment field. J.P.Morgan's market analysis is almost entirely "bottom of the pyramid," derived from investments in businesses that expand access to basic goods and services in "housing, rural water delivery, maternal health, primary education, and financial services for the portion of the global population earning less than $3,000 a year."[7] The J.P.Morgan market size estimates project the industry market share shown in Figure 9.2.

Whether these forward-looking projections are accurate, and they are indeed large and rest on a number of assumptions, a large segment of investors are undoubtedly enthusiastic about putting their capital to

**Figure 9.2** Potential Invested Capital to Fund Selected BoP Businesses

| Sector | Potential Invested Capital Required (US$ billion) | Potential Profit Opportunity (US$ billion) |
|---|---|---|
| Housing (affordable urban housing) | $214–$786 | $177–$648 |
| Water (clean water for rural communities) | $5.4–$13 | $2.9–$7 |
| Health (maternal health) | $0.4–$2 | $0.1–$1 |
| Education (primary education) | $4.8–$10 | $2.6–$11 |
| Financial services (microfinance) | $176 | not measured |

Source: J.P.Morgan, "Impact Investments: an Emerging Asset Class," J.P.Morgan Global Research (November 29, 2010), 12.

socially productive uses. Moreover, the new social entrepreneurs seek to channel this enthusiasm into their work.

To this end, champions of impact investing have begun to refer to it as an *asset class*, less in the traditional instrument sense (i.e., debt or equity) but rather as a kind of investment category (not unlike hedge funds, which have earned their own allocation in many portfolios) that requires a unique set of investment and risk management skills, dedicated industry organizations, standardized metrics, benchmarks, and ratings.

Before that can happen, however, much work needs to be done, not simply on building the infrastructure—ratings and metrics, which we will explore in the next chapter—but further definitional debate.

## Intentionality and Blended Value Redux

Although seemingly unambiguous, intentionality is in fact complex. The *intentional* lens is meant to distinguish impact investing from a straight-up, profit-maximization play. In the BoP context, according to Monitor, "Impact investing does not assume that any investment in a business selling products to poor people inherently creates a social impact."[8] Rather, "impact investing only includes those investments made with the *explicit intention* of having a positive social or environmental impact, such as job creation for low income people. The fact that an investment is made in a poor country is not sufficient to qualify it as an impact investment."[9]

Yet what do we really mean by intentionality? And what kind of social impact are we intentionally trying to achieve? The provision of a good or service? Employment? What does not qualify? Monitor's market size estimates include investments in firms that create employment as a social benefit. This is no doubt an enormously valuable feature of enterprise but begs the question of how much impact investing differs from more mainstream, commercial investment. On the employment ledger, many large firms such as Walmart or McDonald's would qualify, and if the definition of *intentional impact* is expanded even more broadly to include firms that create consumer surplus or welfare, greater social enterprises than Microsoft, Intel, or IBM could not be found.[10] This question holds in both the domestic and emerging-country contexts.

A related and paradoxical question about impact investing has to do with the nature of the returns. By addressing persistent social or environmental challenges, impact investors are seeking to direct their capital to areas of market failure, which should imply some kind of concessionary return. Emerson and Bugg-Levine borrow the *additionality* criterion from the field of international development to argue that impact investments should not be redundant. Rather, they should target businesses in industries, geographies, sectors, demographies, or asset classes that "would not otherwise be capitalized by private investors."[11] Herein lies the conundrum: impact investments, nearly by definition, either do not or should not promise the kinds of market rate returns that mainstream investors seek.

In essence, attracting commercial investment to bear on social or environmental challenges requires some kind of philanthropic subsidy or government-designed incentive. Both will be explored at length when we discuss the role of government in encouraging private capital flows.

# Chapter 10

||||||||||||||||||||||||||||||||||||||||||||||||||||||||||||||||||||||

# INTERNATIONAL
# IMPACT INVESTING

As we saw in the previous chapter, much of the discussion about impact investing centers on the developing world, where the hope and belief is that it is possible to pursue profitable investment opportunities while also providing the poor with basic goods and services. The notion that the private sector is an important engine of social and economic development is hardly new; in fact, it supplies the first principle of market capitalism. Moreover, the practice of deploying capital to stimulate economic growth in poor countries has been the cornerstone of the field of international development for three-quarters of a century.

Our inquiry in this chapter concentrates on the availability and relevance of commercial capital, beyond philanthropy and public sector dollars. We see enthusiasm and momentum for social impact work within the private sector, a hunger to deploy assets in meaningful and productive ways. The question is how large this market really is and whether and how it is possible to harness the flow of commercial capital to public purpose.

## The Field of International Development

The idea that private sector development could be both encouraged and directed to growth in poor countries underpins much of the international development work of the twentieth century. The development field has its roots in the postwar reconstruction efforts of the World Bank, which made loans in Europe and Japan to resuscitate ravaged countries into stable and growing economies. Today, the World Bank continues to make billions of dollars each year in grants and concessionary loans to poor and developing countries.

From its inception, the Bank has also worked to encourage private sector activity on both the host-economy and investor sides of the development equation. In 1956, the World Bank created the International Finance Corporation (IFC) to invest directly in the private sector. The IFC continues in its contemporary incarnation to invest $10 billion annually in projects in more than 100 countries. In addition, most countries participate in local and regional development finance institutions, and most developed countries have their own bilateral finance agencies to steer private sector capital flow to emerging markets. In the United States, for example, the U.S. Overseas Private Investment Corporation (OPIC, founded in 1971) has pioneered many forms of investment insurance, including political risk insurance, to encourage American companies to invest in developing countries. In short, channeling private capital toward global development purposes has a long tradition in the public sector.

## Impact Investing Beyond the Public Sector

Advocates of impact investing hope to expand the field of international development beyond this government-led work to enlisting profit-seeking actors, independently, to the cause. So, just who are these investors?

### Philanthropy, Private Investors, and Family Offices Help Build the Field

As we saw in section I, many of the first private, nongovernment forays into the field of social impact investing, particularly in the developing world, have been nonprofit and from the philanthropic sector: the experimental and increasingly activist use of MRIs and PRIs by foundations such as Heron, Rockefeller, and Gates; organizations such as Google and Omidyar that attempted to create hybrid structures to allow them to invest in businesses alongside charitable grants; and some of the first nonprofit investment firms (e.g., Acumen, Root Capital, and E+Co) that fund businesses but returns profits, if they earn them, back into the firm.

These philanthropic (or quasi-philanthropic) investments in for-profit development serve to ready the field for commercial investors in a number of important ways. First, as in the case of microcredit, early philanthropic investors, including Omidyar, can take risks of capitalizing for-profit investors in untested markets, thereby demonstrating the potential profitability of some of these sectors. Often this is done in collaboration. Recall, for example, the formation of SONG, a $17 million investment fund that supports small and medium-sized enterprises (SMEs) in India, courtesy of the Soros Economic Development Fund, Omidyar, and Google.org, organizations that have also co-invested in other funds, including IGNIA, an impact investing venture capital firm based in Monterrey, Mexico, that supports high-growth social enterprises serving BoP markets in Latin America.

Second, philanthropic or patient capital in for-profit investing has an important role to play in the kind of yin-yang, blended-capital investment structures. As we have discussed, a willingness of these nonprofit investors to accept below-market returns can help incent more mainstream investors to participate in stacked investment deals.

Finally, as we examine next, nonprofit or philanthropic investors can play a critical infrastructure role by building supply chains (e.g., the capacity building that Root Capital and E+Co engage in), measurement and evaluation and rating systems, consultancies, and other structural supports. In this way, they help develop the industry further.

## With Proof, More Profit-Seeking Investors

In recent years, as nonprofit investors demonstrated the viability of profitable investments in these areas, more mainstream and decidedly for-profit investment firms, who use a wide range of investment vehicles from private equity to loan guarantees and bonds to achieve impact, have entered the fray.

### Boutique Firms and Private Equity

Many of these efforts began at boutique firms, whose first social impact portfolios were often invested in microfinance and over time expanded to other sectors. Switzerland-based BlueOrchard, for example, manages $800 million in microfinance portfolios. BlueOrchard's founder, Jean-Philippe de Schrevel, also launched Bamboo Finance, an investment advisory firm specializing in the financing of social enterprises in areas of affordable housing, healthcare, education, energy, livelihood opportunities, water, and sanitation in developing countries. ResponsAbility, another Swiss firm, with $1 billion under assets, invests in nearly 400 companies in BoP markets in 70 countries in the areas of microfinance, SME financing, fair trade, independent media, healthcare, and education. Founded in 2003, responsAbility operates as an independent asset manager; its shareholders include Swiss and German financial institutions, a social venture capital company, a handful of wealthy European investors, and the firm's own employees. In the United States, private equity pioneers of microfinance like Gray Ghost Ventures and Unitus have recently raised new funds for other impact areas that include private schools in poor countries.

‖‖‖‖‖‖‖‖‖‖‖‖‖‖‖‖‖‖‖‖‖‖‖‖‖‖‖‖‖‖‖‖‖‖‖‖‖‖‖‖‖‖‖‖‖‖‖‖‖‖‖‖‖‖‖‖

## Environment and Energy Impact Investing Companies

Although we focus primarily on investors in direct human services that include microcredit, housing, and health, the number of energy and environment impact investors, as we have seen, is large and growing. These firms include Generation Investment Management, EKO, Equilibrium Capital Partners, and SJF Ventures, which often invest in things like green technology and alternative energy (e.g., wind, solar) companies, stranded assets, water or carbon markets or harder to value ecological services (i.e., water purification and carbon sequestration), and the natural capital stocks that produce them. Beyond these boutique firms, more mainstream private capital investors have begun to consider these kinds of investments, including places like Capricorn Investment. For an even larger class of investors, the long-term sustainability of the firms in their portfolio is of increasing concern. Private equity giants Kohlberg, Kravis, and Roberts (KKR) and the Carlyle Group, for example, have partnered with the Environmental Defense Fund to help them achieve sustainable and environmentally beneficial cost reductions within their portfolio companies or to use a kind of EcoValueScreen for upfront investment due diligence.

||||||||||||||||||||||||||||||||||||||||||||||||||||||||||||||||||||||

## Large Investment Banks

A number investment banks and even some of the larger publicly traded firms are beginning to provide products and services to client investors focused on impact. Here, too, much of this investing began with micro-lending. In 2005, for example, Citigroup launched its global microfinance practice. In 2006, Morgan Stanley worked with BlueOrchard to place the first rated microfinance bond offering with European institutional investors, raising more than $100 million for 22 microfinance institutions (MFIs) from 13 countries: Mongolia, Bosnia, Colombia, Peru, Bolivia, Mexico, Nicaragua, Ecuador, Azerbaijan, Albania, Georgia, Russia, and Cambodia. These BlueOrchard Loans for Development (BOLD) represented the first public collateralized debt obligation of loans for MFIs.

That same year, Goldman Sachs helped structure and market the International Finance Facility for Immunisation (IFFIm), a multibillion-dollar bond issue that provided front-loaded finance for emerging market vaccine campaigns. In 2007, J.P.Morgan launched its social finance unit, which aims to build profitable impact business for the bank. In recent years, many others have followed suit, including UBS's Philanthropy and Values-Based investing unit, which it launched in its wealth management business in 2010.

Today, Morgan Stanley has an entire Global Sustainable Finance (GSF) group, responsible for the firm's broader sustainability strategy for investors and clients interested in business models and investment products capable of achieving financial, social, and environmental returns. In the spring of 2012, Morgan Stanley Smith Barney launched its Investing with Impact Platform "designed to help clients align their financial goals and their personal values" by providing a range of investment opportunities in public and private markets "that center on positive social and environmental impact without sacrificing financial performance potential."[1]

# How to Attract More Commercial Capital: Barriers and Solutions

Despite the growing interest of mainstream investors, the impact investing sector faces a number of formidable barriers to further growth. Broadly speaking, these fall into two categories: infrastructure and deal flow.

As we will see, social purpose enterprises, particularly in the BoP context, often begin life as small companies in fragile markets. These companies require technical assistance in addition to loans or equity investment, and because they can take longer to scale than traditional companies, their absorptive capacity is limited: social enterprises of this type often require and can only handle smaller initial investments than many large investors are accustomed to or interested in making.

In addition, because many of these deals are market-, location-, and sector-specific, they need specialized research and due diligence, which is also expensive. And, just as we have seen in the nonprofit and public sectors, proof of impact via a demonstrated track record or a consistent and standardized way of conveying returns, financial, social, or environmental, is often lacking, costly to develop, or simply elusive.

## Barrier 1: Infrastructure: The Measurement and Evaluation Challenge

The question of evidence of financial, social, or environmental impact remains a significant hurdle to further investment in the impact field. We encountered this same issue and the same existential "how do we know" question in the nonprofit sector, even though in this case it is particularly urgent because the quality of returns even more closely informs the quantity of capital available.

Even the most enthusiastic for-profit investor, the one willing to cede some financial return in exchange for social or environmental impact, needs to be convinced of this impact: Has the investment created sufficient social or economic value to offset the opportunity cost of a more financially profitable traditional investment?

In recent years, a number of organizations have developed methodologies and platforms to grapple with this measurement and evaluation challenge. Some have evolved independently, like Acumen's Pulse, a data management and reporting system that is widely used by other impact investors. Others represent concerted efforts such as those by the Rocke-feller Foundation, USAID, and J.P.Morgan to strengthen the infrastruc-ture for this nascent field.

## The Global Impact Investing Network (GIIN): Reporting Standards

Launched in 2009, the GIIN was created to support the activities, educa-tion, and research necessary to accelerate the development of the impact investing field. One of the GIIN's first major accomplishments was the development of Impact Reporting and Investing Standards (IRIS), an effort to standardize the language and methodology for measuring the social performance of impact investments to allow for comparable and credible consistency in how funds define, track, and report on the social performance of their investments.

IRIS offers a standardized approach and has subsector indicators (tai-lored to agriculture, education, energy, environment, financial services, health, housing, and water) that can be used by companies themselves, direct investors who want to track the performance of these portfolios, or fund investors.

The GIIN has also created ImpactBase, an online database of global impact funds. Since its 2011 launch, ImpactBase had attracted hundreds of subscribers and lists more than 125 funds.

## GIIRS: A Ratings System for Social Impact?

Created by the nonprofit B Labs, the Global Impact Investing Ratings System (GIIRS) is a rating system that is analogous to Morningstar invest-ment rankings or the S&P credit risk ratings and attempts to compre-hensively and comparably assess the social and environmental impact of companies and funds. Like IRIS, GIIRS is an effort to bring transparency and standardization to the social impact field and in doing so catalyze further investment. Also like IRIS, with which it is integrated, GIIRS is designed to be used by companies, direct investors, and investors in funds.

## Advisory Intermediaries Help Strengthen Infrastructure

These measurement and reporting standards have helped strengthen the field's infrastructure more broadly, including the work of the growing number of intermediary advisory firms that help to match prospective investors with impact funds and investment vehicles. Imprint Capital, for example, identifies, structures, and manages impact investments for foundations and family offices. Rockefeller Philanthropy Advisors, an organization that has traditionally advised philanthropists on charitable investments, has developed an expertise in impact investing. ImpactAssets, a nonprofit U.S. financial services firm launched in 2010, serves as a kind of translator between mainstream wealth managers and asset owners and the impact world. In 2011, ImpactAssets created ImpactAssets 50, naming top-performing asset managers across asset classes and impact sectors.

## Social Stock Exchanges

A number of efforts to create social impact stock markets, which are a kind of holy grail of efficient social capital market theory, necessitate robust and standardized measures to function as bona fide exchanges.

After some fits and starts, the founders of the Social Stock Exchange in the United Kingdom, which received early feasibility study grants from the Rockefeller Foundation, announced in December 2011 that it would be a recipient of £850,000 of the £3 million in dormant bank accounts the British government was directing to various Big Society Investment Fund initiatives. Although the U.K. stock exchange claims to be the first for social enterprises, similar efforts are taking place around the globe. Some, including the South Africa Social Investment Exchange (SASIX), are really more like philanthropic marketplaces that match nonprofits and donors. Others, however, are in fact part of larger regulated stock exchanges. Ashoka Fellow Celso Grecco, for example, founded Bolsa de Valores Sociais (BVS), which operates within Brazil's largest stock exchange. Tamzin Ractliffe, CEO of NeXii and another Ashoka Fellow, launched iX, which claims to be the world's first impact investing exchange board, in partnership with the Stock Exchange of Mauritius. (The Mauritius exchange is a member of the World Federation of Exchanges and a recognized stock exchange by Her Majesty's Revenue and Customs in the United Kingdom, and can trade in U.S. dollars, euros, or British pounds.) The Impact Investment Exchange–Asia is taking shape in Singapore, and similar initiatives are under way in India, Thailand, and New Zealand.[2]

# Barrier 2: Deal Flow, a Question of Supply

## Scale

The gradual evolution of standardized metrics for reporting and evaluating individual investments and larger portfolio aggregations may go a long way toward advancing the field and removing some of the barriers to attracting more capital, as will the increase in intermediation (advisories and exchange mechanisms) that can reduce the search and due diligence costs associated with understanding complexity and risk.

However, neither of these advances solves the immediate problem of deal flow that many investment banks and other large institutional investors face. The issue here is not one of insufficient capital. Rather, many investors report that a paucity of investment opportunities has stifled growth and enthusiasm, particularly among investors who manage quantities of capital so large they must make commensurately large— multimillion-dollar—investments. The due diligence and other transaction requirements of smaller deals simply do not fit into the economics of their investment models. Even though standardized metrics go some ways to reducing these costs, many social enterprises are small and their absorptive capacity limited.

In addition, as impact investing seeks to harness mainstream commercial investors whose fiduciary responsibility to private investors or even to the public markets requires market rate returns, the impact deals that meet this requirement may be few and far between. In a recent survey of impact investors by J.P.Morgan, investors cited "lack of a track record of successful investments" as the most critical challenge to industry growth.[3] "Shortage of quality investment opportunities" was second, and inadequate impact measurement practice third.

In 2011, two reports out of Monitor assessing impact investments in India and Africa supported this finding.[4] In both instances, they found business models worked when they were "suited to extreme conditions of low income markets," including mobile money transfer, microcredit, microsavings, microinsurance, smallholder farmer aggregation, distribution and sales through informal sales shops, or agent networks or last-mile infrastructure. Many of these models take the form of small, early stage companies. In other words, a disconnect comes between the capital needs of these small enterprises and the investment requirements of large firms. As the Monitor report put it, "An abundance of capital is increasingly chasing too few good investments with an overemphasis on private equity funding models."[5] Sixty percent of the companies Monitor examined sought less than $1 million in capital, and typically even the larger enterprises needed no more than $3 million.[6]

# Chapter 11

‖‖‖‖‖‖‖‖‖‖‖‖‖‖‖‖‖‖‖‖‖‖‖‖‖‖‖‖‖‖‖‖‖‖‖‖‖‖‖‖‖‖‖‖‖‖‖‖‖‖‖‖‖

# CASE STUDY: THE MICROCREDIT STORY

The evolution of the microlending industry offers a compelling case study in the transition from entrepreneurship to enterprise and in the promise and pitfalls of impact investing and of harnessing private capital for social purpose.

It is a story of a sector created when nonprofit social entrepreneurs and public sector development agencies sought to address the market failure characterized by the lack of affordable credit for poor people. Once these early microcredit pioneers built the infrastructure necessary to support successful microlending and demonstrated the profitability of the business model, private and commercial investors followed suit. It is important to understand the issues at stake in the commercialization of microlending, not only because many impact investors believe that much of the growth of their industry lies in this sector (recall the J.P.Morgan market estimates), but also because the questions raised about quantity versus quality of capital, scale, how business models can and should iterate, and the use of subsidy are relevant across industries when it comes to bringing private capital to bear on social problems.

## Background: The Industry's Nonprofit Origins

The appeal of microcredit has always been its elegant simplicity. As a solution to market failure, the story goes like this: Commercial banks do not readily lend to the poor because of lack of profit in it. In the absence of collateral, lenders will make only small loans, yet the cost of administering these loans, including due diligence and ongoing monitoring, remains steep. In response, banks either charge punishingly high interest rates or opt not to lend in the first place. The poor are left with few formal borrowing options and are often at the mercy of loan sharks.[1]

The architects of microcredit argued that by eliminating the profit motive, or at least the steep profit requirements of commercial lenders, small, affordable loans could be made and repaid. Creating this type of self-sustaining credit market for the poor would lead to a virtuous cycle of investment in business and human capital, and a pathway out of entrenched poverty. In 1976, in Bangladesh, Muhammad Yunus launched the Grameen Bank with a series of joint-liability loans to small cohorts of poor women. Fazle Abed, the head of the Bangladesh Rural Advancement Committee (BRAC) created similar programs in the region. Bangladesh was not the only testing ground for microcredit, however. A number of foundations, including Ford, ran demonstration projects of microcredit across the globe. This model soon proved that the poor could be counted on for repayment and helped usher in extraordinary industry growth.

As the industry matured, networks and associations such as Women's World Banking, Small Enterprise Education and Promotion Network, and the Consultative Group to Assist the Poorest (CGAP) grew up to coordinate the work of various microfinance institutions and to help build the industry's infrastructure: undertaking research, promoting standards and rating systems, providing advisory services, and other business planning assistance.

These developments significantly strengthened the sector, attracting additional nonprofit actors as well as the interest of for-profit lenders. As we saw earlier, the early 2000s marked the entry of a number of commercial investors into the industry: recall the 2006 BlueOrchard–Morgan Stanley deal. The same year, Muhammad Yunus won the Nobel for his pioneering work in the field. In those heady days, microfinance was considered a kind of global panacea, one that could combine poverty alleviation with profits. Today, $65 billion in microcredit loans are made to 100 million borrowers worldwide, and much of this growth has been fueled by an infusion of private capital.

## Commercialization

The commercialization of the industry has taken a number of forms, but often it has meant the conversion of nonprofit organizations into for-profit conduits. In one of the first high-profile examples of this trend, Compartamos, a Mexican microlender, morphed from a nonprofit to a for-profit to a publicly traded company. In 2007, Compartamos's IPO raised $467 million in exchange for 30 percent of the company. Not surprisingly, this IPO spurred even greater interest for for-profit lending. In July 2010, SKS Microfinance in India issued 17 million shares to investors like Silicon Valley's venture capital firm Sequoia Capital, raising $50 million in the process. SKS has been particularly controversial, both at the time of its IPO and in the years since. In the lead-up to the public offering, some microcredit analysts warned, "Runaway growth at microfinance companies masks an erosion of lending standards and a lack of regulation that may help spark rising defaults."[2] Earlier that year, high default rates (above 10 percent) in microfinance markets in Nicaragua, Morocco, and Pakistan prompted CGAP to describe the events as a "serious repayment crisis." Many analysts also raised concerns about the Indian microcredit market, the largest in the world.

Andhra Pradesh, the center of India's microfinance industry, has also been a center of controversy. In October 2010, just two months after the SKS IPO, the local government adopted rules to reign in market lenders. This action came in the wake of a significant backlash in India against the IPO and against commercialization as well as more generally to the substantial profits accruing to investors. It also followed 200 suicides in the region, which many poor families and the media blamed on excessive indebtedness and pressure by lenders to repay loans. In the months that followed, default rates on microloans in Andhra Pradesh skyrocketed, and federal lawmakers joined the political fray. By the spring of 2011, shares of SKS Microfinance, which were once heralded as the great success of social enterprise and proof it was possible to serve the poor and earn market rate returns in the process, were down nearly 70 percent from their

IPO price the summer before. Other companies operating in Andhra Pradesh also experienced significant losses.

The larger political backlash against microlending was not confined to India. In May 2011, Yunus was ousted by the Bangladeshi government from his post as managing director of Grameen Bank, rattling the field further. Like SKS stock, the euphoria once surrounding microcredit as a cure-all for global poverty seemed to have plummeted.

Most observers agree that the credit turmoil in India's Andhra Pradesh region can be explained by the rapid growth of microfinance there. Others concur that the allure of market rate returns attracted the flood of private investment in the first place, vastly accelerating industry expansion and risk of collapse. From the early days of microenterprise, concern about commercialization, whether and how much to harness market forces to provide credit to the poor, has animated the debates in the field. After all, capital quantity and quality are closely linked.

Yunus has long maintained that the profit motive, by definition, compromises the integrity of microcredit, since it privileges the needs of investors over the needs of the poor. Yunus explains that he launched Grameen in response to what he perceived to be market failure: large commercial banks could not profitably and therefore would not lend to the very poor. He denounced the IPOs of Compartamos and SKS Microfinance, which both traveled the nonprofit to for-profit path, enriching their company founders and early investors in the process. Writing in the *New York Times* in January 2010, Yunus said, "I never imagined that one day microcredit would give rise to its own breed of loan sharks. But it has. . . . Commercialization has been a terrible wrong turn for microfinance, and it indicates a worrying 'mission drift' in the motivation of those lending to the poor. Poverty should be eradicated, not seen as a money-making opportunity."[3]

Yunus distinguishes the Compartamos and SKSs of the world from Grameen, technically a for-profit business but one in which borrowers are the owners and in which profits are reinvested in the bank. For Yunus, Grameen is a "social business . . . an opportunity to help people out of poverty, which is different than an opportunity to make money."[4] For this reason, Grameen charges 15 percent interest, while publicly traded Compartamos's going rate is closer to 100 percent.

Advocates for and defenders of commercialization counter Yunus's critique with the contention that sharing profits with private investors was the only path to scale, a prerequisite for reaching the billions of the world's unbanked. After all, the SKS and Compartamos public offerings raised hundreds of millions of dollars that could then be loaned to the poor.

Yunus's disagreements did not begin with these IPOs; they echo his earlier disputes with C. K. Prahalad, the economist who popularized the bottom of the pyramid (BoP) approach to poverty-fighting, and with others, like Pierre Omidyar, who endorse the Prahalad view. As we saw earlier, Prahalad believed that the billions of people in the world who live on less than $2 a day represent a gargantuan market opportunity as consumers. By selling them products and services, firms can earn profits *and* serve the needs of the poor. Much to Yunus's chagrin, microcredit is regularly cited as an exemplar of the BoP principle.

In February 2012, Vikram Akula, who resigned as head of SKS the previous fall, made a startling admission to a group of students assembled at Harvard Business School. "Professor Yunus was right," he said. "Bringing private capital into social enterprise was much harder than I anticipated." In his remarks, Akula told students that he "had focused on scaling SKS's model and had not fully anticipated the potential downside of accessing the public market for social enterprise."[5]

Akula's remarks do not necessarily resolve the commercialization debate. They do suggest that Yunus was justified in his concerns about SKS. A recent Associated Press report found that SKS was aware of the fact that its debt collectors were using coercive measures that played a role in some of the borrowers' suicides. However, and despite the egregious practices of one bad company, the fact remains that private capital has been the engine to spread microlending and access to credit to millions of the world's poor.

Which is to say, truth can be found on both sides of the commercialization debate: Profitably brings scale but also potentially unintended perils. The trade-offs inherent in these arguments have important implications for policymakers worldwide. Some of these larger questions related to commercialization, which go well beyond the field of microlending, are explored at length in Chapter 20.

# Chapter 12

|||||||||||||||||||||||||||||||||||||||||||||||||||||||||||||||||||||||||

# IMPACT INVESTING IN THE UNITED STATES

**M**uch of the recent discussion of impact investing centers on the bottom of the pyramid; recall how heavily the market research from Monitor and J.P.Morgan focuses on the developing world. Still, one also finds significant enthusiasm in the United States for true social enterprise, for bringing private capital to bear on entrenched problems here at home. Just what does this field look like in the United States?

Once again, the notion that private sources of capital could be invested domestically to encourage enterprise and promote development is hardly novel. The United States is a country founded on a robust tradition of market capitalism, with hundreds of years of cultural and policy affection for the linkage between private enterprise and national prosperity. When markets have failed or when private solutions ignore particular demographics or geographies, government (and philanthropy) have often stepped in to provide goods and services directly or to create the incentives to encourage private investment. The role of government as a market shaper will be addressed at length in the final chapters. We reference that lens here, however, because it allows us to situate the current impact investing conversation in a much larger history of public policies that steer private capital to public purpose.

# Community Development Field: Housing, Real Estate, and Enterprise Development

## Beginning with Philanthropy and Government

The closest analogy in the United States to the international development work or government-led growth described in the previous section is the field of community development, which has seen a similar sequence of public and philanthropic investment followed by private capital flow.

Most of what we think of as contemporary community development has its roots in the urban renewal activities of the 1950s and 1960s, when neighborhood activists and some philanthropic institutions began to work collaboratively to strengthen poor and distressed communities. Some of the social entrepreneurs of that generation, including the leaders of the Bedford-Stuyvesant Restoration Corporation (Restoration) in Brooklyn, an early community development corporation (CDC), looked to apply business tools and management skills to address social and economic problems and in doing so create greater prosperity for the neighborhood and its residents.

The Ford Foundation was formative in this work. Ford supported organizations like Restoration, which in turned gained the attention of Senators Robert F. Kennedy and Jacob Javits, who sponsored bipartisan legislation to create a federal Office of Economic Opportunity to foster similar community development efforts nationally. The federal government also adopted some of the investment tools Ford had been using to finance the CDCs (direct, below market rate, charitable loans, the first PRIs) into development policy. As we have seen, the 1969 U.S. Tax Reform Act legally defined a PRI as a foundation investment that could generate a financial return but primarily supported a charitable project or activity. PRIs would allow philanthropy to play a major role in the community development field, enlisting foundations as market shapers and demonstrating for more commercial investors that it was possible to pursue social goals while earning financial returns.

In the late 1960s and 1970s, community development became a central component of the federal government's larger national growth strategy for inner cities and a range of new communities across the country. In 1968, Congress passed the New Communities Act, which called explicitly for the "enlistment of private capital in new community development"[1] and would guarantee financing for private entrepreneurs to plan and develop new communities. Refinements to federal community development strategy included block grants that allowed states and municipal governments to channel more funding to CDCs and other nonprofit organizations, which in turn attracted more philanthropic (PRI and other) resources to the field.

Soon a number of regional and national nonprofit development organizations emerged, many of which are still active, including the Maine-based Coastal Enterprises, which today provides financing for job-creating small businesses, natural resource industries, community facilities, and affordable housing; the Neighborhood Reinvestment Corporation (known today as NeighborWorks America); the Enterprise Foundation; and Local Initiatives Support Corporation (LISC), created by the Ford Foundation to pilot financial, technical, and policy support to community development initiatives in three cities. Today LISC operates in 30 cities across the country, drawing on corporate, government, and philanthropic dollars to provide local community development organizations with loans, grants, equity investments, and technical and management assistance.

## The Community Investment Note

Although PRIs have been the primary philanthropic investment instrument for many foundations working in community development, some have expanded their toolbox further. In 1995, for example, the Calvert Foundation pioneered the Community Investment Note, which supports community development activities (e.g., housing, small business development, and the financing of community facilities that include schools, day care centers, and rehabilitation facilities) in the United States and, increasingly, microfinance and fair trade activities internationally. These notes represent an unusual opportunity for *retail* participation in community investment. The Foundation sells these notes directly, and individuals can invest as little as $20 and select an investment term of 1 to 10 years and an interest rate of 0 to 3 percent.

As of 2012, the Calvert Foundation had approximately $200 million invested in 250 community organizations across all 50 states in the United States and more than 100 countries.

|||||||||||||||||||||||||||||||||||||||||||||||||||||||||||||||||||||||||||||

## The Entry of Commercial Capital

The passage of the Community Reinvestment Act (CRA) in 1977, which required banks to extend lending activities to poor communities across the United States, marked a pivotal moment in the field of community development. By providing a mandatory incentive for banks to dramatically increase their investments in poor communities, the federal government paved the way for the growth of a multibillion-dollar industry of affordable housing development and community-based lending.

### Housing and Enterprise Development

In addition to the CRA's compulsory lending requirements, a number of tax credit programs have incented large flows of capital to economic development in housing and enterprise. The Low Income Housing Tax Credit (LIHTC), which was included as a provision of the 1986 Tax Reform Act, is the country's largest affordable rental housing production program. Since its creation, the Housing Credit program has leveraged more than $75 billion in private investment capital, financing the development of more than 2 million affordable rental homes, and includes in its purview a special focus on affordable housing for working families and special needs populations in urban, suburban, and rural communities. It is estimated to finance approximately 90 percent of all affordable housing annually and supports 95,000 jobs.

Similarly, the 2000 New Market Tax Credit (administered by the CDFI at the Department of Treasury) provides tax incentives (tax credits and capital gains tax breaks) to private sector investors who in turn provide capital for business, real estate, and other hard-to-finance projects in poor communities via investment in community development entities (CDEs). To date, the NMTC has mobilized more than $16 billion directly, with an estimated additional $200 billion leveraged from the private sector.

## Growth of Community Development Venture Capital

Most of the dollars in the field of community development flow to the physical infrastructure development of housing, but the field's enterprise component has grown significantly in recent years with the creation and expansion of *community development venture capital*. According to the Community Development Venture Capital Alliance, approximately $2 billion in fund assets (up from $400 million in 2001) provide equity capital to businesses in underserved markets, seeking market rate financial returns while creating good jobs, wealth, and entrepreneurial capacity within the community. Typically, CDVC funds invest cash in exchange for equity stakes in local businesses. The businesses these funds identify are small as are the sums invested, which typically range from $50,000 to $1.5 million.[2]

The first CDVC funds were created in the late 1960s and early 1970s by some of the original community development corporations in response to the lack of private venture capital in many industries and regions generally, and in low-income communities in particular. (The SBIC and a number of state programs attempted to address some of this market failure, though they have not historically targeted venture capital in poor communities.) Some of these early venture funds were capitalized by community development loan funds (CDLF), which typically raised money from socially conscious investors or religious groups willing to accept below market rates of return to advance economic development. However, the number of venture funds focused on poverty relief remained relatively small until the 1990s, when the Clinton Administration created the Community Development Financial Institutions (CDFI) fund at the Treasury Department, some of which went to fund CDVC funds. In 1994, a small group of these funds formed a trade group, the Community Development Venture Capital Alliance, which helped raised the profile of the field.

Today, the CDVC industry comprises approximately 60 funds, about half of which make equity or near-equity investments. Although historically CDVCs received most of their funding from federal, state, and local governments and foundations (often through PRIs, which still account for one-third of the debt dollars invested in these funds), in the 1990s they began to be capitalized by banks and financial institutions, as regulators started to allow banks to satisfy their CRA obligations through CDVC investments.

Over time, many CDVC funds began to broaden their social objectives beyond job creation for low-income individuals. CDVCs were eager to show investors not only how many jobs were created but the quality of those jobs and the broader social and environmental benefits of particular products produced by companies in the CDVC portfolios, which also allowed CDVCs to expand their pool of investors, particularly to wealthy individuals and their foundations.[3]

### Case Study: Pacific Community Ventures

Founded in 1998, Pacific Community Ventures is a nonprofit organization and community development financial institution (CDFI) in California that supports businesses in low-income communities through advisory services and through its partner, Pacific Community Ventures LLC. PCV LLC manages three private equity funds that invest in businesses in underserved areas to create quality jobs for community residents and earn financial returns for investors. Headquartered in San Francisco, PCV manages $60 million and is currently investing out of Pacific Community Ventures LLC III, a $40 million fund that closed in 2007. PCV is a generalist fund but focuses on small, high-growth businesses in specialty food products, ethnic products and services, health and wellness, custom manufacturing, and environmentally friendly products. PCV makes investments of $1 to $4 million.

In 2010, PCV's companies paid $50 million in wages to 3,000 employees. Since its inception, PCV has helped create more than 5,000 jobs for lower-income workers at 250 small businesses.[4] PCV's nonprofit and for-profit work complement each other: PCV's nonprofit arm provides technical assistance to the portfolio companies. This approach, increasingly typical of the CDVC industry, is not unlike that of Root Capital or others promoting social enterprise in developing countries.

# Impact Investing Beyond Community Development

As in the international context, advocates of impact investing ask, beyond the field of government-led community development (broadly defined, and primarily government or philanthropically fostered), whether there are commercial business or enterprise investment opportunities qualify that as *impact*?

As we have seen, a significant increase in interest has occurred in recent years on the demand side, with investors eager to use some of their capital to simultaneously achieve social or environmental impact while also earning financial returns. Yet unlike traditional CDVC, which is primarily trained on poverty alleviation and community development, these new private, social venture funds (e.g., Commons Capital, TBL Capital and Good Capital) often invest in a broader range of areas, from healthcare and education to energy, environment, and "lifestyle" companies.

## Defining Impact Investment Again

Very quickly we see that, despite enthusiasm on the investor side, the definitional parameters remain fuzzy. The questions of *intentionality, market failure,* and *impact* are worth briefly revisiting in the domestic context. Just what firms qualify?

In 2011, on the 100th anniversary of the founding of both IBM and the Carnegie Corporation, Matthew Bishop, author of *Philanthrocapitalism,*[5] wrote a provocative and important piece that appeared in the *Economist* on this question of impact. In the article he asks, "Which has done more for the world, one of its leading companies or one of its most influential charities?"[6]

Bishop makes the company case. "IBM," he writes, "has arguably been a case study in how to create shared value, both through its formalized giving, which is among the most generous in corporate America, but more fundamentally through its everyday business." Bishop suggests that IBM has brought about transformational changes with monumental social impact: the investment in research and invention and promulgation of new technologies with far-ranging benefits (everything from the bar code to the mainframe, the PC, cloud computing, and any number of other advances made by its Nobel laureate researchers); the modeling of important management practices (IBM was a leader in hiring women and giving employees pensions); and employment for many hundreds of thousands of people.

Bishop's point, which is similar to the larger premise of well-functioning market capitalism, is that the greatest impact investment is one made in a responsible, productive, and innovative corporate citizen.[7]

What then of a targeted asset class? Do areas of impact necessarily focus on sectors, geographies, or demographies where markets have failed to attract commercial capital? Does it then also suggest, by definition, at least initially, that these social enterprises will require patient or philanthropic capital while they deliver below-market returns?

The market failure criterion, which is a kind of version of additionality, would likely exclude companies such as IBM from the impact investing universe. It might also exclude a number of the high-profile "doing well by doing good" companies of the 1980s and 1990s: Ben and Jerry's (now owned by Unilever) or Anita Roddick's Body Shop (now owned by L'Oréal), firms well known for their socially and environmentally responsible practices. What about today's ESG corporate all-stars? Starbucks, for example, has a commitment to responsibility that includes significant investment of company resources in local community issues and initiatives, its own environmental and management practices, and ethical sourcing through fair trade and other supports for farmers and their communities (recall Starbucks' various partnerships with organizations like Root Capital). Similarly Patagonia, the privately held company whose CEO, Yvon Chouinard, recently published *The Responsible Company*, devotes 1 percent of its sales to environmental organizations around the world, engages actively in a number of environmental advocacy campaigns, and is vigorous in evaluating the sustainability and energy efficiency of its production processes and those of its suppliers.[8]

These companies are certainly intentional about their corporate citizenship. Further, they seem to subscribe earnestly to the belief that sustainable practices benefit the financial bottom line. But do their core businesses qualify as impact investments? To put a fine point on it, does the world need a $5 latte or a $300 microfleece? And do these definitional distinctions matter?

## The New U.S. Domestic Impact Investments

We return to the "hard to define, know it when you see it" social entrepreneurship premise and examine both a number of companies that impact investors have targeted as qualifying and relevant, as well as firms themselves that self-identify as impact investments. We try to look beyond the traditional field of community development (facilities, infrastructure, and enterprise development) for evidence of new and different investment opportunities.

## Some For-Profit Education

For starters, we follow the money with the foundation PRIs that have been directed toward for-profit companies. Some of these dollars have gone toward education, although the bulk of this funding has gone to facilities development via more traditional PRIs in the form of loans and loan guarantees for charter schools to build new buildings (a PRI favorite). Some education investing, however, has gone directly into for-profit companies. Recall that Gates, for example, invested in Inigral, an education technology start-up. The Kellogg Foundation used a portion of its $100 million mission investing program to make a private equity investment in Acelero Learning, the for-profit Head Start provider founded by serial social entrepreneur Aaron Lieberman, one of the founders of Jumpstart, as well as a $5 million growth capital loan to Revolution Foods, a company that provides healthy school lunches to underserved children in PreK–12 schools.[9]

Recently, the NewSchools Venture Fund, the education venture philanthropy, has opened its portfolio to a few select for-profit investments in education technology and other education companies, including Acelero; Grockit, an online social learning test-prep company; Education Elements, a company that helps schools use technology to improve instruction; and Junyo, a company that works with schools and publishers to collect and use data to improve performance.

To be clear, numerous for-profit education ventures are seeking private capital. Some private equity investors value this market, particularly technology and online, customized learning and professional development and assessment of all kinds, in the hundreds of billions of dollars. But depending on definition, many or most of these would not qualify as intentionally *impact*.

## An Otherwise Eclectic Mix

Companies that have self-identified as *benefit corporations* give insight into the eclectic, growing world of domestic impact investing.

Founded in 2007, B Lab is a nonprofit organization that certifies companies that "use business as a force for good" as *benefit* or B Corps. To become a B Corp, companies must meet extensive standards for their environmental and social performance, scoring at least 80 out of 200 on the B-ratings scale. They must also expand their definition of legal and fiduciary responsibility beyond the interests of traditional shareholders to encompass a broader universe of stakeholders that include employees, suppliers, consumers, community, and the environment. The rigor of the B Corp certification process (companies first self-evaluate and then submit to regular third-party verification) helps ensure against the kind of less meaningful public relations exercise that skeptics call *greenwashing*.[10] In a handful of states, companies can legally incorporate as a B Corp, which is separate from the certification process and represents a new corporate form.

Today, the more than 520 Certified B Corporations across 60 different industries represent $3 billion in revenues. They also range significantly in size and location. The first cohort of B Corps mostly comprised firms that were natural candidates for certification, businesses that already exemplified progressive corporate citizenship. Founding B Corps include Method, a pioneer of "premium environmentally conscious and design-driven" home care, fabric care, and personal care products; King Arthur Flour Company, the country's oldest flour company and one that is 100 percent employee owned; TheGreenOffice.com, an online retailer offering 35,000 green office products and a comprehensive range of sustainability services; Fair Trade Sports, the first sports equipment company in the United States to launch a full line of eco-certified Fair Trade sports balls (it ensures fair wages and healthy working conditions for its workers in developing countries); and TBL Capital, "an intentional, patient capital venture fund" that invests in triple bottom line consumer products, service providers, software, clean technology, green building, health and wellness, and other retail companies. EKO, the private equity firm that invests in environmental markets like carbon, water, and biodiversity, is also a B Corp, as is the Freelancers Insurance Company (FIC). Whether these all satisfy the *intentional* or *additional* criteria in unclear. It's also not clear whether that matters.

## Barriers and Solution to Further Growth: New Corporate Forms Emerge

Although the U.S. impact investing landscape is distinct from some of the BoP investment opportunities, many of the barriers to industry expansion hold in the developing- and developed-world contexts. In the United States, social impact companies and their investors are hampered by issues of infrastructure, including standardized definitions, assessments, and ratings systems. In addition, as the preceding examples suggest, investors in the U.S. context face deal flow challenges. Most of the companies that self-identify as impact are small, with limited absorptive capacity, which explains why firms such as PVC, just like Root Capital in BoP markets, provide both funding and technical assistance to their portfolio companies. Finally, not unlike the BoP case, the companies that satisfy both the size and requisite return hurdles for large commercial investors may be few; at the least, they are hard to find.

As in the developing world context, advances made in the domestic impact investing sphere help to address some of the infrastructure deficiencies. GIIN's tools (e.g., IRIS and ImpactBase) pertain to U.S. as well as BoP companies. Similarly, the GIIRs rating system, developed by B Lab, also includes American impact companies.

On the issue of deal flow, advocates of impact investing in the United States have attempted to address head on the issue of fiduciary responsibility: the desire and legal obligation of investors to seek market rate returns. Although some of these efforts focus on swaying long-held investing conventions to include a longer-term and more sustainable approach,[11] others have sought legal innovations that would allow firms and investors to pursue social or environmental impact, alongside financial returns, without violating fiduciary responsibility.

These new legal forms can be helpful in a number of ways. Consider, for example, a company that has engaged in admirable environmentally and socially responsible practices but then goes public or is acquired by a publicly traded company (e.g., Burt's Bees by Clorox, Ben and Jerry's by Unilever, Body Shop by L'Oréal). In recent years, a number of new legal corporate forms have emerged that attempt to incorporate blended value or double or triple bottom line performance objectives in a company's articles of incorporation. To date, none of these has achieved any kind of critical mass, although statehouses across the country (because businesses are incorporated at the state level) have shown increasing interest.

## Flexible Purpose Corporation

A flexible purpose corporation is a new kind of company, not unlike a C or S corp, that permits its directors to pursue broader objectives than the narrow focus of maximizing financial return for shareholders. They are designed explicitly to shield company managers from potential lawsuits, since the company articles of incorporation state clearly to potential investors that the company has impact-oriented goals in addition to financial objectives.

A number of issues remain unresolved about this new form, including ways for investors to distinguish between those companies that have clear social objectives as a central part of their mission and operations, and those that merely use these stated goals for marketing purposes. Introduced in the California state legislature in February 2011, flexible purpose corporation legislation was passed and went into effect on January 1, 2012.

## The Low-Profit Limited Liability Company (L3C)

The L3C is a low-profit, limited liability company, a legal business entity created for companies that have an explicit and stated mission of achieving a social goal while making a profit, which is returned to shareholders. L3Cs were created as a kind of bridge structure to facilitate investment in socially beneficial, for-profit ventures, allowing the investments to qualify for PRI funding. In order to authorize L3C designation, states must pass legislation to amend the General Limited Liability Company Act (LLC). Thus far, Illinois, Louisiana, Maine, Michigan, North Carolina, Rhode Island, Utah, Vermont, and Wyoming have authorized L3Cs, and legislation has been introduced in a number of other states. Some groups, like Americans for Community Development, are lobbying to pass federal legislation along these lines.

## B Corporations

As part of their infrastructure-building efforts, the B Lab leaders have been lobbying states to formally and legally allow for B-corporation designation as a new corporate form. As discussed previously, benefit corporation status enables company managers and owners leeway to pursue both profit and social and/or environmental impact objectives. To qualify as a B corp, companies must have social purpose as part of their business operations and must embed in their articles of incorporation a stated objective that takes into account the interests of a broad range of stakeholders (e.g., employees, the community, the environment), not only the company owners. In other words, the company value includes financial performance but also its commitment to social objectives. Unlike, say, L3Cs, no potential limits are placed on the company's range of activities or returns. Like L3Cs, however, B-corp legislation is gaining momentum at the state level. New York recently became the seventh state to adopt the new corporate structure, joining California, Hawaii, Maryland, New Jersey, Vermont, and Virginia. B-corp legislation is also pending in Michigan, North Carolina, Pennsylvania, and Washington, D.C. B corps are a legal form, not to be confused with certified B corps, a designation for any company in any state that has passed the B Lab certification process. On January 3, 2012, Patagonia was the first company to take advantage of the new California law, officially becoming a B corporation.[12]

## CICs in the United Kingdom

Alternative corporate forms may be a new feature of the American legal and capitalist landscape, but they have been alive and well in Europe for years (and in some countries, like Germany, for centuries), including numerous kinds of cooperative ownership and governance structures. In 2005, the United Kingdom allowed for the incorporation of community interest corporations (CICs), a national corporate form. Like the flexible purpose corporation, CIC designation means that companies can have explicitly social or environmental objectives that they advance without subjecting themselves to investor charges that they are not fulfilling fiduciary responsibility. As of 2012, there were approximately 6,000 CICs registered in the United Kingdom, and a number of other European countries are examining the model.

# Chapter 13

||||||||||||||||||||||||||||||||||||||||||||||||||||||||||||||||||||||||||

# THE ENTERPRISE PERSPECTIVE: SHARED VALUE CAPITALISM

In January 2011, Harvard Business School economist Michael Porter spoke to the crowd assembled at Davos of his vision for "shared value capitalism." Companies, he said, must create economic value "in a way that *also* creates value for society by addressing its needs and challenges."

Porter, who made his name in the field of strategy—both corporate and national competitive—takes an enterprise rather than investor perspective. Writing with colleague Mark Kramer in the *Harvard Business Review*, Porter argues that most businesses have an "outdated approach to value creation . . . optimizing short-term financial performance in a bubble while missing the most important customer needs and ignoring the broader influences that determine their longer term success." Porter and Kramer focus on what firms can do to restore their role in "creating shared value, not just profit per se." In their view, "Companies must take the lead in bringing business and society back together."[1]

# What Is Shared Value Capitalism?

In Porter's framework, a company can create shared value in a number of ways but primarily by reconceiving products and markets or redefining productivity along the value chain. This first category has to do with creating new products and services to fill unmet needs, whether they are related to things like new energy standards (e.g., GE's energy efficient Ecomagination line) or basic health care, housing, and nutrition of poor people at the bottom of Prahalad's pyramid.

Porter's second category, the value chain, is also broad conceptually, ranging across a wide spectrum of activities. Among the examples he cites are Walmart's packaging reduction and truck rerouting, both measures that saved hundreds of millions of dollars and created environmental benefits, and Nestlé Nespresso's redesigned procurement (the kind it achieved in partnership with Root Capital, described in Chapter 8) in which Nestlé helped improve farming conditions for coffee growers, by providing credit, agricultural inputs, management assistance, to increase its reliable supply of coffee while also paying a premium directly to the farmers for better beans.

## Shared Value Capitalism versus Traditional Corporate Social Responsibility (CSR)

Porter contends that shared value capitalism is about changing the core business of a firm and therefore differs from the decades-old field of corporate social responsibility (CSR), which he posits has traditionally centered on preserving or enhancing a company's reputation. The more optimistic advocates of CSR suggest that, by taking into account the interests not only of shareholders but of all stakeholders (e.g., consumers, employees, communities, the larger environment), CSR will improve a company's bottom line over the long term.

Critics of CSR represent a wide range of disciplines and perspectives. Like Porter, grassroots activists often contend that CSR efforts are a kind of window dressing, carried out by nonbusiness units (marketing or public relations) within firms that do not ultimately reform company practices. A number of policy analysts suggest that CSR diverts attention from the important regulatory work of government. As Robert Reich, labor secretary under President Bill Clinton, puts it, "The message that companies are moral beings with social responsibilities diverts public attention from the task of establishing laws and rules in the first place. The praise or blame for a company's behavior is soon forgotten and barely affects the behavior of consumers or investors."[2]

Many economists, most famously Milton Friedman, who referred to CSR as a "fundamentally subversive doctrine," have argued that CSR is expensive and hard to justify since the purpose of a firm is to maximize shareholder value. Anything short of that explicit objective detracts from the firm's core mission and violates fiduciary duty.[3] Though less polemical than Friedman, Porter adopts a similar "limited connection to business" view of CSR, which he argues is separate from profit maximization. While CSR focuses on doing good, he maintains, shared value focuses on value creation. His is not a moral argument but one rooted in the mutual economic interest of firms and the larger society.

## Is This New? Sharing Credit for Shared Value

How new is Porter's vision? Only two years before at Davos, Bill Gates called for a new kind of *creative capitalism*, one that could harness both the productive and efficient forces of economic self-interest and concern for others. In Gates's words, this was "market-based social change" that helps "ease the world's inequities" by addressing social and environmental problems.[4]

Neither Gates's nor Porter's unified theories of capitalism appear out of an intellectual or policy vacuum. They both draw heavily on a number of earlier contributions to the field, among them Jed Emerson's concept of *blended value*, the idea that all organizations, nonprofit and for-profit, and all investors, produce value "that consists of economic, social, and environmental components" that are "nondivisible."[5]

Porter also makes important points from the literature on measurement time horizons and the *short-termism* that has come to characterize operational and investment decisions,[6] or what Porter calls the "fallacy of short-term cost reduction." The peril lies in the faulty incentives that arise from punishingly brief reporting cycles and compensation structures tied to those cycles, the noxious consequences of which were laid bare by the financial crisis.

All of these themes are explored by a number of Porter's colleagues, who have examined, in different ways, the social financial value nexus. Rosabeth Moss Kanter, for example, illustrates how vanguard companies like IBM, P&G, Publicis Group, Shinhan Financial Group, Banco Real, and Cemex simultaneously create "innovation, profits, growth, and social good."[7] Lynn Paine's most recent research on companies that meld high ethical standards with strong financial results includes *Capitalism at Risk: Rethinking the Role of Business*. In this post-crash analysis, Paine and her colleagues Joseph Bower and Herman Leonard insist that "business must stop seeing itself as merely a self-regarding participant in a system that is largely 'given' — or shaped by others — and start seeing itself as a leader in protecting and improving the system that gives it life."[8] While they argue that government has an important role, they, like Porter, also insist that business must take the lead in securing the future of capitalism.[9]

## Externalities, Public Goods, and Sustainable Capitalism

At their heart, the *creative* or *shared value* paradigms attempt to address the problems of market failure and externalities: social or environmental costs or benefits (public goods) that are not fully priced by the market. In the environmental community, scholars and advocates have grappled with these issues as they relate to the "commons" — how society addresses externalities, both positive and negative — when external costs such as pollution, which the producer does not bear, are typically overproduced and external benefits, such as education, public safety, clean air, or clean water, are usually not produced by private markets.

The literature on the treatment of public goods is vast. When it comes to public policy, society tries to address negative externalities like pollution with regulations, taxes, fines, or market mechanisms of some kind or another (e.g., a cap and trade regime for pollution) that helps price a good or service and allows firms to internalize the externalities. Positive externality *public goods* such as education are often provided directly by the government, or, as we have seen increasingly in the United States, the government pays for the public good or service, which is delivered by private, often nonprofit third-party organizations.

*Sustainable capitalism* is a kind of ecological version of shared value capitalism, both premised on the idea that, over the long term, some social and environmental costs will ultimately create internal costs for firms, and the firm will realize greater value by mitigating or addressing these costs. Generation Investment Management, a firm founded in 2004 by Al Gore and Goldman Sachs's David Blood, describes sustainable capitalism as "a framework that seeks to maximize long-term economic value by reforming markets to address real needs while considering *all* costs and stakeholders."[10]

Sustainable capitalism, according to its proponents, "*does not represent* a trade-off with profit maximization but instead actually fosters superior long-term value creation."[11] From a corporate strategy perspective, sustainable capitalism means taking into account environmental, social, and governance costs in operations and risk assessment. For investment purposes, it means identifying things like stranded assets, those with a value that would change significantly, either positively or negatively, were a reasonable price on carbon or water imposed (or regulation of labor standards improved) in emerging markets. As we have seen, a number of firms, from the boutique to the mainstream, have attempted to incorporate the sustainable paradigm into their investment strategies.

Increasingly, researchers are examining the performance of companies that take this long view and try to turn sustainable practices on a number of environmental, social, and governance dimensions into strategic advantages, either through enhanced revenue or reduced cost. In addition to valuing the benefits of positive social or environmental activities, these researchers attempt to quantify the impact of negative activities that may result in brand degradation, investor flight (and resulting increased cost of capital), difficulty in finding cooperative suppliers, or the challenges associated with recruiting and retaining talent. A number of recent studies found evidence that sustainable companies outperform their nonsustainable peers in the long run.[12]

## Global Firms, Local Partners

The shared value paradigm typically concentrates on large companies. For example, participants in a 2010 shared value roundtable at Goldman Sachs included representatives from Cisco Systems, Hewlett-Packard, IBM, Western Union, Alcoa, InterContinental Hotels Group, Dow Chemical, Medtronic, and PG&E. What is notable, however, is that much of this work, particularly in the developing-world context, relies on partnerships between sizable corporations and local social entrepreneurs. "Moving into emerging markets has caused us to look at health differently," explained the executive from Medtronic, the medical device company. "It's a whole different market when you start looking at models of care that exist and don't exist, and the expertise that doesn't exist, and how you can play a role in complementing that with shared value."[13] Many companies look to social entrepreneurs for relevant expertise. Such is the case for example, with Nestlé, Root Capital, and the Guatemalan coffee growers.

## Ashoka's Hybrid Value Chain (HVC)

These kinds of collaborations have long been pursued by social entrepreneurs. Bill Drayton has worked with companies for decades to create partnerships that bridge the business and civic sectors. At Ashoka, these *hybrid value chains* allow for important symbiosis: businesses offer scale, expertise in operations, and financing; social entrepreneurs offer lower costs, strong social networks, and a deep understanding of local customers and communities. Together, says Drayton, they can "remake global economies and create lasting social change."[14]

Consider, for example, the housing industry, where much of Ashoka's HCV work is targeted. Approximately one-sixth of the world's population lives in slums and squatter cities. In the HVC view, approximately 1 billion people who are potential consumers for cement companies, tile and brick makers, banks, utilities, and others are shut out of the formal housing market. Ashoka believes that in housing, like so many other sectors, collaborations between firms and nonprofits could help unlock this market and social-impact opportunity.[15]

In Colombia, for example, Ashoka introduced Colceramica, a Colombian subsidiary of a South American building materials retailer, to Kairos, a human rights organization that works with people displaced by armed conflict. Together they produced a business plan and mutually beneficial partnership: Colceramica provided the tiles and business expertise, and Kairos recruited a salesforce of women who were paid from sales proceeds from customers while still reducing Colceramica's distribution costs by a third. The program launched in 2006 and by 2009 had sales of $12 million across six Colombian cities, improving the living conditions of nearly 30,000 families and giving 200 saleswomen an important monthly income.

Ashoka has pursued similar HVCs across the globe. In India, Ashoka brought together mortgage companies, for-profit housing groups, and local citizen sector groups to create affordable apartments for the informal and local workforces. (India's housing deficit is estimated at approximately 25 million.) This partnership promises to create thousands of homes, both for buyers and for laborers and their families, and $100 million in sales for the companies.

Ashoka's HVC initiatives are not limited to housing. In an innovative healthcare partnership in India, Ashoka helped incubate Healthpoint Services, a for-profit company that joined businesses, citizen-sector groups, venture capital and social investors to deliver high-quality healthcare to rural villages. Its clinics, called E Health Points, use telemedicine such as video technology and electronic medical records so that patients do not have to travel extensively to see a doctor. On the basis of the success of Healthpoint's pilots, the finance minister for Punjab asked that 600 E Health Points be built in that state.

## Muhammad Yunus's Social Business

Muhammad Yunus calls these kinds of initiatives *social businesses*.[16] For Yunus, a social business is one in which the company is focused on providing a social benefit rather than maximizing profit for owners. Social businesses are typically owned by investors who "seek social benefits such as poverty reduction, healthcare for the poor, social justice, [and] global sustainability" but who reinvest profits into the firm or use them to provide more goods and services. In Yunus's view, the Grameen Bank he founded is a social business, as are its Grameen Family of Companies affiliates, which provide a wide range of goods and services to poor people, from credit and healthcare to telecommunications and Internet service.

In 2005, Yunus says that Grameen made a giant step for social business by partnering with French yogurt maker Danone to make a fortified yogurt for Bangladeshi children that the poor could afford. As in the HVC model, Grameen and Danone worked together closely, researching options in the yogurt lab and in local bazaars, where traditional mishit doti, Bangladeshi yogurt that is stored in clay pots, does not require refrigeration. Without refrigeration, which keeps the cultures in Danone's products alive, Danone could not guarantee consistency of flavor or texture. But because most rural Bangladeshis are off the electricity grid, refrigeration was not going to be possible. Therefore, Grameen and Danone designed a distribution system using "Grameen ladies." These borrowers of the Grameen Bank live in the villages Grameen serves and sell the yogurt, moving it rapidly from factory to consumer. Yunus has since gone on to form social business joint ventures with Intel, Adidas, and BASF, among others.

◖

In some ways, the *shared value, creative*, and *sustainable capitalism* perspectives are more sweeping and radical than those of the impact investing school, which is trained on a distinct asset class of intentionally social purpose businesses. Shared value, on the other hand, looks to reform the way all businesses participate in society. What is noteworthy, however, about both approaches, and particularly the enterprise view, is how little they emphasize the role of government; Porter and Paine and her colleagues all suggest that business must take the lead in "fixing market capitalism." The following chapters suggest instead that public policy can and should play a vital, robust role in enabling firms and their investors to become more responsible, profitable actors in our market capitalist system.

# III

IIIIIIIIIIIIIIIIIIIIIIIIIIIIIIIIIIIIIIIIIIIIIIIIIIIIIIIIIIIIIIIIII

# SOCIAL INNOVATION IN THE PUBLIC SECTOR

At the dawn of the twenty-first century, the social entrepreneurship revolution has made important inroads into the public sector. Although the movement's pioneers, particularly in the United States, were comfortably rooted in the nonprofit sphere—recall those social entrepreneurs who had founded new organizations in reaction to the perceived failure of both the public and private sectors to meet pressing human needs—their influence is now manifest in a number of government reform efforts. Many of these social entrepreneurs, as we have seen, have come to recognize that government plays a crucial role in enhancing the scale and impact of their own work, in fostering innovation and entrepreneurship, social and otherwise, and in shaping markets to serve the public good.

This more affirmative view of the positive and catalytic role of government has convinced some social entrepreneurs to forge closer ties with their public sector allies or to take up posts within government. A new breed of activist, a kind of *civic entrepreneur*, is now informing governing philosophies and practices at the local, state, and federal levels with many of the tenets of social entrepreneurship. In the public sector context, we call this the *social innovation* school.

## What Do We Mean by Social Innovation in the Public Sector?

What, exactly, do we mean by *social innovation* in the public sector? Like social entrepreneurship, the concept eludes any one definition and bears different significance in different contexts. However, a number of common themes have emerged across polities. At its root, social innovation is an effort to *improve* the way the government addresses deeply entrenched social problems, to shape markets to serve common purpose where they have traditionally failed (i.e., externalities and public goods), and to ensure that either public or private actors produce value when meeting human needs.[1]

A priori, then, nearly all of the contemporary social innovation efforts focus in some way on *proving* that value through measurement and evaluation and then directing government resources to scale these proven and evidence-based solutions to social change. To this end, as we will see, governments at local, state, and federal levels are using more sophisticated data collection and assessment for performance measurement and management purposes.

In some places, social innovation concentrates on the workings of government itself. Here, the *innovation* school draws on earlier reform efforts, including the "reinventing government" work of the Clinton administration, which primarily aimed to make the internal operations of government more efficient and federal agencies more externally or customer oriented. Today's social innovation agenda, however, is fundamentally more sweeping in ambition and practice, creating policy laboratories to nurture new approaches to program design and implementation and open innovation initiatives to enhance the transparency of governmental activities.

Other social entrepreneurs in government focus on adapting a new set of tools that includes prizes, challenges, targeted funds, and big data initiatives, among others, to promote greater innovation either within government itself or within the entrepreneurial third-party entities, both nonprofits or private sector companies, that deliver social services on government's behalf.

This question of *delivery* is a central one. Recall that over the past 20 years, the contours of the social sector have shifted dramatically as government's role has morphed from one of direct service provision to pro-curement, contracting with third-party organizations to provide an array of social goods and services. Most social innovation advocates believe to varying degrees that competition between and among these private pro-viders and their government counterparts is central to the innovation pro-cess and to ensuring the value of the goods and services provided.[2]

Some of the more strict adherents of the Schumpeterian creative destruction school believe that this kind of competition (i.e., breaking government hold where it has a monopoly on the delivery of a good or service, such as in education) is the only way to achieve innovation. In this view, the citizen is customer, and, per the market analogy, consumer choice will necessarily drive improved quality and efficiency in the deliv-ery and value of social services.[3] Others are less dogmatic about the pri-macy of the market model for social innovation, instead honing in on what works and bringing it to scale. According to Kim Smith, who has studied social innovation and is an expert in its application to education policy, "While innovation often connotes shiny, brand new, and wildly different, all it really means is new ways of doing things that bring about an improved result."[4]

Harvard Business School's Clay Christensen characterizes this distinc-tion as one between *disruptive innovation* (new products or services that break with current practice and displace established competitors) and *sustaining innovation* (improving the value of products or services within the existing system).[5] Advocates of social innovation embrace both kinds in identifying and spreading what works. This pragmatic, evidence-based view holds that although competition in some form is important, govern-ment can foster innovation and entrepreneurship, social and otherwise, in any number of ways and places, often in the form of federal support for local or community solutions.

The social innovation school, therefore, represents more than a benign conception of government; it imagines a resoundingly more affirmative array of responsibilities for government that are active and catalytic, wherein government becomes a market shaper that can create the infrastructure, architecture, and conditions to support the way private actors, both non-profit and commercial, meet needs where previous efforts have failed.

Over the past generation, an artificial states-versus-markets ideologi-cal segregation has calcified our political dialogue. The newer social innovation school rejects this either-or bifurcation and instead posits that government is necessary for entrepreneurship (social and commercial); and in turn, healthy and entrepreneurial markets are necessary for a well-functioning economy and society.

# Chapter 14

THE CASE OF NEW YORK
CITY: SOCIAL INNOVATION
THE BLOOMBERG WAY

If there is a one-man embodiment of public servant as CEO, it is New York City's Mike Bloomberg. A brilliantly successful media and technology entrepreneur, Bloomberg ran for mayor on the leadership achievements of his business career and promised to bring his "bottom line insights" to the public sector. In his inaugural State of the City Speech, Bloomberg told New Yorkers,

> I was elected largely on the basis of my business background. I think New Yorkers expect me to run city government in much the same way I ran my company. I am doing exactly that. I built a successful, worldwide media company by making employees part of the team—with the incentives and desire to do more, do it better, and do it with less.[1]

Well into his third term as New York's chief executive officer, Bloomberg remains both a revered and controversial figure in the city, in large measure because of his private sector approach to governance.

Bloomberg is not always consistent in how he applies business jargon. For example, the billionaire mayor alternately refers to New York City as a company, product, or brand. On the other hand, clear tenets of his approach exemplify important elements of the larger social innovation school. Choice, competition, and greater accountability to citizen-consumers are defining qualities. Similarly, rigorous measurement through exhaustive data collection and the evaluation of these data to inform policy design and agency management lie at the heart of the Bloomberg paradigm. "In God we trust," the mayor is known to say. "Everyone else bring data."

Bloomberg has also hired many innovators, some (and sometimes controversially) from the corporate world, but others with a strong mix of public and private sector experience, like Shaun Donovan, or career civic entrepreneurs with extraordinary track records of innovation within government, like Linda Gibbs.

Some elements of the "Bloomberg Way" are well known to New Yorkers and policy makers the world over. The high-profile hallmarks of what some call "New York Inc." include the introduction of customer service surveys at city agencies; an overhaul of NYC websites and other consumer-oriented communication technologies; the reform of the Mayor's Management Reports, the city's report card, to focus more scrupulously on outcomes; and ambitious and business-friendly redevelopment efforts, from the city's Olympic bid to the Hudson and Atlantic Yards.

However, some of the more profound governing innovations of the Bloomberg administration have occurred in the daily work of the city's agencies, where a sometimes different approach to government has been brewing. A number of these activities have played out on a public and often contentious stage, such as former school chancellor Joel Klein's effort to bring the education reform platform to New York City. Yet many less heralded policy experiments are taking place across city government, particularly in the delivery of social services.

In this chapter, we examine how measurement, evaluation, and a proactive use of data collection and analysis have transformed the work and policy objectives of a number of the city's social welfare agencies, including the Human Resources Administration and the Department of Homeless Services; the education reform agenda of Joel Klein at the Department of Education, where he sought to introduce competition and choice in different forms to improve the performance of failing schools; the policy laboratory approach of the newly created Center for Economic Opportunity; and the market-shaping maneuvers of Shaun Donovan, Commissioner of Housing Preservation and Development, who looked to harness private capital for public purpose to ameliorate the city's affordable housing crisis. Collectively, this work represents the significant influence of social entrepreneurship in the public sphere.

## ■ The Value of Evaluation: CompStating New York's Social Services

In *The Tipping Point*, Malcolm Gladwell popularized the story of the dramatic shifts that occurred within the New York Police Department; these cultural changes toward creativity and innovation led to a significant reduction in crime. Among the levers of change was the use of CompStat, a data collection and analysis tool that has been widely credited with helping to significantly reduce all categories of crime across New York City. A similar but lesser-known tale of data, performance management, and radical improvement in quality of life for New Yorkers involves the field of human services.[2]

The Bloomberg administration didn't invent data collection for evaluation and management. For years, city agencies have attempted, with mixed success, to track clients, the services provided to them, and the value or impact of those services. Under the Rudolph Giuliani administration, significant gains were made in this area, particularly as many agencies invested in new technological resources. Just as important as the tools, however, is the leadership's ethos and their commitment to the use of measurement and evaluation, the funding, and the appointments necessary to make assessments meaningful. For better or worse, Mike Bloomberg has shown himself to be one of the greatest of advocates for data analysis in city government.

As the cases of the Human Resources Administration (HRA) and the Department of Homeless Services (DHS) show, effective use of measurement and evaluation not only allows an agency, and even a city, to understand how and where it is having social impact, but it can also lead to a *fundamental reconception of agency purpose* by identifying outcomes the organization is really trying to achieve and what indicators best measure its success in meeting those objectives.

## Human Resources Administration: Using Data to Improve Welfare Reform

New York City's Human Resources Administration (HRA) is the nation's largest municipal social service agency. With 15,000 employees and a $5.6 billion budget (and more than $15 billion in contracts), HRA provides social services including welfare-to-work programs, temporary public assistance, food stamps, Medicaid, HIV/AIDS support services, domestic violence prevention, homelessness prevention, and emergency interventions to more than 3 million people.

In 1996, HRA was charged with managing the city's welfare reform efforts, which had begun well before federal legislation took hold. During the Giuliani administration, HRA's mission changed from an agency primary concerned with providing income supports and social services to one that would offer temporary economic and social service support and whenever possible help its clients to achieve economic independence. This welfare-to-work shift came with an evaluation challenge: while moving people "off welfare" can be clocked by a simple reduction in the rolls, helping them to achieve economic independence is both harder to measure and less accurately reported.

In response, HRA began to develop a number of new data collection tools that were similar to the police department's CompStat to help them better assess and fulfill this new mission. One of the first of these was Job-Stat, launched in 1998 by HRA Commissioner Jason Turner. JobStat was designed to increase agency accountability for reducing the city's welfare caseload *and* for finding people jobs by focusing Job Center staff on indicators related to job placement, enrollment, and retention rates (not just dropping people from the rolls).

Under Commissioner Verna Eggleston, appointed by Mayor Bloomberg, the HRA further refined this approach of using data to inform policy decisions. Among her other initiatives, Eggleston instituted new measures to track *sustainable* employment: duration, retention, and quality of job. VendorStat, for example, allows the agency to better track contractors who must place clients in employment and ensure they remain employed. HRA now relies on a variety of data tracking tools (Homecare VendorStat, HASAStat, and AdminStat, among others) to enhance its performance management and inform changes to service design and delivery.

One of Eggleston's most innovative programs, WeCARE, offers a more customized approach to the employment needs and abilities of HRA's clients. WeCARE grew out of extensive research and evaluation showing that most of the individuals who received public assistance for more than five years had considerable medical and mental health barriers to work, and that enormous sums of money were being spent on these clients who were not getting healthier or any closer to self-sufficiency. The more customized approach to placement and self-sufficiency has proven enormously cost effective.

## Department of Homeless Services: New Focus on Ending Homelessness

In 2002, Bloomberg hired Linda Gibbs as commissioner of the Department of Homeless Services (DHS) to oversee the city's ambitious strategy to end chronic homelessness. This effort was notable for many reasons, not the least for the way Gibbs helped the agency to fundamentally reconceive the issue of homelessness and solutions to it. When Gibbs arrived at DHS, she found an agency passionately and capably committed to serving the city's homeless. "In terms of the ability of the organization to meet its basic mandate—which is to provide good, decent shelter—it was very good," she says. However, "they served [the] homeless; they didn't solve homelessness."[3]

Gibbs led a massive strategic planning process within her agency to examine this issue and ultimately determined that housing, not shelter, should be the long-term goal of the agency.[4] As in the changes in welfare-to-work metrics at HRA, this new direction meant measures of success at DHS could not simply be getting people off the streets or numbers of people served in shelters. Rather, the agency's new goal represented a fundamental shift from outputs to outcomes, which then required investment in programs and policies such as homelessness prevention.

With this new objective, data collection and evaluation also changed, beginning with the city's first count of the street homeless population.

Permanent housing placements became a new data point tracked, and incentives were put in place to make these placements possible. DHS also began to look more closely at homelessness at the neighborhood level, using data and GIS maps to hone in on the community districts that were experiencing the greatest number of homeless families. Not surprisingly, but not previously known, more than one-quarter of homeless families each year came from a small number of neighborhoods, which DHS then began to target with more preventive services.

The legacy of this work is still being defined as New York City and State work to build new supportive housing in economically challenging times. However, DHS remains an unequivocal example of how data collection and analysis, a recalibration of performance evaluation from outputs to outcomes, and a change in the selection of programs and indicators to measure success against those desired outcomes can help shift the mission of an agency and transform the way it addresses an entrenched social problem.

In 2006, Bloomberg appointed Gibbs deputy mayor for Health and Human Services, where she would oversee nine city agencies with a combined budget of more than $20 billion.

## Pay for Performance: Performance-Based Contracts

The shift to a more outcomes-based focus of evaluation has also, in some agencies, involved greater use of performance-based contracts with the city's vendors. These kinds of contracts are mostly as they sound, arrangements that link payment to the provider's ability to meet agreed-upon performance targets. Under performance-based contracts, the third party contractors bear the risk. Historically, performance-based contracts have been used with private sector vendors for things like infrastructure building (e.g., roads, construction) where outcomes are clear and specific.

In recent years, a number of the city's human service agencies have experimented with performance-based contracts with their social service vendors. This approach is easier in some areas of social service than in others, where outcomes are easier to define and measure. For example,

HRA may use performance-based contracts to link vendor payment to certain clear outcome milestones such as job placement, retention, or, as we have seen, retention in higher-wage jobs. DHS, too, has a large number of contracts, and increasingly, it has used bonuses for high-performing vendors. However, for other agencies, performance contracts can be difficult to design or implement, particularly when outcomes themselves are murky. Take, for example, the case of foster care, which is overseen by the Administration for Children's Services. Is the desirable outcome adoption, reunification, creating a stable environment for the child, making sure the child stays in school, or ensuring that the child gets proper medical attention, or all of the above?

Clearly, performance-based contracts lend themselves more readily to some circumstances than others. Their increased use, however, particularly in the way they shift risk to vendors and insist on outcomes (not unlike prizes), is part of the larger pay-for-performance approach of the social innovation school.

## ■ Competition: Joel Klein and the NYC Department of Education

Michael Bloomberg was swift to act on his campaign pledge to overhaul New York City's challenged school system. He razed the independent Board of Education, created instead a Department of Education and a Panel for Education Policy, whose members required mayoral approval, and appointed as chancellor Joel Klein, a man who embodied Bloomberg's reform vision. Klein's stint as head of Bertelsmann gave him private sector bona fides. Moreover, his battles as antitrust attorney at the U.S. Department of Justice, where he successfully broke up Microsoft, appealed to the new mayor. When it came to monopolies, Klein was one of the nation's fiercest dragon slayers.

Though a product of New York's public schools, Klein had no educational experience, and for this reason his chancellorship required a special state waiver. This exception roiled his detractors, as did his many private-sector hires, but Klein believed it was an asset to reform. "The DOE was fundamentally a monopoly," he said. "The mayor wanted someone who was *not* a career educator, not captive to the organization."[5]

Klein explained his philosophy thus:

> Whether a school does well or poorly, it will get the students it needs to stay in business, because most kids have no other choice. And that, in turn, creates no incentive for better performance, greater efficiency, or more innovation—all things as necessary in public education as they are in any other field. . . . A full-scale transition from a government-run monopoly to a competitive marketplace won't happen quickly. But that is no reason not to begin introducing more competition.[6]

Like Bloomberg, Klein believed that competition meant creating more choices for parents, which would ultimately improve the performance of individual students and schools and close the achievement gap. In policy terms, this approach resulted in the testing of a number of new approaches meant to ensure or create higher-quality schools, and these experiments drew directly from the education reform playbook: small schools; charter schools; community-designed and -led schools; experiments with curriculum; teaching models; technology; changes to the length of the school day; merit pay where possible; closing failing schools; and training for teachers and principals, who were often given greater latitude over school management (budget, hiring and firing, and curriculum) in return for accountability for student performance and outcomes, as measured by test scores and school report cards. Ultimately, Klein opened 125 new small high schools, 100 charter schools in high poverty neighborhoods, and closed dozens of others.

Klein also relied on a number of partners outside the DOE to advance his reform agenda, including social entrepreneurship nonprofits (TFA, City Year, New Leaders for New Schools, New Visions for New Schools, The New Teacher Project, and others) and the movement's philanthropic heavy hitters, like Gates and Broad. Klein's private sector allies included McKinsey & Company, which assisted with the initial DOE reorganization from a 32-district to region system, and GE's Jack Welch, who helped create the NYC Leadership Academy for school principals, modeled on GE's corporate training center and, according to Klein, intended to train school leaders to think less like "an agent of the bureaucracy" and more like "the CEO of his or her own school."[7] These supporters were also important advocates for the chancellor's broader reform platform. When Klein and Bloomberg lobbied New York State to raise the cap on the number of charter schools, for example, Klein reports that "philanthropic and business interests raised millions to support the mobilization effort, run ads, and hire lobbyists. We prevailed, and the cap was raised substantially."[8]

Klein's critics are many, and his struggles with the educational establishment and the unions in particular are legendary and instructive. Many veteran educators believed he distrusted them, as evidenced by his consistent preference for private sector hires (including some particularly unsuccessful ones, like Cathie Black) and his hostility toward a number of entrenched practices. Some have argued, too, that his data-driven intensity, especially regarding test scores, was as likely to improve management efficiency as the quality of teaching and learning (i.e., "assessment is a tool, not the solution"[9] concerns). Concern came not just from union leadership but often from school leaders and teachers who took issue with the antiseptic laboratory approach.

Education reform, in New York City and beyond, is the subject of rich and intense debate and discussion, though beyond the scope of this book. It is still early to render a verdict on Klein's legacy and the success of his social entrepreneurship approach, though some recent data show education gains, particularly in four-year graduation rates and some elementary and middle school test scores in reading and math.[10] It is also true that large systems like New York City's have a long way to go to substantially improve education.

What is clear is that Klein's work represents a new kind of approach to social change. Although he often described his mission of improving New York City and the nation's public schools as "the civil rights battle of our time," it is as much a revolution in how we think about waging that battle. Rather than use the courts (the approach of the *Brown v. Board of Education* era), Klein and others use the tools of policy design, informed by a new view of the public sector and of the power of markets to shape the delivery of public goods.

Klein's social entrepreneurship legacy should also be assessed in impact beyond New York City. Jonathan Mahler, who has studied Klein's work and education policy more broadly, observes, "Now that education reform has become established as a national movement, backed by countless millionaires and endorsed by President Obama himself, it's easy to forget that Klein was once a lonely pioneer, if not the first chancellor to try to overhaul his schools, then surely the first to undertake such an ambitious effort to do so, and in the city with the largest—1.1 million students—and most complicated school system in the country."[11]

Klein not only emboldened like-minded reformers like Michelle Rhee, the no-holds-barred schools chancellor in Washington, D.C., he raised a new generation of education social entrepreneurs. Alumni of Klein's administration include Christopher Cerf, now the state superintendent in New Jersey; Andres Alonso, superintendent in Baltimore; Garth Harries, assistant superintendent in New Haven; J. C. Brizzard, superintendent first in Rochester, then in Chicago; Marcia Lyles, superintendent of Delaware's Christina school district; and John White, who in 2011 took over the New Orleans schools. This next generation of change makers is advancing the social innovation agenda in relentless pursuit of what works in education.

## ▨ The Laboratory: New York City Center for Economic Opportunity

When it comes to innovation, Michael Bloomberg's greatest achievement may be the work of a small and mostly unheralded office, the Center for Economic Opportunity, an in-house poverty-fighting laboratory that has made remarkable strides in influencing how the city, as well as the country, addresses entrenched social and economic problems. After all, the mayor notes, "the world's leading science and technology companies have set up research and development divisions to pioneer new products. Why not do the same in the fight against poverty?"[12]

In 2006, while New York City was generally prosperous, poverty persisted. In response, Bloomberg created the Commission for Economic Opportunity, a group of leaders from government, the nonprofit sector, business, academia, and foundations that included people like Dick Parsons of Time Warner, Jeff Canada of the Harlem Children's Zone, and Rockefeller's Judith Rodin to analyze the causes, scope, and consequences of the city's chronic poverty.

The commission's two major findings were both related to what the city did not know. The first involved flaws in the federal poverty measure, which resulted in an imperfect understanding of how many people actually lived in poverty in New York. The second had to do with how the city attacked poverty, both its causes and effects. The commission called for a much clearer sense of what worked programmatically. In response, the mayor established the Center for Economic Opportunity (CEO) and charged it with reducing the number of people living in poverty in New York City through innovative and results-driven initiatives.

The CEO was to be headed by Veronica White, who had served as COO of the New York City Partnership and CEO of the New York City Housing Partnership and who would report to Linda Gibbs, now deputy mayor for health and human services. Like Gibbs, White was passionate about the power of data, analysis, measurement, and evaluation to improve public policy. The driving force behind the CEO, in spirit and practice, is this question of proven results.

While some of the CEO's small staff focused on devising a more accurate and useful poverty metric, most became engaged in program work, which began with the creation of one of the country's first innovation funds. The CEO uses this fund to provide financial support to 20 city agencies implementing programs that both reduce poverty and increase self-sufficiency among city residents. In particular, the CEO focuses on programs that fill service gaps and improve education, skills, and job opportunities for low-income New Yorkers, with emphasis on the needs of the working poor, young adults, and children. Perhaps more important than the dollars, however, is the technical support the CEO provides, serving as partner to the agencies it funds to design, implement, and evaluate programs.

## What Is Innovation?

According to White and Kristin Morse, the CEO's director of program development evaluation, *innovation* does not always mean *new* as much as identifying what works. While some interventions are based on new ideas, others rest on evolutions of local programs and established, evidence-based models. The fund therefore supports a wide range of programs, including, among others, literacy, higher education access, improved approaches to pregnancy prevention or employment, expanded access to job placement and training, or increased child care and early childhood opportunities for poor children.

### Measurement and Evaluation

Proving what works lies at the heart of the CEO's approach, as ongoing financial support from the innovation fund depends on positive, demonstrable results. The CEO works with each partner agency to design individualized evaluation programs. In addition to an in-house evaluation team, the CEO employs four independent external research organizations (MDRC, Westat, Metis Associates, and Harvard's Education Innovation Laboratory) to monitor and evaluate each program.

Morse explains that the customization of the evaluation is important. Accordingly, the CEO has no one-size-fits-all approach, and the rigor and level of investment of each evaluation take into account variables that include the quality of available data, the timing of expected outcomes, the availability of appropriate comparison groups, and the existing knowledge about a particular intervention. Even though much of the analyses are highly quantitative, the CEO also uses focus groups, surveys, and other kinds of narrative reports from evaluators to provide comprehensive context and depth. RCTs are used to evaluate some programs, though they arc not a universally applied gold standard.

Morse also notes that the CEO is constantly evaluating its own evaluation. "What are the right metrics?" she asks. "Take workforce development. Are we just looking at job placement, or do we need to examine the quality of the job placement? How far above minimum wage does the job pay? Was there a wage improvement? Did it change people's lives?"[13]

## The Laboratory Model: Experimentation and the Case of Opportunity NYC

Identifying what works can also mean bold experimentation. In 2007, the CEO launched Opportunity NYC, the country's first conditional cash transfer program, an initiative that sought to reduce poverty by making payments to families who fulfilled a combination of workforce, education, and health commitments. Opportunity NYC was modeled on international development efforts that have used conditional cash transfers (CCTs) to encourage socially and economically productive behavior in poor households. The original CCT program, pioneered in Mexico, has been enormously successful; it now includes 20 million families and has been replicated in more than 20 countries.

The New York City pilot, however, represented the first CCT initiative to be tested in the United States or Europe. Families participating in the three-year pilot could receive payments for, among other things, regular health and dental visits; maintaining full-time employment or attending education or job training programs; children's superior school attendance; and sustained or improved academic performance.

The CCT offers a number of valuable lessons in social innovation. First, the initial MDRC evaluations, which involved a control group, show which elements of the program worked well and which less so, allowing MDRC to rework the interventions accordingly. Second, the CCT illustrates one important role for philanthropy in promoting innovation: While most programs at the CEO are funded with city money, this $63 million pilot was underwritten almost entirely with foundation funds from Rockefeller, the Annie E. Casey Foundation, MacArthur, the New York Community Trust, the Open Society Institute, the Starr Foundation, and Robin Hood. Because Opportunity NYC, Veronica White notes, was particularly "out of the box" it benefitted from private sponsorship: philanthropy that can take risks on unusual programs that initially lack public support.[14] Now that the CEO has established the CCT's evidence base, and has refined the model further, it can be substantiated with public money. As we will see in Chapter 16, the federal Social Innovation Fund is now expanding Opportunity NYC to seven other pilot cities.

In true laboratory form, the CEO also acknowledges when programs do not post desired or expected results, and terminates funding accordingly. Out of 40 projects launched, CEO has discontinued or completed 12. Some were intended as time-limited pilots, but White says that "others were worthwhile experiments that didn't ultimately earn their keep. One important lesson that we have learned is that, especially in an era of budget cuts, identifying and terminating failing programs allows good programs to receive the funding they need to thrive."[15]

## Research and Policy: Impact Beyond NYC

The CEO recognizes that many of the issues it works on cannot be addressed at the city level alone and require larger policy reforms and resources. Therefore, policy advocacy at the state and federal levels is central to CEO's poverty-fighting agenda. Often it involves sharing or exporting the CEO's own proven program models or research findings, like its recalibrated poverty measure. Developed by the CEO's Poverty Research Team, this methodology has served as the basis for the new Federal Supplemental Poverty Measure and is now used by a number of municipalities.

The CEO itself has also been an important laboratory model. During the 2008 election, the CEO advocated for the creation of a kind of Federal Urban Innovation Fund to fight poverty by supporting innovative and evidenced-based initiatives along the CEO lines. As we will see, this proposal helped bring about the creation of the White House Office of Social Innovation and the first federal social innovation fund. (In 2012, Kristin Moore succeeded Veronica White as executive director of the CEO when White was appointed commissioner of the Department of Parks and Recreation.)

## ■ Shaping Markets: Shaun Donovan and the NYC Acquisition Fund

Although distinct in his approach from that of Joel Klein at the Department of Education, or from the work of various social service agencies, Shaun Donovan, the young and entrepreneurial housing commissioner, represented another in New York City's new breed of social innovators. Tapped in 2004, Donovan was charged with fulfilling Mayor Bloomberg's ambitious pledge to create vast amounts of much needed affordable housing, at the height of the city's (and the country's) housing bubble. Like Klein, Donovan had experience in both the social and private sectors, although his career and reputation as an innovator was rooted firmly in the field of affordable housing.

Donovan's work as commissioner was innovative in a number of ways, particularly when it came to finance. By using city and philanthropic dollars to mitigate risk for private investors, Donovan was able to bring the energy and capital of New York's commercial real estate developers to bear on the affordable housing crisis.

In the heady days of New York's soaring real estate market, exceedingly high land values and construction costs, an increasing population, and a rapidly dwindling inventory of city-owned property all resulted in an affordable housing crisis. In response, Mayor Bloomberg pledged to preserve or build 165,000 units of low- and moderate-income housing by 2013 and hired Shaun Donovan to oversee this ambitious New Housing Marketplace Plan.

Donovan understood that although the "hot" real estate market was a cause of the acute shortage of affordable housing, it could also be part of the solution. The key lay in creative financing and in bringing together actors from the public, nonprofit, and private sectors to work on the problem. Donovan explained his philosophy in pragmatic terms: "There are lots of folks more skeptical of the market and working with the market than we are. There are groups that would argue that we should only work with nonprofits. I believe we should work with both. Because at some fundamental level, I believe in competition. I believe that by having a broader pool available, having for-profits in the mix, we may get a lower price or be able to manage it more efficiently."[16]

"I would never believe that the private sector, left to its own devices, is the best possible solution," he continued. "I'm in government because of the role of government in setting rules and working in partnership with the private sector. On the other hand, there's no way you could ever get to a scale that can really affect the housing problems in this country without working with the market."[17]

Donovan was unusual in the way he considered the interests of all players and how they could be aligned in mutually beneficial ways. For example, he was a champion within the Bloomberg Administration of inclusionary zoning, which would allow developers to build multi-family structures of more density (greater number of units for the space) in return for setting aside a portion of their projects for lower-income residents. The administration embraced this idea and helped it win public support for the rezoning of several large former industrial areas with the expectation of producing nearly 10,000 new low-cost units over a decade.

In a 2006 *New York Times* profile of Donovan, Janny Scott describes a similar approach in the development of the Nehemiah Spring Creek Houses at Gateway Estates in East New York. The deal, which Donovan brokered, is the social innovation school at work. The Related Companies, the most active developer in New York, bought city-owned land to build a 625,000-square-foot retail center. The city used proceeds from the sale to pay for streets, sidewalks, and sewers—the "public goods" components. Financing for the first phase of home building came from a combination of lenders: a Community Preservation Corporation loan, local church organizations, and a private lender. The city also subsidized the cost of the single-family homes.

"This is something you would never have had the opportunity to do 20 years ago," Donovan told Scott. "This is one of the signal shifts in our strategy—how you think of ways to harness the marketplace and channel that to keep housing affordable. But," he added, "you're always trying to work within the bounds of what the market is going to do. It's clearly a huge challenge: Can you keep up?"[18]

Donovan's chief legacy in New York City, and the work that brought him national attention as a housing innovator, was the creation of the New York City Acquisition Fund. In 2006, to launch this affordable housing finance facility, Donovan assembled a number of New York's major philanthropies and commercial investors. The fund was designed to use public and philanthropic dollars to remove risk for private investors, eventually attracting $230 million to help nonprofit housing groups and small developers compete for private land sales and ultimately produce or preserve 30,000 low-cost apartments over the course of a decade. The fund is unique in the way it allowed developers to access early financing or bridge loans in a timely way to acquire private land and buildings. The fund also works because the city guarantees permanent financing, if necessary, for projects that would be unable to secure construction funding from mainstream financial capital markets.

Donovan succeeded through a kind of blended capital approach, which he achieved in part because of the financial commitments of foundations like Ford, Rockefeller, MacArthur, Heron, and Robin Hood that made PRIs, often in the form of subordinated, low-interest loans and loan guarantees, which in turn helped attract senior debt commercial investors like Bank of America, J.P.Morgan, and HSBC.[19]

In 2008, Donovan took a leave of absence from the Bloomberg Administration to advise Barack Obama's presidential campaign in the face of sweeping national foreclosures and national economic crisis. On January 26, 2009, Obama tapped Donovan as HUD secretary, where he would become one of the leading social innovators of the new administration.

In time we will gain richer insight into the legacy of the Bloomberg administration; just how enduring its governing philosophy and practices prove to be, and what kinds of social change they ultimately achieve. The "Bloomberg Way" is not without its critics, some enmeshed in the debates of a particular area of policy, such as education reform, others who object more broadly to the infusion of a kind of *corporate rationality* into our civic values.[20] And while unintended consequences have certainly been part of some of the administration's social innovation policies (e.g., fraudulent job placement numbers resulting from the pressures of performance-based contracts[21]), the overall direction in the delivery of services, particularly those enhanced by data collection, analysis, measurement and evaluation, is one of improvement. Furthermore, as a larger laboratory of social policy that imports pilot programs (e.g., conditional cash transfers) and exports successful findings (e.g., an improved poverty measure), the wide influence of Bloomberg's social innovation approach is considerable.

# Chapter 15

||||||||||||||||||||||||||||||||||||||||||||||||||||||||||||||||||

# THE OBAMA ADMINISTRATION IN THEORY: SOCIAL INNOVATION GOES TO WASHINGTON

At the federal level, social entrepreneurship found a natural ally and advocate in Barack Obama, who—first as candidate, later as president—championed innovation as a linchpin of economic renewal: public investments in infrastructure and systems that would in turn foster technological and scientific innovation from private sector investments in research and development. It was Keynes-meets-Sputnik: public investment in a time of recession to catch us up and make us a leader in the twenty-first-century technologies.

The innovation agenda also infused the Obama administration's architecture and vision of social policy in a way that distinguished it from both the prior Bush administration (which imagined a vibrant nonprofit sector, but as a substitute for, not partner with, government, and comprising largely faith-based initiatives) and that of his Democratic predecessor, Bill

Clinton. Early stirrings of the social entrepreneurship movement were evident in the Clinton administration's domestic policy agenda; it was, after all, the administration that founded the Corporation for National and Community Service and AmeriCorps, which in turn nurtured the growth of some of the hallmark entrepreneurship nonprofits of the 1990s. Still, the wholesale adoption of an innovation agenda in all areas of government, and in social policy in particular, would not emerge until Obama took office.

This shift was both generational and experiential. Obama himself had been a grassroots organizer, a veteran of the nonprofit sector. Michelle Obama left her law practice to become a social entrepreneur, founding the Chicago office of Public Allies, the service organization created by Vanessa Kirsch in the days before New Profit.

This social innovation mind-set was also reflected in the intellectual and policy allies Obama looked to during his campaign and whom later he tapped for top posts within the administration: social entrepreneurs who spread the social innovation mantra within the White House, across various agencies, and more broadly within the social sector. Much has been written about the influence of behavioral economics and economists in the administration. Less understood is the influence of this cohort of social or civic entrepreneurs and advocates of the social innovation school whose imprint is evident across the government.

The underpinnings of the social entrepreneurship movement included a vigorous emphasis on measurement and evaluation and the evidence base in policy design; the use of competition (prizes, challenges, special funds, big data initiatives) and policy laboratories to incent innovation; and a renewed and creative use of financial and other instruments to nurture entrepreneurship and attract private capital to bear on social problems. These characteristics of the social innovation agenda took an unprecedented profile and influence across agencies within the Obama Administration, marking a significant change in the way the federal government approached social policy.

## ■ The Value of Evaluation: Peter Orszag at OMB

President Obama entered the White House with an economic crisis well underway and, accordingly, a deep scrutiny of the federal budget and budgetary process. To head the Office of Management and Budget, Obama appointed Peter Orszag, the 39-year-old director of the Congressional Budget Office. The president charged Orszag with crafting the budget and overseeing the effectiveness of each federal program composing it at a moment of both severe constraints *and* the need for massive stimulus expenditures.[1]

For Orszag, this directive meant funding only "what works" in government programs and therefore making social investments in education, healthcare, and other social services in a "smarter" way. His vision of social policy, driven by both the fiscal realities of a cratering economy and a social entrepreneurship world view, both represented and infused the administration's social policy philosophy with an emphasis on innovation and the tools (i.e., rigorous measurement and evaluation and the increased use of competitive prizes and challenges) to design and implement new social programs and reinvigorate existing ones.

## An Evidence-Based Approach

Like many in the administration, Orszag believed his budgetary mandate required evidence-based evaluation of which programs did and did not work. This intense focus on evaluation early on would help define Orszag's tenure and the administration's larger approach to social policy. In a June 2009 OMB blog post entitled "Building Rigorous Evidence to Drive Policy," Orszag articulated this vision:

> One of the principles motivating the President's Budget is that, as a nation, we haven't been making the right investments to build a new foundation for economic prosperity—and we need smarter investments in education, health care, and social services. But, in making new investments, the emphasis has to be on "smarter." Many programs were founded on good intentions and supported by compelling anecdotes, but don't deliver results. . . . Rigorous ways to evaluate whether programs are working exist. But too often such evaluations don't happen. . . . This has to change, and I am trying to put much more emphasis on evidence-based policy decisions here at OMB. Wherever possible, we should design new initiatives to build rigorous data about what works and then act on evidence that emerges—expanding the approaches that work best, fine-

tuning the ones that get mixed results, and shutting down those that are failing.[2]

Accordingly, Orszag outlined a two-tiered funding scheme with increased dollars for proven programs and support for those with a promising track record and a readiness for further assessment. "This design differs from the typical approach," he said.

"We haven't simply created a block grant and told states they can do whatever they want, nor have we dictated a particular program design and told everyone to follow it. Instead, we've said that we're flexible about the details of the program; we only insist that most of the money go toward the programs backed by the best available evidence, and the rest to programs that are promising and willing to test their mettle."

According to Orszag, the two-tiered approach had two advantages; it would inform the administration about which programs to invest in, and it would create appropriate incentives for the future.

## The Application of RCTs to Social Policy in the Public Sector

Orszag's vision for social policy was not uncontroversial, and his pronouncements set off a flurry of debate about just what constituted *evidence based* and about the larger role of measurement and evaluation within the social sector. Particularly sensitive was his endorsement of the randomized control experiment (RCT) approach. In his original June blog post, Orszag had linked the word *smarter* to the Coalition for Evidence-Based Policy, a nonprofit organization founded in 2001 that strongly advocates for and advises government agencies on the use of randomized control trials to evaluate programs.

Although Orszag himself did not go so far as to explicitly embrace RCTs as the only means of program evaluation, his nod to the Coalition was sufficiently inflammatory and threatening, particularly to those organizations that faced potential defunding. It ignited heated discussion in the social sector about whether RCTs could and should be the gold standard for evidence-based proof of efficacy. As we have seen, this debate was not entirely new, but it had never been so central to mainstream domestic policy discussions.

Having laid the foundation, Orszag would continue to build a policy framework to implement this measurement and evaluation agenda. In 2009, OMB launched a voluntary but agency-wide evaluation initiative that helped and encouraged agencies to publish their ongoing evaluation research, allocated substantial funds for evaluation purposes, and created an interagency working group to promote greater evaluation across the federal government.[3]

## ■ Competition: The Theory—Using Prizes and Challenges to Spur Innovation

In September 2009, as the economy worsened and the unemployment numbers posted higher, the president released his *Strategy for American Innovation*, which defined the government's role in promoting innovation through investing in human, physical, and technological capital, and catalyzing breakthroughs in targeted industries. This innovation agenda, which would be most fully articulated in the 2011 State of the Union address, called on government to "promote competitive markets that spur productive entrepreneurship" and included a mandate to focus on government itself, in an effort to "improve public sector innovation and support community innovation." An important part of public sector innovation involved fostering greater use of high-risk, high reward policy tools along the lines of the prizes and challenges we saw in Chapter 6.[4]

In early 2010, the push for prizes and challenges took on even greater momentum from a number of the administration's innovation champions. In March, OMB Deputy Director Jeffrey D. Zients, who would later be appointed to the newly created post of chief performance officer, issued a memorandum with "guidance on the use of challenges and prizes to promote open government."[5] Zients, along with Thomas Kalil, deputy director of the White House Office of Science and Technology Policy (OSTP) and an expert on competitiveness, prizes, and technological innovation, explained the advantages of prizes for the government: they establish important goals without having to pick a winner (they do not prescribe the best team or approach); they stimulate private sector development significantly greater than the cash value of the prize; and they transfer risk to the innovator because they pay only for success.[6]

In April 2010, the White House convened many of experts in prizes including Jean Case of the Case Foundation, Peter Diamandis of the X Prize, the head of Ashoka Changemakers, Jonathan Bays of McKinsey & Company, as well as public sector prize veterans, like those from NASA, to discuss the potential of prizes in the social policy setting.[7] The meeting helped further shape the administration's thinking on the use of these tools and led to the creation of Challenge.gov, a "platform for crowdsourcing U.S. government challenges." Challenge.gov, which looks a lot like Ashoka's Changemakers, lists various competitions occurring across government agencies and invites the public to participate in what it calls an open-source "one-stop shop where entrepreneurs, innovators, and citizen solvers can compete for prestige and prizes by providing novel solutions to tough national problems, large and small."[8] The innovation advocates at OSTP and OMB also created a community of practice to promote the use of prizes and challenges across the government and pressed for legislative clarity to encourage their adoption. In December 2010, Congress passed the America COMPETES Act, which granted all federal agencies broad authority to conduct prize competitions.

Not surprisingly, the innovation agenda has been broadly embraced at agencies with a long history of prize use, particularly in areas of science and technology. NASA, an innovation veteran, recently launched a challenge-style Tournament Lab to source solutions to real-world challenges facing NASA researchers and created the Center of Excellence for Collaboration Innovation (COECI) to promote "new models of problem solving using collaborative innovation methodologies such as crowdsourcing and open innovation" across government agencies. The Department of Energy has created its own Advanced Research Project Agency (ARPA-E), modeled on DARPA, the Defense Department's Advanced Research Projects Agency, which was authorized under the COMPETES Act to spur innovation in energy research and often works with the clean tech and venture capital industries to foster commercial application of this research. Similarly, the National Institute for Standards and Technology (NIST) is using a kind of open innovation approach to develop interoperable standards for the twenty-first-century Smart Grid. These agencies also regularly list on Challenge.gov. In 2011, for example, the Air Force Research Laboratory (AFRL), in conjunction with InnoCentive, launched the Vehicle Stopper Challenge to figure out how to stop vehicles fleeing conflict zone checkpoints without destroying the vehicle or harming its occupants. DARPA has posted a number of challenges on topics ranging from combat support vehicles to vulnerabilities in the military's document shredding process.

Perhaps a more striking feature of the social innovation movement, however, is the enthusiasm for competitive tools like prizes and challenges in areas of human service. As we have seen, outcomes in social services in areas such as health and education can be much more complex to define than, say, a particular technology, and can take much longer to achieve. That has not stopped the innovators in this field, however, from experimenting along these lines. One glance at Challenge.gov shows a range of prizes and challenges addressing topics from obesity and diabetes to community college competitions and small business creation in poor communities. In the chapters that follow, we explore how the social innovation agenda has made its way, large and small, into the ethos and workings of government agencies that address any number of human needs, with innovation and entrepreneurship as the levers of social change.

# Chapter 16

# THE OBAMA ADMINISTRATION IN PRACTICE: UNLEASHING THE INNOVATION MOJO

The most high-profile application of innovation principles to social policy occurred at the Department of Education, where Secretary Arne Duncan represents a new kind of change maker. From the beginning, Duncan, whose track record as CEO of the Chicago school system pleased both the ardent market-oriented reformers and the more traditional educators, was not shy about flexing his cabinet muscles. Although most education policy and debates play out at the state and local levels, Duncan dramatically expanded the reach and influence of his office, in large measure because of the resources granted to him. In 2009, Congress approved $100 billion of emergency education money through the stimulus bill, which doubled the size of the Department of Education's budget and allowed Duncan to become deeply involved in almost every area of education policy. It was the moment to put the social innovation theory to practice.

# Race to the Top

In July 2009, Duncan announced what would be the signature program of his tenure, the Race to the Top Competition, a $4.35 billion competition designed to spur innovation and reform in state and local district K–12 education, and the first large-scale application of the competitive prize-challenge model to social services. At the Department of Education, innovation meant asking, "How do you achieve dramatically different results at scale?"[1] As we discussed earlier, finding an answer did not necessarily mean inventing new programs as much as it meant identifying evidence-based interventions and taking them to scale.

Race to the Top was designed "to encourage and reward States that are creating the conditions for education innovation and reform." Its goal then translated into demonstrating improvement in student outcomes, closing achievement gaps, improving high school graduation rates, and ensuring student preparation for success in college and careers. States that applied were awarded points for their plans for education reform in four areas: adopting standards and assessments that prepared students for college and the workplace; building data systems that measured student growth and success and informed teachers and principals about how to improve instruction; recruiting, developing, and retaining effective teachers and principals, particularly in underserved areas; and turning around low-achieving schools. Two phases of the initial grants took place in 2010 followed by a third round in November 2011. (The administration's 2012 budget proposal also included a $900 million request for a district-level Race to the Top Competition.)

# Government as Catalytic Force

Yet the legacy of Race to the Top will be as much about the catalytic role of government as it was about dollars awarded: how program design in general and the competitive granting process in particular can incent innovation. The high bar for entering the competition required states to make fundamental and often structural reforms, including changes to state laws and regulations or the introduction of state-wide standards, even before a single dollar of grants was awarded. In round one, of the 40 states that applied, 20 changed laws, policies, and standards in preparation for their applications; dozens more would make similar changes as a result of the competition. Many have suggested that this Race to the Top competitive granting model could be used in other policy and regulatory spheres.

# Investing in Innovation (i3) Awards

While Race to the Top was its most visible competition, the Department of Education employed a number of others. In 2009, Duncan created an Investing in Innovation (i3) Fund with $650 million in stimulus dollars to promote "innovative and evidence-based practices, programs, and strategies" that would improve K–12 achievement and close achievement gaps, decrease dropout rates, increase high school graduation rates, and improve teacher and school leader effectiveness. Unlike Race to the Top, the i3 grants could go to individual school districts, nonprofit organizations working with districts, or some kind of consortium of schools.

At its heart, i3 was really about scale and thinking about scale in new ways. This was particularly true in the way it linked funding to levels of evidence or proof of concept. The i3 Fund would award development grants to support new concepts deemed worthy of further study, validation grants for programs that showed promise but were wanting in additional evidence of effectiveness, and scale-up grants for programs of proven efficacy and large effect. The i3 Fund had all the hallmarks of the social entrepreneurship revolution and its conception of social innovation, particularly in the way it functioned like a venture philanthropy firm, explicitly linking funding amounts to levels of evidence (recall the EMCF model) and requiring each applicant to match federal funds with private dollars.

## Partnership with Philanthropy

The i3 Fund was administered by the Department of Education's Office of Innovation and Improvement (OII), often described as the agency's entrepreneurial arm or in-house laboratory. The OII was headed by Jim Shelton, another of the administration's innovation champions, whose career had included stints at McKinsey, the NewSchools Venture Fund, and the Gates Foundation, where he had run U.S. education programs. Not surprisingly, Shelton had little trouble enlisting a number of major foundations (among them Gates, Ford, MacArthur, Hewlett, and Kellogg) to help design and support i3. These philanthropies committed an additional $500 million to the fund and worked closely with many nonprofits and schools to help them apply.

## Government as Scale Capital

The i3 grants demonstrate the role that government funds and policy can play in scaling successful programs. Forty-nine winners were selected from 1,700 applicants. Among the four winners of the $50 million scale grants, as we have seen, was Teach For America, which, in partnership with 148 local education organizations, will use the funds to expand its teacher corps by more than 80 percent (28,000 new teachers) by September 2014. Validation grants of up to $30 million went to a number of unusual consortia, including Talent Development–Diplomas Now, the collaboration between Johns Hopkins Center for Social Organization of Schools, Communities in Schools, and City Year, to work with some of the country's most challenged middle and high schools to increase the number of students who graduate. The 30 development grants of $5 million for promising ideas were sourced from a variety of places: schools, school districts, and local nonprofits. The administration also granted second- and third-round i3 awards.

## Promise Neighborhoods: Innovation at the Community Level

The Department of Education, often through its OII, also implemented a number of other smaller initiatives to spur innovation in education. Promise Neighborhoods, for example, is a $30 million competitive grant program modeled on the holistic and multipronged approach of programs like the Harlem Children's Zone (HCZ). Promise Neighborhoods, like HCZ, is premised on the notion that strong schools need to be supported by their communities and that, conversely, schools can anchor community-wide change.

In 2010, the initial Promise Neighborhood grants went to nonprofits in 21 of the country's most distressed neighborhoods to plan for a continuum of cradle-to-career solutions of educational programs and family and community supports, with schools at the center. Though many grants went directly to educational organizations, some, like the Brooklyn Promise Neighborhood award, went to a family health center that oversaw a plan that included the local community service and child welfare agencies, early childhood education programs, schools, and the community board. In 2011, the Department of Education awarded a second round of planning grants and a first round of implementation grants. Promise Neighborhoods are now in 18 states and the District of Columbia.

In addition to its competitive granting characteristics, the Promise Neighborhood's *community solutions* approach marks an important component of the social innovation agenda. It not only reflects a collective or more collaborative approach to entrepreneurship in which many people and organizations must work together to achieve enduring social change (discussed further in Chapter 18), it also demonstrates a kind of design-thinking approach in which, with federal support, solutions are community generated and specific.

## ▥ Open Innovation and Big Data

While some social entrepreneurs in the Obama administration have used prizes and challenges to spur or scale innovative programs at the state or local level, others are using them in an open-source way, particularly when it comes to harvesting the potential of existing government resources like big data.

## Gov 2.0, Open Government, Open Innovation

On President Obama's first day in office, he signed the Memorandum on Transparency and Open Government, which outlined a number of initiatives to foster "a new era of open and accountable government," among them, opening up vast amounts of data to private citizens and businesses.[2] In 2009, the Obama administration launched Data.gov, a web portal that makes prodigious amounts of government data available to the public, and named Vivek Kundra, the country's first chief information officer, as overseer. Kundra would work closely with newly appointed Aneesh Chopra, the first chief technology officer of the United States.

This open government initiative is sometimes referred to as Gov 2.0, and it was not the first time the government opened data reserves to private or commercial innovators. In the 1970s, for example, the National Oceanic and Atmospheric Administration (NOAA) started releasing daily weather data to the public; today, hundreds of companies, from weather .com to small makers of smartphone apps, use those data for commercial and public benefit. Similarly, in the 1980s, the government made available GPS data, which helped create an entire industry of new companies that deploy this information across millions of devices.

The innovation innovation, as it were, extended Gov 2.0 to the world of human services, where the potential benefits of releasing data to the public and to commercial innovators are vast. Take the case of healthcare, where, according to McKinsey's Big Data estimates, the value of opening up federal data could be $300 billion a year.[3]

## Todd Park at HHS: CTO and Entrepreneur in Residence

One of the country's most important health and data entrepreneurs is Todd Park, who joined the administration as chief technology officer of the Department of Health and Human Services (HHS), an "entrepreneur in residence" job created especially for him.[4] A veteran of Silicon Valley, Park was keen to apply his private sector experience to the larger social welfare agenda and has become one of the administration's most entrepreneurial innovators.

At the age of 24, Park cofounded Athenahealth, a healthcare technology company he took public with a $1 billion market cap. In the years that followed, Park invested in a number of other healthcare companies, including Castlight Health, a kind of "Travelocity of healthcare" that allows consumers to compare prices for medical services. For Park, Castlight demonstrated the broader power of data and information and their potential to address some of the problems of cost and inefficiency in the U.S. healthcare system. At HHS, Park hoped that by opening up enormous amounts of data, he could foster innovation both within government and the marketplace.

## Health Data Initiative, the Health Data Challenge

In March 2011, Park began to release data across agencies under HHS and invited leaders in the tech and healthcare industries to spend 90 days creating technology tools around that data. The successful innovators would present in June at the first Community Health Data Initiative Forum, or what Park calls a Datapalooza.[5]

The winning technologies revealed the larger potential of this project. Microsoft, for example, incorporated hospital quality and patient survey information into its Bing search engine. Bing hospital searches now include patient satisfaction versus the state average. Another example is iTriage, an app that allows users to type in medical symptoms or treatments and search for the closest providers, which now also indicates where the uninsured can go for free or inexpensive treatment. More than 100,000 iTriage users have found community health centers this way.

One of the more popular tools created came from MeYou Health, a game called Community Clash, which works like blackjack for community health data with users competing against rival cities. Different health indicators are displayed on cards, and users switch out indicators in their city that they believe are weaker than in their rival cities. Park believes this approach has any number of functional applications. "There's a burgeoning thread of activity happening that says maybe the way to educate people on health is not to tell them to eat their spinach," he says. "In a world where Farmville goes from zero to 70 million users, I think the person who starts 'Healthville' and gets 50 million users, that person will be one of the most important health care figures in the twenty-first century, because they'll do more in that one stroke to advance health care education than all the public health announcements combined."[6]

In June 2012, Park hosted the second annual Health Data Initiative Forum. This time, more than 75 companies competed for 45 slots. Park hopes that these competitions will help raise awareness about the existence of the data. "About 95 percent of innovators across the country who could turn our data into products and services don't even know we have it," he says.[7] He also believes that the success of these Datapaloozas is important for encouraging others in government who might otherwise be hesitant to "liberate" their vast collections of data.

# The Promise of Open Innovation and Big Data Across Agencies

HHS is not the only federal agency looking to marry open innovation and big data for social good. The Department of Labor (DOL), for example, has made much of its data public and has posted a series of challenges to encourage software developers to produce user-friendly tools. These challenges have produced a number of web-based applications, including Where Are the Jobs and OES Map, which use occupation employment statistics to help job seekers and others better understand the labor and job market. Similarly, Eat, Shop, Sleep is a free iPhone app that allows users to see which stores, hotels, and restaurants have health, safety, or wage violations. Seth Harris, the deputy secretary at DOL whose staff is trying to link this information to larger search engines, calls it a kind of "employment law YELP."[8]

In March 2012, Todd Park succeeded Annesh Chopra as CTO of the United States. Park said that he had every hope of "cloning" the health data initiative in other sectors more broadly, from energy and education to public safety. To that end, the administration launched Safety.Data.Gov and released 700 data sets related to safety of all varieties (transportation, product, industrial, community), and in June, the OSTP and the Department of Transportation hosted a Datapalooza along these lines, the first Safety Data Jam, which featured 40 innovators.[9]

"That's what I want my legacy to be," says Park. "To demonstrate that government can act in lean start-up mode to make change happen, and to unleash the innovation mojo of the many talented innovators across government."[10]

## Big Potential for Big Data

Much has been written about the commercial potential of big data and the enormous opportunities for firms working in this area. The U.S. federal government is only one of many public sector entities exploring the social value of harnessing big data. Different countries use data differently. India's Unique Identification Number database, for example, is the world's largest biometric database, with 1.2 billion identities.

While controversial in many ways (privacy among them), this system was designed to help move people out of poverty, to help them gain access to welfare benefits, and to allow them to open a bank account or get a cell phone anywhere in the country, circumventing the traditional and often corrupt village-based identity systems.[11] One could imagine any number of possible beneficial uses of the data, from mining credit history to expanding financial services for the poor to identifying public health problems, along the lines of Google's Big Data trend tracking and mapping, Google Flu Trends, and Google Crisis Response. These kinds of real-time data analyses inform the work of Global Pulse UN, the United Nations' innovation laboratory, intended to use digital data and analytics to better understand changes in human well-being and to design tools for more effective policy work. The World Bank, too, has increasingly been making its data available to the public.

||||||||||||||||||||||||||||||||||||||||||||||||||||||||||||||||||||

## ■ The Laboratory: The White House Office of Social Innovation and Civic Participation

The social entrepreneurship imprint in the public sector is perhaps most evident in the creation of an entirely new White House Office of Social Innovation and Civic Participation, which serves as a kind of innovation laboratory for the Obama administration. The OSICP was premised on the idea that it could help catalyze entrepreneurship, both within government and more broadly in the larger universe of nonprofit providers that deliver social services on the government's behalf.

## The Social Entrepreneurship Blueprint: An Office of Social Innovation

Calls for a dedicated office to promote social entrepreneurship have been percolating for some time in the social sector. In 2007, Michele Jolin of the Center for American Progress, who had also served on Clinton's Council of Economic Advisors and as a senior vice president at Ashoka, outlined a kind of social innovation blueprint for the White House that described exactly what an office of social entrepreneurship might look like and called both for greater use of prizes and a grow-what-works or social innovation fund.[12]

Similarly, America Forward, the coalition of nonprofit and philanthropic organizations led by Vanessa Kirsch and her colleagues at New Profit, advocated for government to promote innovation and scale-what-works by investing in foundations (like New Profit) that were experienced in identifying and supporting evidence-based solutions to social problems. During the 2008 presidential campaign, America Forward lobbied candidates across parties to make its case. According to Kirsch, "Our incentive was to get the decision of what nonprofits to fund outside of government. The idea is that there is an intermediary—the foundation—that can make those decisions and isn't politically driven."[13]

A handful of innovation laboratory models also lent themselves to federal replication. Recall that New York City's Center for Economic Opportunity (CEO) already had in place its own social innovation fund, designed to encourage and scale evidence-based and proven programs. During the presidential transition, the CEO recommended the creation of a national urban innovation fund that would be focused in particular on the challenges facing urban communities. Although ultimately the new White House Office of Social Innovation would have a wider purview, it resembled in practice the New York City precursor.

## OSICP Launch: The Innovators

When it was launched in 2009, the new Office of Social Innovation drew heavily from the ranks of this social entrepreneurship cadre, now champions of social innovation in the public sector. The office was headed by a team comprising Sonal Shah, a former member of the Treasury Department in the Clinton administration, who in the intervening years had worked on environmental strategy at Goldman Sachs and then as the head of Global Development Initiatives at Google.org; Michele Jolin, who had served on the presidential transition team and helped design the new office; Marta Urquilla, a former Echoing Green Fellow and youth development expert who had also worked in the Corporation for National and Community Service; and Divya Kumarayaia, a young policy analyst. From its inception, the new office also had strong support from Melody

Barnes, director of the Domestic Policy Council, who was a committed champion of the social innovation agenda.

## Philosophy: Scale What Works

For Shah, the office and its purpose and programs were all about scale. "Social innovation," she said, "is the intersection between entrepreneurship and public innovation," and the office was designed "to take the best ideas and take them to scale."[14] This goal meant redefining both social problems and opportunities to solve them, often by reconceiving traditional public and private sector partnerships in broader collaboration terms: "What is the problem we want to solve," asked Shah, "and what consortium can we put together to solve it?"

Like so many of her entrepreneurial allies, Shah believed innovation meant *what works*, not necessarily something new. Her office, in essence *government as scale capital*, would look for outcomes, not define process. "Not new things, proven methodologies, give them scale and profile," she said.

At OSICP, social innovation translated into rigorous use of measurement and evaluation, although Shah was less dogmatic about the RCT approach than others in the administration. She noted that good evaluation was expensive; government, like its private sector counterparts, needed to make large investments in data and evaluation. (Shah had observed how well evaluation practices served companies like Google and Goldman.) RCTs, however, were not necessarily the only way; in many areas the public sector still had to define what *evidence* meant and what *outcomes* should look like. According to Shah, moving from compliance-oriented to outcome-oriented evaluation was itself a mark of progress.

Although the OSICP hoped to nurture the innovation agenda more broadly within the administration through approaches such as establishing a social innovation working group across agencies, most of the emphasis would be on spurring and scaling innovation externally. According to Jolin, "The goal of the agenda is to have greater impact with limited government resources; to learn from and invest in what is working in communities around the country; to catalyze action rather than assume government has the answers; and to use greater competition and other market mechanisms to foster innovation and implement lasting solutions."[15]

# Edward M. Kennedy Serve America Act, Expanding National Service

The initial work of the OSICP focused on civic participation and the promotion of national service. For years, the AmeriCorps program had provided much of the lifeblood and scale capital to social entrepreneurship organizations like Teach For America, City Year, and Jumpstart, and the new Edward M. Kennedy Serve America Act, which the president signed into law in April 2009, provided for sweeping expansion of national service, including a threefold increase in funding for AmeriCorps.[16] By supporting the Corporation for National and Community Service's (CNCS) rollout of the new legislation, the OSICP could help ensure that federal funds and supports would be directed to local needs and innovations via organizations with proven records of social impact.

# Tools: The Social Innovation Fund: A Catalytic Force

The CNCS would also house the signature initiative of the OSICP, its Social Innovation Fund (SIF). In April 2010, the CNCS named Paul Carttar as the director of the SIF. Like his colleagues, Carttar was also a social entrepreneurship veteran, having cofounded the Bridgespan Group (the nonprofit consulting arm of Bain) and having worked for New Profit, Inc., the Monitor Group (Monitor's nonprofit arm), and the Ewing Marion Kauffman Foundation, "the world's largest foundation devoted to entrepreneurship."[17]

The Social Innovation Fund was a relatively small competitive grant program of $50 million, but it was intended, like the much larger Department of Education competitions, to be catalytic. Like i3, the SIF was decidedly venture philanthropic in design, seeking evidence-based programs that required second-stage or growth funding to scale further. Rather than granting directly to service providers, the SIF determined it would work with partners accustomed to identifying innovation.

In July 2010, SIF awarded grants to 11 intermediary organizations, which in turn regranted the funds via their own competitive application processes. In the initial selection process, reviewers judged applicants on the basis of program design, organizational capacity, cost effectiveness, and budget. In the subgranting process, the SIF made evidence of impact a criterion for investment. In addition, for every dollar invested by the SIF, intermediary and community organizations would have to match with funding from private sources at a ratio of 3:1. In other words, the $50 million investment of federal money would ultimately direct $150 million toward social service organizations.

The 11 inaugural grants went to intermediary organizations that worked in the areas of economic opportunity, healthy futures, youth development, and school support. One went to the Pathways Fund, a partnership among the Blue Ridge Foundation of New York, the Carnegie Corporation, J.P.Morgan Chase, Open Society Foundations, Robin Hood, SeaChange Capital Partners, and New Profit, which in turn made multiyear grants to youth development organizations dedicated to improving high school graduation rates, college enrollment, and access to jobs paying a living wage. In addition to funds, Pathways also provided technical assistance (particularly for measurement and evaluation) and created a "portfolio learning community," allowing its grantees to share best practices with each other.

For other grantees, the SIF represented a new chapter in the way philanthropy worked with and approached government. The Edna McConnell Clark Foundation, for example, was one of the original intermediaries, and the SIF award marked the first major collaboration and co-funding EMCF had undertaken with government (EMCF was matching 1:1) to scale evidence-based programs. According to Nancy Roob, the EMCF president, "If successful, it might change the way the philanthropic sector in the U.S. thinks about capital allocation by blending together public funds with private resources aligned with proven social solutions."[18]

## SIF Meets SIF

One of the other original SIF awards was a $5.7 million grant to New York City's Center for Economic Opportunity (CEO) to replicate five of its antipoverty programs, including Family Rewards, a modification of its original conditional cash transfer program, to eight other cities, including Kansas City, Memphis, and Tulsa. Recall that New York's CEO was itself a social innovation laboratory; its pioneering social innovation fund and its insistence on an evidence-based approach to funding social interventions offered a model for the White House OSICP. In that first round of 11 grantee intermediaries, the CEO was the only government entity selected.

Veronica White and Kristin Morse of the CEO note that they did not select the "usual suspects"—places like Boston, the birthplace of City Year, Jumpstart, and a major node of social entrepreneurship—when it came to roll out partners. Rather, the CEO looked for cities where public officials and local philanthropies were "intellectually aligned" with the mission and objectives of both the federal and NYC innovation funds but likely lacked the kind of resources to implement these programs on their own. In this sense, the New York and federal SIFs, and the laboratories that created them, have helped to scale not just proven programs but the social innovation movement itself.

# Chapter 17

||||||||||||||||||||||||||||||||||||||||||||||||||||||||||||||||||||||||

# SHAPING MARKETS: SOCIAL IMPACT BONDS ABOUND

In the fall of 2011, the White House Office of Social Innovation and Civic Participation, under its new director and champion of social innovation Jonathan Greenblatt, hosted Pay-for-Success: Investing in What Works, a gathering of representatives from foundations, academia, nonprofit service providers, federal agencies, and Congress, plus a large contingent of state and local government leaders, to discuss the potential of *social impact bonds (SIBs)* and the broader set of pay-for-success initiatives for which SIBs have become a kind of shorthand. In the past few years, SIBs, which were described by *Harvard Business Review* as one of the top "audacious ideas to solve the world's problems,"[1] have attracted the attention of policymakers at all levels of government, across the United States and the world. As such, they represent not only the broad sweep of social entrepreneurship in government, but also an important innovation in collaborative social change efforts among the nonprofit, private, and public sectors.

## What Are Social Impact Bonds?

Social impact bonds are one of a number of pay-for-success instruments emerging in the field of social finance that aim to fund prevention services with private sources of capital by monetizing the value these investments create. The concept is relatively simple: the government agrees to pay for preventive programs that reduce long-term public expenditures or generate new tax revenue by financing against the expected cost savings or increased receipts; private investors underwrite these investments up front. To date, pay-for-success contracts have taken the form of social impact bonds and human capital performance bonds (HUCAPS), both in pilot stage.

Specifically, SIBs, which are better known and more widely explored than HUCAPs, are outcome-based contracts in which the public sector agency commits to pay for a significant improvement in a social outcome for a defined population following a particular intervention. In that sense, an SIB is not a traditional bond, because investors are paid only for successful outcomes and therefore bear all the risk of the investment. SIBs include within their financing model an incentive to dramatically improve outcomes, and returns are graduated according to levels of impact. If an intervention fails, the investor gets nothing. If an intervention succeeds beyond a predetermined benchmark, the investor gets an even higher rate of return.

In many ways, SIBs epitomize the social innovation school of public policy, emphasizing measurement and evaluation of near RCT dimensions and focusing on *outcomes* rather than *outputs*. Similar to the pay-for-performance contracts we saw in New York City, government pays only for performance or success and therefore shifts the risk; in the case of the SIB, the risk is shifted onto the investor. The aspiration is that SIBs will help bring more private capital to bear on social problems.

### The Peterborough Pilot

The United Kingdom's 2010 SIB pilot, designed by Social Finance, a British nonprofit funding intermediary, centers on reducing recidivism in a prison population in Peterborough, England. In this case, Social Finance arranged a contract between the British Ministry of Justice, private investors, and four nonprofit service providers to reduce re-offenses among male prisoners who leave Peterborough prison having served their relatively short terms of one year or less. During the six-year period of the pilot, the nonprofits provide intensive support to 3,000 prisoners, first inside prison and then following their release as the prisoners return to their communities. The better the reductions in recidivism, the better the returns: if the nonprofits succeed in reducing recidivism rates by 7.5 percent or more, the British government will pay investors out of the long-term social savings, up to 13 percent. Below the 7.5 percent threshold, the investors get no returns. The re-offense rate will be evaluated in close to RCT terms, comparing it to recidivism in a control group of 30,000 prisoners who do not receive intervention services.

The Peterborough test case is a good one because the prison houses short-term prisoners who currently receive little or no support from Britain's probation services when they are released from prison; have relatively high reoffending rates (60 percent) within one year of release; and whose reincarceration is enormously expensive. In this situation, the social costs are both high and well known; an obvious control group is available; and it is possible, in a relatively short time period, to measure the effect of the intervention. It also helps that proven nonprofit providers are available to deliver services and capable evaluators can provide reliable measurement and evaluation. Politically, this kind of issue area lends itself to SIBs: typically, support to publicly fund intervention for convicted criminals is low, even when the potential for social savings is vast.

The hope is that the SIB model may lend itself to other areas of social service. Investments in the prevention of chronic homelessness, for example, could and typically do produce improved social outcomes (e.g., increased residential stability and better health) and reduce the need for costlier crisis responses (e.g., repeated emergency room visits, hospital admissions, incarceration, and use of shelters) in relatively manageable time frames. A recent landscape analysis from McKinsey found that, although the entire range of potential applications has not yet been fully explored, SIBs seem especially well suited to scale interventions for behavior change.[2] Conversely, some interventions may be less well suited to SIBs where outcomes are hard to define or time horizons are particularly protracted. For example, even though we know interventions in early childhood produce prodigious long-term cost savings, the time frames for realizing these returns are obviously long.

## SIBs Broad Sweep: Innovation at All Levels

Not surprisingly, the Peterborough pilot has attracted the attention of governments from across Europe to Canada, Australia, and even the Middle East. Many champions of innovation are under severe budgetary constraints in the wake of the financial crisis and are keen to bring in new sources of private revenue.

### Federal Innovation

In January 2012, the Obama administration announced that the Department of Justice and the Department of Labor would support SIB-like pay-for-success pilots through 2012 funding competitions: in the case of DOJ, as a feature of an existing antirecidivism program, and in the case of DOL, funding for programs focused on employment and training outcomes as part of its Workforce Innovation Fund. In his 2012 budget request, President Obama included $100 million for pay-for-success initiatives across seven program areas, including workforce development, education, juvenile justice, and care of children with disabilities.[3] Although Congress voted it down in the larger budget battles, the DOJ and DOL pilots will proceed, and the administration is pushing again for the broader effort across agencies.

### State Interest

In the United States, interest in pay for performance has been particularly strong at the state and local levels, where budgets are in crisis and preventative services, even those that will reduce costs and improve social outcomes over the long term, are often the first to be cut.

In 2011, Massachusetts became the first state to formally pursue SIBs by issuing first a Request for Information (RFI), then in 2012 a formal Request for Proposals from social entrepreneurs working in the areas of homelessness and juvenile justice. The state's $50 million Social Innovation Financing Initiative will pilot SIBs, with the help of two nonprofit providers (Massachusetts Housing and Shelter Alliance and Roca Inc.) and the advisory intermediary Third Sector Capital Partners, to try to stem chronic homelessness and to support youth who leave juvenile correction and probation systems.[4]

Among those promoting the understanding and use of SIBs in the United States is Social Finance U.S., a nonprofit sister organization of U.K. Social Finance. Social Finance U.S., headed by Tracy Palandjian, has identified a number of promising SIB applications including permanent supportive housing for chronically homeless individuals and families and community-based alternatives to juvenile detention along the Massachusetts lines as well as home- and community-based aging-in-place programs for elders and alternative community corrections for adult offenders, among others.

Like Social Finance in the United Kingdom, Social Finance U.S. plans to provide nonprofits with working capital it raises from investors. However, while the initial U.K. pilot raised money from philanthropic sources only, Social Finance U.S. is looking to attract both foundations and investors seeking higher yields, perhaps by dividing returns into tranches or the kind of stacked or blended capital.[5] Social Finance U.S. has been exploring SIB collaborations with more than 30 state and local governments, including Rhode Island, Connecticut, New York, and Michigan. Palandjian believes that the next wave of social impact bonds, what she calls "SIB 2.0," may pave the way for other kinds of innovative social finance instruments. The Nonprofit Finance Fund, headed by Antony Bugg-Levine (formerly of the Rockefeller Foundation), has also been a leader in this field.

## Minnesota and the Human Capital Performance Bond

In Minnesota, Ashoka Fellow Steve Rothschild has taken a slightly different approach with something he calls *human capital performance bonds* (HUCAP). Rothschild is the CEO of Twin Cities RISE!, an organization that helps poor people and convicted felons find gainful employment. In HUCAP, Rothschild has devised a pay-for-success contract in which the state raises funds by issuing general obligation bonds, directs those funds to nonprofits that have generated positive social outcomes and created government savings, and uses cash unlocked by those savings to repay the bondholders. Like the social impact bond, savings to the state come in the form of increased tax revenue and reduced costs for incarceration. However, in this model, the state provides money to the nonprofit only when its clients find jobs and when they have secured employer-provided health insurance for a year. Minnesota's Governor Mark Davis allocated $10 million for human capital performance bonds in his July 2011 budget, making Minnesota the first state to pass legislation on pay-for-success contracts. The Minnesota budget will award contracts to a number of nonprofits across service areas, using Twin Cities RISE! as its model.

The differences between the social impact bonds (SIBs) and the human capital bonds (HUCAPs) are subtle but important. HUCAPs function more like real bonds; the state backs them, and private investors are guaranteed their money back. The expected rate of return, about 4 percent (akin to AA), is relatively lower than the SIB, which is really more like an equity investment with the investors' capital at risk and with returns that vary, depending on the success of the intervention (recall that in the Peterborough pilot, investors can lose all their money but can also get returns as high as 13 percent). Advocates of the HUCAP suggest that the lower but guaranteed rate of return will help prove the model and generate investor confidence, because nonprofits are likely to beat the expected rate.

The timing on the payments of the two instruments is distinct. With SIBs, organizations like Social Finance raise the money from investors and front working capital to the nonprofits. With HUCAPs, the nonprofits bear the risk because they are paid only if they perform. Although the challenge here lies in securing working capital for the project (which the nonprofits might raise via philanthropic PRIs or other forms of patient capital), these service providers have more of a performance incentive themselves.

Other incentives also differ. In the case of SIBs, private investors must engage in due diligence to evaluate the effectiveness of the intervention. With the HUCAP, an intermediary would likely evaluate the potential efficacy of the intervention. In the SIB model, it is assumed that an intermediary, like Third Sector Capital Partners or Social Finance, manages all the coordination of the transaction between the government, private investors, and (likely nonprofit) service provider. With HUCAPs, the state itself manages the financial instrument, floating the bonds and creating a performance pool of dollars to pay for successful intervention.

## SIB and the City: The Test Case

In August 2012, the Bloomberg administration announced that it would pilot a social impact bond to finance a program aimed to reduce recidivism, making New York the first American city to test the SIB model. The program is a four-year intervention designed to lower the re-offense rate, currently near 50 percent, of adolescent men who leave Rikers Island prison. It has garnered a great deal of attention for a number of reasons, among them that its lead investor, who is putting nearly $10 million into the effort, is Goldman Sachs. MDRC will structure and oversee the program, and the Vera Institute of Justice will evaluate it. In some ways, the New York SIB is much like its Peterborough predecessor: if the program reduces recidivism by 10 percent, Goldman is repaid its full investment. If recidivism drops further, Goldman could earn as much as $2 million in additional profit. And if recidivism does not drop by 10 percent, Goldman stands to lose as much as $2.4 million.

The New York City SIB is also notable for its own innovations. For starters, an investment bank, and not a consortium of philanthropic investors, is chief underwriter. The money is coming from Goldman's Urban Investment Group, which helps the firm meet its CRA obligations; it is not Goldman's charitable arm. In addition, Mayor Bloomberg's personal foundation, Bloomberg Philanthropies, which already made a $30 million commitment to the city's Young Men's Initiative (of which this SIB is now a part) is providing a $7.2 million loan guarantee to MDRC, mitigating risk for Goldman, which will not lose its full investment. If the program does not succeed, MDRC will use the Bloomberg foundation money to repay Goldman for most of its investment; if successful, Goldman will be paid from the city's Department of Correction, and MDRC may use the money for other social impact bonds. Jeffrey Liebman, a public policy professor at the Kennedy School at Harvard, told the *New York Times*, "This will get attention as perhaps the most interesting government contract written anywhere in the world this year. People will study the contract terms and the New York City deal will become a model for other jurisdictions."[6]

## SIBs in Perspective

Despite the great enthusiasm for these pay-for-success pilots, many challenges are inherent to their broader adoption. For starters, SIBs and HUCAPs depend on accurate and precise measurement and evaluation in identifying the right outcomes, an issue that is not limited to social finance but is a prerequisite for the field's expansion. Sorting out the business of intermediation and deal design involves determining which nonprofits can provide the services and which can undertake the evaluations is no small task. The complexity of this process, and others, can make pay-for-success instruments expensive to administer, in some cases, perhaps more expensive than if the government paid for the service directly.

More broadly, whether SIBs or HUCAPs can attract large sums of commercial, profit-seeking capital that in turn brings scale remains an open question. The £5 million Peterborough pilot was underwritten primarily by philanthropic sources, as will be the Massachusetts pilots. For this reason, the New York City–Goldman Sachs partnership is a pioneering effort and one that will be closely watched. Finally, it is worth remembering that many social challenges simply do not lend themselves to this pay-for-success model. All this suggests that while SIBs may not a panacea for all the world's problems, they have the potential to be an important tool in the poverty-fighting arsenal.

The excitement from so many parts for the social impact bond financing model reminds us that governments everywhere are under severe fiscal strain. It also suggests that the movement we have called *social innovation* in the public sector is widespread. The examples from the Bloomberg and Obama administrations are in no way exhaustive (even within the New York City and federal governments, we omitted many fascinating case studies in innovation); rather, they offer some insight into a new approach to governance.

Of course not all these innovation initiatives are without criticism, and not only for their purported market orientation. For example, even champions of social entrepreneurship in the public sector have questioned the decision criteria of some of the recent innovation fund competitions, noting the inherent tension between the twin objectives of innovation and scale, particularly when funds for scale are premised on proven results. For example, some have argued that the graduated evidence framework of i3, with its narrow eligibility requirements, precluded applications from some truly innovative proposals from early-stage organizations.[7] In addition, and nearly by definition, i3 and SIF did not consider organizations making deep impact in communities but with little interest or relevance for national scale. Indeed, and not surprisingly, the design of these first innovation competitions reflected the worldview of their architects, which represent one particular vision of social entrepreneurship.[8] We will discuss these issues further in the next chapter, but they need to be addressed directly by innovation advocates within the public sector.

What is powerfully evident is that these tools, and the larger social innovation agenda of which they are a part, represent a new way of governing, guided by the belief that public policy has an important role to play in spurring innovation in the social sector and beyond.

||||||||||||||||||||||||||||||||||||||||||||||||||||||||||||||||||||||||||||||

## Social Innovation in the United Kingdom: Promoting Social Entrepreneurship Across the Sectors

After focusing almost exclusively on social innovation in the United States, an example from the United Kingdom helps illustrate the global nature of the social entrepreneurship movement. In Britain, the government's social innovation agenda, which is designed to foster social entrepreneurship and social enterprise, has been part of the broader movement in that country to reform its public sector, and to shift to more of a third-party government model of social service delivery.[9]

As we have seen, the late 1990s marked a surge in the interest in and practice of social entrepreneurship in Britain. Keen to harness this enthusiasm, Prime Minister Tony Blair became an active proponent of expanding and enhancing Britain's social sector, both social purpose business (social enterprise) and social entrepreneurship in the nonprofit, or charitable, sector. Blair's government launched two of its early social investment funds in the late 1990s, and in 2000 created a Social Investment Task Force to examine ways in which the United Kingdom could improve economic growth and general welfare in its poorest communities. This task force, and much of the pioneering work in what it would call *social finance*, was led by Sir Ronald Cohen, the chairman of Apax Partners and widely considered to be the father of venture capital in the United Kingdom (in 2002 Cohen also founded Bridges Ventures, an "innovative sustainable growth investor" that brought the field of community development to the United Kingdom).

In 2006, the British government created the Office of the Third Sector (OTS) within the Cabinet to "support the environment for a thriving third sector (voluntary and community groups, social enterprises, charities, cooperatives, and mutuals), enabling the sector to campaign for change, deliver public services, promote social enterprise, and strengthen communities."[10] The following year, Cohen's Social Investment Task Force made a number of recommendations along the lines of American community development and included proposed legislative, regulatory, and tax policies that would encourage greater private sector and philanthropic investment in poor communities. It also proposed the creation of a social investment bank. Although the Blair government did not realize the vision for the bank, in 2007 Cohen created his own version of it in the form an investment advisory shop, Social Finance, which also pioneered the first social impact bond via the Peterborough pilot.

In 2010, under Prime Minister David Cameron, the OTS was renamed the Office for Civil Society, and the following year announced it would create an investment bank for social enterprises. In April 2012, chaired by Cohen and capitalized with £600 million from dormant bank accounts, the bank, Big Society Capital, opened for business. The bank will finance charities, community groups, and social enterprises that prove they can repay an investment through the income they generate. It is being closely watched as an innovation in social finance and important cross-sector collaboration.

# IV

‖‖‖‖‖‖‖‖‖‖‖‖‖‖‖‖‖‖‖‖‖‖‖‖‖‖‖‖‖‖‖‖‖‖‖‖‖‖‖‖‖‖‖‖‖‖‖‖‖‖‖‖‖‖‖‖

# ROOM FOR DEBATE

In 2008, the world convulsed. Although we are still sifting through the rubble, trying to assess the toll of the economic collapse, it is evident that the legacy of the financial crisis and the punishing recession in its wake will also be one of ideological reappraisal. This inflection point—a moment to pause, reflect, and reconsider—that applies broadly to politics and policy also holds for social entrepreneurship.

Of course, many of the debates explored in the following chapters preceded the crash. But the recent economic dislocation, with its enormous human cost and a rattling of our faith in markets, lends both urgency and heft to their examination. First, we explore some of the nuanced reconsiderations of social entrepreneurship: how we define it, the value and limits of the business orientation, and the ways in which its impact is understood, measured, and evaluated.

Second, in recent years, many social entrepreneurs have expressed and demonstrated reconceived views of both government and philanthropy and the respective roles they play in advancing social change. For starters, it has meant a more affirming view of government and the power and necessity of government's resources to scale nonprofit efforts. Consequently, it has also meant a more philosophical discussion of the promise and limits of philanthropy, both in its relative size to government and the sway and influence that the very wealthy should have on our political and policy discourse.

The book concludes with a return to the discussion of states and markets. We discuss some of the tensions inherent in commercialization and privatization, and the regulatory role government must play when private actors engage in public purpose activities. Beyond the regulatory function, however, we discuss the important historical as well as future looking ways in which government shapes markets to serve the public good and in which the three sectors (nonprofit, private, and public) can work together to achieve social change. All these elements drive and shape social entrepreneurship for the twenty-first century.

# Chapter 18

||||||||||||||||||||||||||||||||||||||||||||||||||||||||||||||||||||||||||||

# SOCIAL ENTREPRENEURSHIP REVISITED

**E**very attempt to define social entrepreneurship stirs debate about the nature of that definition. This is particularly true when it comes to the discussion of the business orientation of social entrepreneurship, and to the extent and value of this sway in the social sector. Of course the backlash against some of the field's business bias started well before 2008, but the economic collapse and its challenge to some of the fundamental assumptions of the market paradigm provide a natural point to (re)assess the relevance of this model to social entrepreneurship.

## Social Entrepreneurship Reconsidered: The Value of the Business Approach

### How New?

Much of the debate about the merits of *philanthrocapitalism*—a shorthand borrowed from a 2008 (precrash) book of the same name that extols the "new" philanthropy and the influence of business in the social sector—

has its roots in a kind of culture clash.[1] What Omidyar, Gates, and others praised in themselves as bold new thinking, others read as hubris and a deliberate attack on the nonprofit sector and its veterans, who had for years been grappling with many complex social and economic issues. Many of the philanthrocapitalists, successful in one sphere and new to another, saw inefficiency in the nonprofit sector but seemed to overlook the knowledge and experience residing there.

Omidyar, who described himself as "pro-market, anti-big government, skeptical of traditional philanthropy"[2] acknowledged the discord. "Every business person who first engages in the nonprofit sector goes through a lot of growing pains, disappointments," he said. "It is a very different kind of sector, a different cultural environment."[3]

To those who had spent careers in the field battling things like entrenched poverty, the *new* proposed solutions often seemed overly ambitious or naïve, and often not that new. Phil Buchanan, the president of the Center for Effective Philanthropy, notes that the near obsession with "the shiny new cure-alls when they're neither new nor cure-all"[4] ignores, among other things, the long history of *scientific* philanthropy, which dates back to the early twentieth century (the root cause approach that Judith Rodin hoped to refashion from Rockefeller's founding principles); the hard and hard-nosed work of measurement and evaluation that many foundations, including places like Ford and Robert Wood Johnson, had undertaken for decades; and the simple recognition that assessing, much less achieving, long-term social change is extremely complex.

Susan Berresford, who spent 37 years at the Ford Foundation, including her last 10 as its president, cautioned against a dangerous dichotomy between old and new philanthropy. "I don't think there is anything more ambitious about new philanthropy than old philanthropy," she told the *Financial Times*. "Hundreds of foundations for decades worked to address apartheid, hundreds of foundations worked to support the civil rights movement in this country, there is nothing more ambitious than those noble aims. They were extremely results-oriented—they wanted the end of apartheid, they wanted fairness for minorities—and the use of business principles has been in the foundation world for a long time."[5]

(Of course the preoccupation with newness in social entrepreneurship is confined to venture philanthropy; often forgotten in the innovation conversation are large, well-established nonprofits: organizations like Save the Children, Worldvision, Goodwill, and so many others that for years have had enormous social impact but are often not associated with entrepreneurship.)

## Markets Are Means, Not Ends

In *Just Another Emperor: The Myths and Realities of Philanthrocapitalism,* Demos scholar and former Ford Foundation executive Michael Edwards challenges a number of presumptions of the inherent superiority of the market model, a kind of "business knows best" fallacy. For starters, Edwards makes a useful and basic distinction between some of the tools of business, many of which can improve the effectiveness of nonprofit organizations, and a wholesale adoption of free-market ideology, a point more recently reiterated by political philosopher Michael Sandel in *What Money Can't Buy: The Moral Limits of Markets.*

Some private sector principles, Edwards contends, simply do not translate. Long-term "social transformation," he points out, is neither easy to measure nor always cost-effective in profit-maximizing terms. "Despite their admirable energy and enthusiasm and genuine intent, the philanthrocapitalists risk misfiring when it comes to much more complex and deep-rooted problems of injustice."[6] Buchanan, Sandel, Edwards, and many others are simply reminding us that nonprofits, often by design, work in areas of market failure that defy the logic, pace, and measurability of market models.

"Would philanthrocapitalism have helped to finance the civil rights movement in the U.S.?" Edwards asks. "I hope so, but it wasn't 'data-driven,' it didn't operate through competition, it couldn't generate much revenue, and it didn't measure its impact in terms of the numbers of people who were served each day, yet it changed the world forever."[7]

The point is that, in some instances, the *process* of social change itself does not lend itself to the corporate analogy. "In business," Edwards writes, "the pressure to quickly go to scale is natural, even imperative, since that is how unit costs decline and profits margins grow, but in civil society things have to move at the pace required by social transformation, which is generally slow because it is so complex and conflicted."[8]

## Social Change Is Incredibly Complex

With time and experience, some of the philanthrocapitalists themselves have come to acknowledge the importance of this earlier work, reevaluate their own efforts, and recognize just how challenging social change is. According to Mario Marino, the technologist and venture capitalist turned philanthropist, "What we thought [was] so simple, obvious, and ready for our 'business-like approach' proved incredibly complex and involved—needing skills well beyond our business expertise. What we learned is that true impact comes not only from what we do but also is the result of the thoughtfulness, empathy, humility, and yes, effectiveness of how we do it."[9]

Recognition of that complexity and how much it weighs on the challenges of the social sector is in part why Jim Collins, of *Good to Great* fame for his insights in the corporate sector, asserts, "We must reject the idea—well-intentioned, but dead wrong—that the primary path to greatness in the social sectors is to become 'more like a business.'" Collins argues that the "culture of discipline" required for high-performing organizations across sectors "is not a principle of business; it is a principle of greatness."[10]

Further, Collins suggests that the greater complexity of managing in the nonprofit sector—where money serves only as an input, not an output, and where leaders must contend with nuanced governance and diffuse power structures—might produce better, more disciplined leaders than their executive counterparts in the commercial sectors.

# Social Enterprise versus Entrepreneurship Redux

## The Limits of Enterprise: The Empirical Record

The recognition that social change is complex and often defies ready solutions has come in part from the mixed track record of some of the enterprise endeavors that many nonprofits have undertaken. This awareness has occurred in ways large and small. The original aspirations of Google.org, for example, were significantly reappraised as the company replaced some of its more sweeping climate change and poverty initiatives with engineering and data-driven projects more consistent with the company's core competencies (things like Google Flu). In "Google Finds It Hard to Reinvent Philanthropy," *New York Times* reporter Stephanie Strom writes of these curtailed, or reassessed, ambitions, "The hyperbole looks more like hubris."[11]

At a smaller scale, a number of scholars and practitioners in the United States have found that the pressure on nonprofits to generate revenue can be seen as distracting and ineffective. In their examination of organizations that had traveled the start-a-business route, Bridgespan's Jeffrey Bradach and William Foster found that "the general enthusiasm for business, which reached a fever pitch during the booming 1990s, has had a profound impact on nonprofits and the institutions that support them." Yet most organizations they studied had limited success with these experiments: "The potential financial returns are often exaggerated, and the challenges of running a successful business are routinely discounted. Most important, commercial ventures can distract nonprofits' managers from their core social missions and, in some cases, even subvert those missions. We're not saying that earned-income ventures have no role in the nonprofit sector, but we believe that unrealistic expectations are distorting managers' decisions, ultimately wasting precious resources and leaving important social needs unmet."[12] In its 2007 report, "The Limits to Social Enterprise," Seedco also found that many nonprofits, pressured to launch commercial enterprises, had their work derailed by the distractions of running businesses. "The differences between nonprofit organizations and for-profit enterprises were increasingly viewed as flaws in the nonprofit paradigm that could be cured by a more business-like approach. . . . We believe it is time for a more balanced vision of social enterprise."[13]

Of course, the basic fee-for-service model is not new. Recall that public charities, particularly large ones like nonprofit hospitals, schools, and arts institutions, already receive between 50 percent and 70 percent of their income from fees for goods and services. What Seedco and others found was that while nonprofit social enterprise along these lines could work when operations were closely aligned with the organization's charitable purposes (e.g., Goodwill thrift stores and its employment objectives), the pressure to do so proved particularly problematic on nonprofit service providers in more traditional human services that typically did not generate much revenue.

Their conclusion—no one size fits all, no silver bullet—is simply one of reappraisal, or a more nuanced consideration of when and how business models lend themselves to social change efforts and when they do not.

Interestingly, and perhaps reflecting a pendulum shift away from the enterprise emphasis of entrepreneurship, the term *innovation* has begun to take greater hold to describe the work of change makers in the nonprofit sector. In 2008, the *Stanford Social Innovation Review*, an intellectual weathervane for the field, featured an article calling for a more realistic assessment of the achievements of venture philanthropy,[14] noting the limits, as well as the achievements, of this approach, followed by a long and much discussed essay advocating for the use of the term and concept of *social innovation*[15] rather than *social enterprise* as the lens for "understanding and creating social change in all of its manifestations." Some of the original social entrepreneurship funders—New Profit, Echoing Green, and Blue Ridge Foundation, among others—now include *social innovation* as a term of art to describe their work, and as we saw earlier, this is the language used by the new school of social entrepreneurs in the public sector.

## Scale, Weighed Again

The reassessments of the business paradigm for nonprofits and social entrepreneurship more broadly have also encouraged, in some quarters, more refined thinking about scale.[16] Some have suggested, for example, that the venture capital analogy, with its sights set on organizational capacity building and scale, may have inadvertently led to a muddying of purpose, an emphasis on increasing an organization's size rather than its impact.[17]

In recent years, a number of funders have begun to rethink scale definitions and targets, considering ways in which impact can be enhanced, not just through organizational growth or wholesale replication of programs but instead by expanding an idea or innovation, technology or skill, advocacy or policy change.[18] Or, as Bradach puts it, "The question now is 'How can we get 100× the impact with only a 2× change in the size of the organization?'"[19] Recall that one of the critiques of the Obama administration's innovation fund competitions like i3 was their insistence that awards go to nonprofits ready to scale, perhaps inadvertently excluding organizations making large and local impact with little interest in scaling.

Dove®

Share a
sunset.

Dove®
RED VELVET
SWIRL
1330106 CC
®/TM trademarks
©Mars, Incorporated

## A More Democratic and Sometimes Collaborative View of Social Entrepreneurship

Related to scale, a definitional "push-back" in social entrepreneurship from across the political spectrum has occurred, with renewed attention to the role of more ordinary citizens (not Ashoka's one in 10 million) in the work of social change. William Schambra of the Hudson Institute challenges what he believed has become an elite view. The real social entrepreneurs, he says, are often unheralded, improving their communities in local but important ways.

"The glory of American civil society," Schambra explains, "is precisely that it permits and encourages everyday citizens to build countless smaller, limited, local projects to address the problems before them. . . . This kind of social entrepreneurship—let's call it *citizen* entrepreneurship—is not a rare, exclusive form of social practice that seeks to revolutionize entire systems at once or to stride boldly back and forth across the boundaries of philanthropy, the marketplace, and politics. But as Alexis de Tocqueville pointed out, the sum of countless such efforts spread across the face of society generates an astonishing level of social energy, cultivating the values essential for democratic freedom along the way."[20]

For others, this more democratic vision of social entrepreneurship challenges some of the fierce individualism of the social enterprise school; recall Omidyar's faith "in the potential of individuals and the power of markets" to propel social change. Instead, says Michael Edwards, "What lies at the heart of civil society is collective action and mutuality, which challenge the atomization and individualization of society."

## Ashoka's EACH Vision, Collaborative Entrepreneurship

In recent years, Ashoka has embraced a wholly new vision of social entrepreneurship, an "EACH" world in which "Everyone is a Changemaker," not only the most trailblazing social entrepreneurs, and in which all change makers work in collaboration with each other. Drayton believes that this shift in understanding and approach is such a "fundamental change, that it affects everything" far beyond Ashoka, including the basic architecture of organizations that "move from walled hierarchies to teams of teams" and the generative sources of knowledge and information that can be open-sourced and widely shared. "Once you see that," he notes, "the rest is pretty simple."[21]

Although Ashoka remains firmly committed to identifying and selecting the world's most exceptional social entrepreneurs for its Fellowship, the organization has also recently developed a number of programs and initiatives aimed to promote what it calls *collective entrepreneurship*. Ashoka relies on a "mosaic model" in which a scan of the common themes across Fellows' work is used to identify "tipping point issues" and focus Ashoka's own programs. Ashoka calls this approach *venture collaborative entrepreneurship* (VCE), and it informs all new initiatives: Ashoka's focus on teaching empathy to young children; its youth ventures programs aimed at providing young people with opportunities at change making in their communities; and its profitable hybrid value chain collaborations between businesses and civic society organizations. Even Changemakers, Ashoka's online, open-source competitions, is meant to encourage a participatory and collaborative approach to problem solving.

Ashoka is not the only social entrepreneurship organization to adopt a more collectivist definition of social entrepreneurship, although often this collaborative view extends the unit of analysis beyond individuals to organizations. The Skoll Foundation, for example, now talks about investments in the broader ecosystem in which its social entrepreneurs operate.[22] Mark Kramer and John Kania of FSG Social Impact Advisors call this "collective impact: The commitment of a group of important actors from different sectors to a common agenda for solving a specific social problem." Writing in *SSIR*, Kramer and Kania explain, "Unlike most collaborations, collective impact initiatives involve a centralized infrastructure, a dedicated staff, and a structured process that leads to a common agenda, shared measurement, continuous communication, and mutually reinforcing activities among all participants." They cite as examples the significant educational gains made in Cincinnati when leaders across sectors came together and committed to improving educational achievement and a community-wide push to clean up the Elizabeth River in southeastern Virginia.[23]

## Reevaluating Measurement and Evaluation: Shift from Returns to Learning

This broad reconsideration of social entrepreneurship has had a number of profound implications, among them important refinements to measurement and evaluation in the sector. These refinements have translated into a correction to some of the unintended consequences of the business-knows-best approach to assessment. They have also resulted, in some quarters, in a shift in understanding of the basic purpose of evaluation, from one concerned with returns per se to one centered on learning and continuous improvement.

## Contribution versus Attribution

As we saw in Chapter 4, some of the new funders have focused intently on divining *attribution*, that is, measuring the precise and specific proof of the impact of each dollar they have invested: the Robin Hood effect. Similarly, grantees must demonstrate to these funders how their work, in isolation, has impact. Both can discourage collaboration.[24] The new thinking about "collective impact" instead looks to assess *contribution* and may be a more relevant evaluative lens when it comes to organizations working in concert, even if it is harder to measure specific variables influencing outcomes.

## The Problem of Metric Drift

The attribution requirement is related to a larger insistence on measurement, which, unquestioned, can skew the mission of a nonprofit. Because of the truth in the adage "what gets measured gets done," an unrelenting focus on measurability can lead organizations to pursue only activities that can be measured, perhaps jettisoning others that are important but hard to evaluate.

The management literature is replete with cautions about mission drift: nonprofits changing course, sometimes unwisely, in pursuit of a particular funding source. The analogous danger here is metric drift. Recall, for example, REDF's original SROI metric, useful for programs that can be readily monetized such as job training, for example, but less so in other areas. Funders, too, may inadvertently eschew investments in harder-to-measure work. At Edna McConnell Clark, for example, 75 percent of funding goes to single-service organizations. These nonprofits provide only one service, such as mentoring or nurse visits, rather than a mix of supports. Although EMCF argues that it is selecting grantees based on their effectiveness, it is true that proving efficacy is simpler in the case of single service.

Laser-like focus on all things measured can also lead to project-based funding (e.g., distributing mosquito nets) that delivers short-term, measurable "bang for the buck." At the same time, as we have seen, most nonprofits have an increasing need for unrestricted funding for capacity building.

It is not only a risk for philanthropic funders. While seemingly agnostic about process or provider, the scaling *what works* approach of the public sector social innovation school insists on measurability and is often highly quantitative.

## Drowning in Data

These measurement problems can be exacerbated by the lack of consistency in the field when it comes to metrics, even across rigorous funders. The scramble to gather data to demonstrate impact is expensive and onerous for grantees, particularly when different funders demand different information.[25] (Recall that Robin Hood and Tiger, for example, both fund antipoverty work in New York City, but with different data reporting requirements.) As a result, nonprofits and funders often find themselves "drowning in data," regardless of whether they can *prove* impact.[26]

## What Can Be Measured: Numbers as Metaphor, and Accountability versus Quantification

Some of these unintended consequences reveal confusion: of measurement and quantification and about the basic purpose of evaluation. As the saying (often misattributed to Einstein) goes, "Not everything that counts can be counted, and not everything that can be counted counts." This does not mean that things cannot be assessed and measured; certain things just cannot be quantified for financial models. According to Edwards, "Business metrics and measures of success privilege size, growth, and market share, as opposed to quality of interactions between people in civil society and the capacities and institutions they help create."[27]

Jim Collins reminds us that as long as we focus on the right inputs and outputs, "It doesn't really matter whether you can quantify your results. What matters is that you rigorously assemble evidence—quantitative or qualitative—to track your progress."[28] And as we have seen, many organizations (funders and service providers alike, in the nonprofit and public sectors) *have* made this important shift from measuring inputs to measuring outputs.

Ultimately, social impact is achieved through long-term *outcomes*, which sometimes, though not always, and not always accurately, can be measured through single outputs. (An output might be a test score; an outcome might be improved educational achievement over the long term.) Often, but not always, it is possible to identify the right proxy or indicator for the desired outcome. Collins's point suggests that measurement, even of outcomes, is as much about the exercise as the answer.

In this sense, the legacy of the social entrepreneurship revolution on measurement and evaluation is as much about accountability and goal setting as it is about *proving* impact. This notion is somewhat at odds with the strict *efficient social capital markets theory*, which demands rigorous and comparable metrics to parse high-performing organizations from the less-efficient of their cohort.

This goal is laudable, of course, but the theory also presumes a kind of rationality in donor intent. It is worth remembering that the vast majority (nearly 75 percent) of the approximately $300 billion in philanthropic giving in the United States comes not from large, professional institutions but from millions of individuals, and the bulk of this giving goes to religious institutions (35 percent), alma mater educational institutions, or other local community organizations. These donations are often personal, emotional, and subjective, and not necessarily swayed by relative efficiency concerns.[29]

This fact should not lessen the efforts to improve metrics and measurement methodologies, but it does reinforce the point that the purpose of measurement and evaluation should be for internal management purposes (i.e., improving the operations of an organization, which can be expressed in goal-setting, qualitative terms) and for accountability as much as for quantifying some kind of universal returns.

## The Importance of Learning in Evaluation

Indeed, the evolution in some quarters has moved away from a *judgment* attribution or strict ROI-style *returns* orientation toward measurement for organizational *learning* purposes.

The Center for Effective Philanthropy (CEP) has played a central role in advancing this more nuanced view of evaluation. Founded in 2001 on the premise that foundation performance and efficacy are just as important as the performance of grantees in creating social impact, CEP has devised a range of research, assessment, and evaluation tools for foundations to gauge their own effectiveness, including its Grantee Perception Report (GPR), which uses upward feedback that includes quantitative and qualitative data to assess philanthropic performance. Many foundations, including Gates, Rockefeller, and Ford, now use GPR findings to guide the nature of their relationships to grantees and often to change programmatic strategy. CEP has also developed a number of other related stakeholder measures to enhance the feedback mechanisms.

CEP is not alone. A number of funders have begun to shift to evaluation focused on "improvement, not just proof" or what McKinsey calls "learning for Social Impact."[30] A recent report from Grantmakers for Effective Organizations offers a number of compelling examples, among them the Skillman Foundation's ambitious, multiyear community change initiative in six Detroit neighborhoods, which uses real-time evaluation to "respond to results on the ground"; a new "Making the Case" evaluation methodology from the 70-member Women's Funding Network that emphasizes contribution over attribution to "tell a fuller story" about the role all stakeholders have played in the community's social change initiatives; and several participatory evaluation initiatives, like the one from the Health Foundation of Central Massachusetts designed to include grantees, foundation staff, and external evaluators in the collective work of grant program planning, monitoring, and evaluation.[31]

## Learning from Failure

Another related frontier in performance evaluation has to do with failure and how social entrepreneurs increasingly view missteps as a kind of "learning for social impact." (Ironically, learning from failure might represent the most market-oriented approach to evolution in Schumpeterian, creative destruction terms.)

Historically, the philanthropic sector has been criticized for its opaque decision making, lack of accountability, and hesitation about admitting errors. Yet, wrote Joel Fleishman in 2007 in *The Foundation*, "If foundations are doing what they are supposed to be doing—maximizing social value by solving hard social problems—they are bound to suffer failures.

Instead of hiding them, they should be exalting them alongside the successes, because it is the failures that prove that foundations are not simply picking the low-hanging fruit. Most of all, foundations should wear them like the badges of honor they are, so that other foundations and the entire nonprofit sector can learn from their failures."[32]

In the few years since Fleishman's writing, several foundations have more openly embraced programmatic stumbles as learning opportunities — for their own organizations and for the sector more broadly. In 2007, both the James Irvine Foundation and the William and Flora Hewlett Foundation published widely read reports about "failed" philanthropic investments. James Irvine describes a massive midcourse correction in an eight-year, $60 million effort to improve educational achievement in underperforming schools in California. Hewlett commissioned and then published a postmortem on a $20 million, 10-year Neighborhood Improvement Initiative (NII) in the Bay Area that fell significantly short of expectations.[33]

In 2010, the Robert Wood Johnson Foundation devoted several chapters of its *Anthology* to a discussion of programs that "did not work out as planned"[34] either because of a flaw in strategy, challenging environmental context, or simply poor execution across a range of its health-related initiatives.[35] Also that year, Jean Case shared thoughts about what she called a "Painful Acknowledgement of Coming up Short" on the Case Foundation's blog, describing mistakes Case had made in supporting PlayPumps, a merry-go-round water-pump system (the pumps, they found, work only when there are large numbers of children playing on them).[36] More recently, the Gates Foundation has pledged more transparent discussion of its own investment learnings. Some of Gates's more high profile "failures," including its controversial small school initiative, are discussed at length in the next chapter.

In January 2011, Engineers Without Borders (EWB) launched AdmittingFailure.com, a website that is designed to encourage nonprofits, including service providers and funders, to share their programmatic hiccups as a broader learning exercise. Aimed primarily at the international development community, the site was created to ensure "we learn from failures instead of repeat them—that we are failing forward."[37] Says Ashley Good of EWB, "Failure's only bad when it's repeated. . . . When a project fails, that's not necessarily a bad thing—it allows us to cross something off the white board."[38] Or, in the words of Warren Buffett, who has pledged $30 billion of his fortune to the Gates Foundation, "If we don't fail, if we hit it out of the park every time, then we're not going after the right problems."[39]

# Chapter 19

||||||||||||||||||||||||||||||||||||||||||||||||||||||||||||||||||||||||||||

# NEW VIEWS ON PHILANTHROPY AND GOVERNMENT

The 2008 crash and the ensuing recession have raised fundamentally existential questions about social welfare, shared prosperity and about how states and markets help achieve each. As we saw in the last chapter, it has meant a reassessment of the business sway in social entrepreneurship, and how we think about and measure impact. So, too, has the economic collapse begged a reimagination of the role of government, not just as a regulator but as a proactive force for good. For many social entrepreneurs, who undertook their work in reaction to perceived government failure, this shift in outlook is an important one.

In this chapter, we discuss two relatively new features of the social entrepreneurship movement stemming from our reconsideration of the purpose of government. First, we ask whether private resources, philanthropic or otherwise, are sufficient to address our broad range of social needs. The answer, many social entrepreneurs have concluded, is no, and accordingly they are now engaged in vigorous advocacy efforts to enlist the power of government dollars and policy to achieve impact. Second, we ask more normatively, who should define our priorities when it comes to public policy, and are we comfortable with the degree of influence our generous and powerful philanthropists exercise? For a number of social entrepreneurs, the latter has sparked a more candid, if sometimes uncomfortable, discussion about wealth, influence, and policy choices.

## Advocacy: Government Is Necessary for Scale

In recent years, many social entrepreneurs, who initially tried to scale their organizations primarily through private resources, have (re)discovered the unmatched reach of government in terms of dollars and policy and have tried to harness that reach through increased advocacy efforts (philanthropic resources are simply not enough). Furthermore, the government-as-partner view is part and parcel of the more *collaborative* view of social entrepreneurship and impact.

### What Is Advocacy?

Advocacy can refer to a broad range of activities, such as voter mobilization, media coverage, and direct political persuasion, among others. Policy advocacy (lobbying) efforts to influence specific legislation or regulation, or secure government funding for a particular program is now a billion-dollar industry, and nearly three out of four nonprofit organizations engage in some kind of efforts along these lines.

By law, foundations cannot engage in direct lobbying (one of the reasons Omidyar and the Google founders chose hybrid forms for their philanthropic organizations). However, they can and increasingly do try to influence policy through grant making or support of issue campaigns.

### Valuing Advocacy's Impact

Advocacy can be hard to measure, and the increased pressure on organizations to show quantifiable impact for every dollar invested can discourage advocacy efforts. In "The Elusive Craft of Evaluating Advocacy," Steven Teles and Mark Schmitt show that many of the social sector measurement challenges described previously, which include long-term time horizons necessary to achieve social change, nonlinear advances, muddied causality, diffuse effects, and collaboration between groups, apply in spades to advocacy.[1]

Nevertheless, when they work, advocacy efforts can be highly transformative. Teles and Schmitt point to the recent expansion of charter schools or healthcare reform in the United States as examples of changes resulting from tenacious and successful advocacy efforts. "Good ideas like these did not catch on widely just because they worked," they explain. "They happened because of creative investments in public persuasion, legislative action, and political activity."[2]

Increasingly, entrepreneurial nonprofits have recognized the value of these investments. A recent study from the National Committee for Responsive Philanthropy examined 110 social welfare organizations across 13 states and found that, in aggregate, these nonprofits spent approximately $230 million on advocacy for minimum wage laws, expanding tax credits for the working poor, and other programs. In turn, these efforts helped produce more than $26 billion in direct and indirect benefits, a return on investment in individual and community benefit of about 115 to 1.[3]

In their 2007 bestseller *Forces for Good*, Leslie Crutchfield and Heather McLeod Grant show that successful nonprofit organizations often start out providing strong programs, but eventually their leaders realize that they cannot achieve large-scale social change through service delivery alone and add policy advocacy to secure government dollars or change legislation. "Ultimately," they write, "all high-impact organizations bridge the divide between service and advocacy. They become good at both. And the more they serve and advocate, the more they achieve impact."[4]

## Social Entrepreneurship Service Providers: TFA and City Year

As we have seen, Teach For America combines both service and advocacy, as the organization has expanded its programs primarily through government money and has sought to influence public policy relating to education reform more broadly. Although Wendy Kopp relied initially on private (corporate, foundation, and individual) funds to launch and sustain TFA, its more recent and aggressive growth has depended upon expanded use of federal funds like the i3 grant from the Department of Education. In policy terms, TFA has been among the most high-profile nonprofits advocating for education reform and often undertakes this work through the political and educational leadership of its alumni. To this end, TFA explicitly develops programs like its Political Leadership Initiative to foster and advance its alumni's advocacy work.

City Year's success has also relied on both direct service and advocacy. From its inception, City Year was built on a diversified funding mix, with approximately half of its financial support coming from the private and philanthropic sectors and half from public programs like AmeriCorps. Today, as City Year has further expanded its national footprint, it derives approximately two-thirds of its funds from government (federal, state, and local) and one-third from private sources.

From the beginning, City Year's leaders also recognized that the federal government represented more than public dollars. The realization of a truly national service platform would require what Alan Khazei, City Year's first CEO, calls *action tanking*, creating a model for national service programming that others could follow and lobbying for the larger policy efforts needed to sustain the movement. In 1990, City Year served as a model for the National and Community Service Act of 1990, and again in 1993 for the creation of AmeriCorps and the Corporation for National and Community Service. In 2003, when AmeriCorps experienced federal budget cuts of nearly 80 percent, Khazei led a Save AmeriCorps coalition of nonprofits and citizen activists and successfully rallied Congress to restore and add $100 million to its funding.

In some ways, Khazei's professional trajectory exemplifies how the social entrepreneurship movement has come, over time, to positively reassess and engage the public sector as a force for good. Recall that City Year was a nonprofit founded in reaction to perceived failures in both the public and private sectors. Brown and Khazei engaged in advocacy; indeed, it was AmeriCorps' funding that allowed City Year to grow, while they also kept close ties to the private and philanthropic sectors. Khazei suggests that it was his 2003 lobbying work to save AmeriCorps that whetted his appetite for national grassroots organizing and awakened his deeper sense of the power and potential of government to do advance large scale social impact. "The Save AmeriCorps campaign was a turning point for me as well as for the national service movement," he says. "[It] rekindled my interest in politics, policy, government, and in participating in larger movements for change."[5]

Khazei left City Year in 2006 to form Be the Change, an advocacy organization that creates national issue campaigns by organizing coalitions of nonprofits, social entrepreneurs, policymakers, private sector leaders, academics, and citizens. In 2008, Be the Change launched its first campaign, ServiceNation, which aimed to put national service on the platform of each presidential candidate in the 2008 election and played a central role in the enactment of the bipartisan Edward M. Kennedy Serve America Act, legislation that designated hundreds of millions of dollars for national service programs. That fall, Khazei took advocacy one step further and actually ran for the office in the special election for Ted Kennedy's open Senate seat. Khazei did not win, although he went on to enter the primary again in the fall of 2011 to unseat Scott Brown.

## Social Entrepreneurship Funders Get into the Advocacy Act

ServiceNation was not the only 2008 campaign targeting the presidential candidates. Much of this kind of work came from social entrepreneurship funders, who have more broadly adopted the view that government is necessary to achieve social impact. As we saw earlier, Vanessa Kirsch, founder of New Profit Inc., helped launch the America Forward Coalition, a campaign that created a blueprint for ways in which the federal government could help foster greater social entrepreneurship in the social sector and that served as a kind of playbook for the Obama administration's Office of Social Innovation and Civic Engagement and its Social Innovation Fund. (In addition, New Profit added advocacy organizations like Stand for Children to its grantee portfolio.) Also in 2008, the Gates and Broad foundations launched Strong American Schools, or Education in 2008, to make education reform an issue in the presidential race.[6] In the lead-up to the election, and through 2009, the Atlantic Philanthropies invested $25 million in healthcare reform efforts via Health Care for America Now, an advocacy campaign that played a critical role in the passage of healthcare reform.

Advocacy has grown, even beyond the election cycle, at many large foundations. In 2011, the Bloomberg foundation made a $50 million bet on climate change work, considered by some to be the largest single advocacy grant to date.[7] The Gates Foundation now has a dedicated 11-person policy and advocacy team and spends hundreds of millions of dollars a year on this work.[8]

## Influence, at What Price?

Of course, one man's advocacy is another's plutocracy, and the extraordinary growth in wealth over the past generation, and the activist philanthropy that has sprung from it, necessarily begs age-old questions of power and influence.

### The Gates Effect

In the history of modern capitalism, no one's fortune or philanthropy has been more spectacular than that of Bill Gates. Gates's $37 billion foundation gives away $3 billion a year ($8 million a day) to global public health, development, and education) and calls upon his fellow billionaires to follow suit. Yet, for all his magnanimity, Gates is not without critics.

### Gates as Government

The Gates Foundation has focused primarily on international health and development. To date, it has spent nearly $13 billion on public health initiatives in some of the world's poorest countries. By some estimates, Gates makes nearly 50 percent of all international grants made by U.S. foundations,[9] and because of the foundation's size and influence, global health now represents the largest category of international funding by U.S. foundations (nearly 40 percent of the total).[10] In fact, the foundation's spending is on par with the development assistance budgets of most large countries, just behind Italy and ahead of Switzerland.[11] By any stretch, this extraordinary generosity and good work occurs in a field that is often underresourced. However, it also means that Gates has unparalleled influence in setting global public health policy and priorities.

### Steering the Public Health Agenda

Take the case of malaria eradication. Before Gates targeted this disease, malaria received approximately $100 million in attention each year globally. Between 2000 and 2008, Gates spent over $1 billion on it. In 2007, Gates made malaria eradication a priority and convinced other funders to join, including the World Health Organization (WHO). Yet the head of malaria research at the WHO and other scientists complained that the foundation's dominance of the issue risked negating the WHO's policy role.[12]

This concern in part has arisen because of Gates's insistence on eradication; some believe containment is a more cost-effective strategy. Gates holds the same view on polio and began regularly investing in polio eradication in 2005 and in 2009 substantially increased funding and advocacy. To date, Gates has spent $1.3 billion on polio eradication efforts, including research and vaccinations, and he regularly meets with heads of state in countries like India, Nigeria, and the Arab states of the Persian Gulf (polio now affects mostly Muslim children) to call attention to the disease.

The debate over the cost versus potential benefit of the last-mile investment in polio eradication has been fierce. Efforts have reduced the number to fewer than 200 cases a year. Critics of the eradication strategy, who point out that the effort has cost $9 billion to date and each year consumes another $1 billion, suggest that the $1 billion a year should be spent on preventing death from pneumonia, diarrhea, measles, meningitis, and malaria.[13] Gates and other eradication proponents argue that without the current level of applied pressure, polio could cause up to 200,000 deaths per year. The WHO recently created a panel of scientists to monitor progress through 2012 and make recommendations.

Some in the public health community lament that the Gates Foundation's money attracts researchers to its particular interests and draws them away from other diseases or areas of investigation.[14] Richard Horton, editor of the medical journal *The Lancet*, argues, "It's his money and he has the absolute right to spend it how he wishes. But because the amount of money is so huge, it has the potential to distort the research field and government priorities. If Bill Gates has a particular priority and invests hundreds of millions of dollars in that priority, then people will follow the money."[15]

A related concern about Gates's influence is raised by those who believe that international development dollars for public health and poverty fighting should focus on root causes of diseases, the entrenched and challenging political and economic disparities in a society, of which disease and destitution are merely symptoms. According to Laura Freschi and Alanna Shaikh, Gates's preference for technological solutions like vaccines "lets world leaders off the hook. It allows them to avoid grappling with corruption, human rights abuses, war, geopolitical calculation, and social inequality as causes of global poverty and human suffering. It's easier to develop a diarrhea vaccine than to get the feces out of the water supply, but clean water provides benefits far beyond diarrhea prevention."[16]

## Steering the American Education Reform Agenda

Although the lion's share of Gates funding goes to global public health, the foundation has also played an increasingly robust role in funding and advocating for education reform initiatives in the United States, where it spends about $450 million a year. Here, too, Gates's significant influence on public policy has fueled extensive discussion about agenda setting.

Gates is an easy target in areas where the foundation has stumbled. These failures have been most pronounced in the foundation's work on small schools. Between 2002 and 2008, the foundation spent more than $2 billion to advocate for and then underwrite efforts to disaggregate large public high schools into smaller ones, on the theory that more intimate "communities of learning" would lead to educational gains. The idea was not unheard of, and Gates's decision to fund the small schools initiative involving more than 2,600 schools across 45 states was informed by a number of social scientists and other experts in the education field. Yet by 2008, despite some notable successes in New York City, it was apparent this strategy was not working, and it was all but dropped by the Gates Foundation, leaving the small schools movement rudderless.

Frustrations over the small school miscalculation are numerous. For many, the full-throttle embrace and then sudden abandonment represents not only the hubris and undue influence of Gates but also of a number of other mega funders who have supported various planks of the education reform movement. Critics take issue with the message and the messenger. They are frustrated not only that the elements of reform (choice, charter schools, national curricula, merit pay for teachers, greater testing and measurement and evaluation, closing schools) smack of business principles and are anti-union, but also that the agenda has been advanced by what Diane Ravitch called "the billionaire boys club,"[17] which, in addition to Gates, includes Eli Broad (of the Eli and Edythe Broad Foundation), the Walton Family Foundation, and others.

The concern is as much about tactics as ideology, as Gates, Broad, and others similar to the philanthropists we saw in the previous section have taken to advocacy to advance their policy agenda. It is perhaps here, in the realm of advocacy, that plutocrat watchers most fear the rise of undemocratic forces. Edward Skloot notes that of the $373 million the Gates Foundation spent on education in 2009, $78 million went to advocacy. By some estimates, Gates and other large foundations spend more than four times as much of their budgets on advocacy as their smaller foundation peers.[18]

The question is, what happens when Gates, having exerted enormous sway, is wrong? Ramon Gonzalez, the principal of Middle School 23 in the South Bronx profiled in "The Fragile Success of School Reform in the Bronx" in the *New York Times* in 2011, asks this question about education reform more broadly. "I'm just afraid that our kids are being sacrificed while everyone is learning on the job," he says. "This is not some sort of urban experiment. These are kids' lives we're talking about."[19]

## Accountability and Transparency

Gonzalez's point raises larger issues about accountability in American philanthropy. One of the virtues of philanthropy—that it is unconstrained by voters or stockholders and therefore can take programmatic risks—also means there is little public reckoning, which is remarkable at a foundation like Gates, given the dollars and influence at stake. All funding decisions are ultimately approved by a board of directors consisting of four people: Bill Gates; his wife, Melinda; his father, Bill Gates, Senior; and now Warren Buffett.

Concerns about accountability in the philanthropic sector have increased as the total dollars in the sector have grown, particularly as philanthropists have used advocacy to advance their philanthropic and political interests. In 2008, for example, when Gates teamed up with Eli Broad and others for Education in 2008, the education reform campaign was, at $60 million, one of the most expensive single-issue campaigns ever launched in a presidential race.

## Political Philanthropy and the War of Ideas

As we have seen, advocacy takes many shapes. Often it has taken the form of movement building, not just as Gates and others have done in support of specific issues like education but in seeding the broader political ideologies that have shaped our politics over the past generation.

For the most part, conservatives have led the way on funding influential research organizations (dedicated to ideas such as small government, deregulated industry, and low taxation), beginning with political philanthropists like Richard Mellon Scaife and the John M. Olin Foundation (the "venture capital fund for the conservative movement"[20]) and led today by the $35 billion of brothers Charles and David Koch. The left, however, is not entirely bereft of political philanthropists. George Soros, for example, whose philanthropy in Eastern Europe has done more than any state or market to foster post-communist civil society there, also funds important work in the United States on education and campaign finance reform and was particularly active in financial support to defeat George W. Bush in 2004. But as a number of political scientists and analysts have noted, in terms of total dollars and discipline and focus, investments in political philanthropy from the left pale in comparison to those from the right.[21]

The fascinating and complex war of ideas is beyond the scope of this book, but it is worth noting that, in recent years we have seen greater scrutiny of the use of philanthropy to directly purchase political influence. By law, charitable foundations cannot engage in direct political lobbying and must conduct exclusively nonpartisan activities that promote the public welfare. However, a number of recent reports find otherwise—for example, that the Koch brothers use their foundations as vehicles in the service of their corporate interests, namely Koch Industries, particularly on energy and environmental issues.[22]

## Public Money and Alternative Models of Social Welfare

Concerns about power and influence, however, extend well beyond the legality of political philanthropy. In light of the gaping inequalities laid bare by the economic crisis, one important question is whether our economic model based on relatively low taxes, spectacular riches, and significant influence of the wealthy on social policy through their philanthropy is the one we want for the provision of social welfare.

Some calls for greater accountability of philanthropic spending center on claims that philanthropic assets are a form of "public money" because government gives up revenue by exempting charitable organizations from taxation and by giving tax deductions to donors. The amount of revenue forgone by the U.S. government, the calculation of which depends on a number of assumptions about discount and payout rates, the vibrancy of the stock market, and whether the donation is to an endowment or to a direct service provider, has been estimated to be as much as 75 cents for every dollar foundations give to nonprofits.[23]

The general idea of philanthropy, then, is one of quid pro quo: charities should provide a public good or service equal to the amount of revenue the government has surrendered in tax revenue. Although legally this claim is difficult to make,[24] a legitimate debate centers on the best use of resources. By granting a tax subsidy that encourages giving directly to public charities or to a foundation, we are making a choice. By implication, we believe that private individuals and organizations will make better social welfare use of the money in allocation and service provision than the government would through taxation and direct spending. This notion may be so, but it is not a universally held belief. The Europeans, with higher levels of taxation and higher levels of direct government spending, have made different choices about the provision of social welfare. (It is worth remembering, more generally, that the imperative to "do more with less" stems from the presumption that improving the revenue side of the budgetary ledger through increased taxes is not a policy option. That, too, is a choice.)

In the end, philanthropy has a vitally important role to play in our society. In fact, as discussed throughout this book, the roles for philanthropy are many: providing capital for any number of social purpose projects in general, and in particular taking risks with unproven programs and establishing the evidence base for government to scale; providing capacity building assistance to grantee organizations and analogous infrastructure supports for nascent industries in the form of measurement and evaluation, rating systems, research, and advisories; demonstrating the viability of returns in areas such as microlending that commercial investors might overlook; providing subsidy or mitigating risk through instruments like guarantees or first-loss investments alongside government to attract commercial investment in public-good projects; and exercising voice on corporate and public policy through public interest advocacy campaigns. But an increasingly vigorous conversation is taking place about the extent of this sway and how philanthropy can complement, not substitute for, the work of our democratically elected governments.

# Chapter 20

||||||||||||||||||||||||||||||||||||||||||||||||||||||||||||||||||||||||||

# COMMERCIALIZATION
# AND ITS DISCONTENTS

The 2008 crash and its economic, political, and philosophical after-shocks have revealed two paradoxical truths: our faith in private, commercial actors, particularly when it comes to concern for the common good, is shaken, and our need for them to participate in the provision of public goods and services, because government coffers are so strained, is even more pronounced.

Although there were many causes of the financial crisis, we know that insufficient regulation of a number of high-risk activities in the banking sector played a large role in destabilizing our economy. Therefore, as we consider ways to bring more private capital to bear on social purpose activities, we need to be smart in our approach. Being smart means not only determining the right level of oversight for private actors, but also a much more nuanced discussion of just what constitutes a public good, and where and when those goods are best provided by nonprofit, private, and public actors.

## Commercialization

Let's begin by revisiting the case of microlending and the Yunus-Prahalad-SKS debates (detailed in Chapter 11). Yunus argued that commercialization had compromised the quality of lending and had led to the crisis in microcredit in India and beyond. In contrast, Prahalad and other commercialization champions (including, initially SKS's CEO) countered that commercial investment was necessary for scale. In some ways, both sides are right. Which is to say, profitability brings scale but potentially also unintended perils, particularly when capital flows and industry growth are inadequately regulated.

The unavoidable trade-offs of quantity and quality also remind us that no one-size-fits-all answer addresses entrenched and complex social problems. Often, the world's poorest are not well served by the BoP paradigm; in the microcredit industry, the 50 largest microfinance institutions are not located in the world's poorest countries. Consider also that the Consultative Group to Assist the Poorest changed its name to the Consultative Group to Assist the Poor. It may be, for example, that for loans to the poorest, a nonprofit or Grameen-like model works best. However, the structure required to make larger loans and more of them might function better as a profit-seeking venture, like an SKS or Compartamos, albeit a highly regulated one. The importance of this kind of variegation holds for the provision of a broad set of goods and services.

No-one-size-fits-all has an interesting corollary when it comes to innovation: while there may be no silver bullet for the problems of poverty, nonprofit sponsored iteration, experimentation, and investigation along the lines that have taken place within the field of microlending can help us to better understand what works and under what circumstances. For example, some of the RCT-type evaluations conducted by Esther Duflo and her MIT colleagues suggest that credit may be necessary but not sufficient to raise people out of poverty.[1] Researchers, practitioners, and funders are now looking into what kinds of additional products and services, when combined with credit (particularly savings, health insurance, and crop insurance — in short, a wraparound approach) can help to raise the world's poorest out of poverty. Further insight into the necessary services has been provided by economist and field researcher Jonathan Morduch, whose use of *financial diaries*[2] of the poor to answer the question, "What are the necessary goods and services poor people need?" reminds us of the enormous value of local problem solving — a kind of design thinking or community solutions approach to fighting poverty.

Perhaps the most important lessons to come out of the microlending debates have to do with the respective roles of government, the nonprofit sector, and commercial investors. In the early stages of the industry's development, governments and nonprofits worked to shape a market that was not adequately served by for-profit lenders, paving the way for future commercial investment by creating the kinds of infrastructure supports through research, advisories, and ratings systems that would improve profitability and demonstrate proof of these profits. As we have seen, it can happen in a number of fields in which market failure occurs; government and philanthropic entities fund the infrastructure of the physical (roads, electricity, supply chain models) or institutional (legal protections, research, standards, ratings schemes) variety. This kind of infrastructure is often necessary to reduce risk and transaction costs sufficiently to attract private capital. In addition, as we have seen, government and philanthropy can prime the pump for private investment by participating in yin-yang or blended capital structures, where the nonprofit or public entities requiring lower hurdle rates directly subsidize the returns to private investors.[3]

In each instance, it is fair and necessary to ask whether public or private philanthropic resources should be used to subsidize the profits of private investors. Some frame this question as a moral or ideological one, but perhaps it is more useful to consider it in utility terms: do the social benefits from the increased scale of the public good or service provided (in this case, credit) justify the use of tax dollars or philanthropic resources? This is a vital question and role for government.

# Privatization

Although not entirely analogous to the commercialization tensions in the BoP context, the debates in the United States about privatization, and about the provision of public goods and services by for-profit actors, also center on this issue of the place of private capital in common purpose.

## What Do We Mean by Privatization?

Privatization can mean different things in different places. In Europe for much of the twentieth century, state ownership of various large, major, and often heavy industries, including steel, airlines, oil, and gas, was the norm. In general terms, privatization in those countries has meant the transfer of ownership from government to private companies. In the United States, privatization is much more about contracting out to non-profit or for-profit providers services once provided by government, the kind of third-party government discussed in section I. Even though the circumstances of privatized goods and services in the United States differ from pure commercialization (e.g., the case of microlending in which privately backed commercial lenders are selling to consumers in a relatively free market, not contracting with government to provide a good or service), much of the promise and many of the unintended pitfalls that come from harnessing the profit motive also attend privatization in the United States.

## Why Privatization?

The growing enthusiasm for privatization has two primary rationales. The first has to do with theories of government failure that, broadly speaking, suggest that private (nonprofit or commercial) actors provide public goods and services more efficiently and with potentially greater social impact than public bureaucracies. Some argue this greater impact is particularly true of companies, because the profit motive drives a closer examination and potential reduction of costs, resulting in a more efficient delivery of goods and services. The second argument rests on simple fiscal math: empty government coffers can no longer provide all the goods and services that people need, and the government either cuts a service entirely or contracts with a third party to provide it more cheaply.

In *What Money Can't Buy: The Moral Limits of Markets*, Michael Sandel argues that over the past three decades, our enthusiasm for markets, what he calls *market triumphalism*, has so deeply infused our thinking and values that "we have drifted from having a market economy to being a market society."[4] Sandel suggests this circumstance is potentially nefarious for two reasons, first because of inequality (in a society where so much has been commercialized and is for sale, lack of means matters even more), and second because of the corrosive tendency of markets. "Putting a price on things in life can corrupt them. That's because markets don't only allocate goods; they express certain attitudes toward the goods being exchanged. . . . Sometimes market values crowd out nonmarket values worth caring about."[5]

Sandel, like so many others (including the case made by Michael Edwards in Chapter 18), argues that we have lost the distinction between the market as a tool "for organizing productive activity" and the market as a way of life. Sandel explains that this situation is morally problematic: "Some of the good things in life are degraded if turned into commodities," he says. "Paying kids to read books might get them to read more, but might also teach them to regard reading as a chore rather than as a source of intrinsic satisfaction. Hiring foreign mercenaries to fight our wars might spare the lives of our citizens, but might also corrupt the meaning of citizenship." The other moral concern typically raised is the same one voiced in the commercialization debates: some of the fiercest controversies regarding subsidy have to do with providers making profits on taxpayer-funded services.

Is it possible to use this logic to ask the question on nonideological, social-utility grounds? In other words, when does commercialization bring efficiency, scale, and reach to populations or communities that have not been adequately served by government agencies or nonprofit providers? When does the profit motive sufficiently diminish the quality of a good or service that we decide it is an inferior mode of delivery? Here is Yunus's point about microfinance: commercialization may have attracted vast sums of capital to extend credit to millions who might not otherwise have it, but in the process, in some cases, commercialization has vastly distorted incentives for lenders (not unlike the subprime situation in the United States).

When we privatize services in the United States, do we ask the same set of questions? Again, no one-size-fits-all answer is possible, but the evidence suggests we are not asking the question urgently or frequently enough. The breadth of these long-running debates exceeds the scope of this book. However, it is worth considering the following examples.

## Housing Credit

Fannie Mae and Freddie Mac, originally GSEs (government-sponsored entities) that helped provide credit for homeownership, failed spectacularly during the financial crisis. But their failure was not because they were public. Rather, they failed precisely because they had been privatized and had taken on the riskier behavior of some of their fellow profit-maximizing firms; they did not act like public utilities. Interestingly, Ginnie Mae, which remained a GSE, did not engage in that kind of high-risk lending.

## Prisons

In the world of human services, ample evidence shows that privatizing prisons in various places in the United States has not only compromised the quality of conditions in those facilities, it has led to greater rates of incarceration where local economies have come to depend on the prisons and the large number of prisoners as a source of income and employment. In May 2012, the New Orleans *Times-Picayune* ran "Louisiana Incarcerated," an eight-part series investigating how the state's mostly private prison system benefits from high incarceration rates (and the perverse sentencing that leads to them), and that rural sheriffs, or "prison entrepreneurs," have a financial stake in these enterprises and are elected by people whose jobs depend on this now $180 million industry.[6] The problems of privatized security are not limited to Louisiana; we have witnessed the unintended consequences of outsourcing security from Arizona (where private prisons "cherry pick" healthy prisoners[7]) to Abu Ghraib.

## Healthcare

Prisons may offer a clear-cut case against privatization, even if the treatment of convicts does not engender enormous public sympathy. Reports out of other human services, however, are a different story and suggest again that on the nonprofit versus for-profit spectrum, no one size fits all. The extensive data and research about hospitals (e.g., two-thirds of American hospitals are nonprofit, and the remaining third are either government-run or for-profit) are not definitive about the superior performance of any one model. In areas of cost and profit margin, they do not seem to be statistically all that different. Where they do seem to differ is on case mix. For example, evidence indicates that for-profit hospitals are located in areas with relatively well-insured patients. In addition, data suggest that for-profit hospitals tend to provide more in the way of profitable services (i.e., open heart surgery) and avoid relatively unprofitable ones (i.e., psychiatric emergency services). Again, different models may lend themselves better to different circumstances and target populations.

Within the healthcare field, innovations in delivery models, when implemented and regulated appropriately, can balance well the reach and scale private capital provides with the necessary quality of social service. For example, new approaches to preventative dentistry, particularly those serving poor children, have attracted the interest of private equity investors. For years, public health advocates have decried the crisis in dental care and pointed out the enormous cost savings that accrue from investments in prevention. Yet even when Medicaid spending increased to cover dental care, many poor children in rural areas could not reach a dentist. A number of for-profit management companies have emerged to provide back office and other supports to mobile dentists, similar to doctors who work for mobile health clinics, who treat children onsite in school, making the economics work for both the dentist and the private investors to serve large numbers of Medicaid-eligible children. And despite some instances of companies engaging in unsavory practices (notably, Medicaid fraud), others have reached large numbers of children—hundreds of thousands, in some cases—who otherwise lacked access to dental care. As in the case of microcredit, this example suggests a real role for private investment to bring scale and reach to others who have not been served, but government regulators must be ruthless in their scrutiny.

These debates in the areas of higher education, the financing of that education, or the investment of social security retirement accounts, among many others, run wide and deep in the social sector. And again, rather than fighting them on ideological grounds, one could assess each on a case-by-case, utilitarian basis, beginning with a first-order question about just what we consider to be a public good. And of course this discussion goes well beyond social services. In 2010, for example, ProPublica, an independent, nonprofit newsroom, was founded on the conviction that investigative journalism had become a kind of public good, no longer adequately produced by commercial market forces. The second-order question is then about the mode of delivery, and whether, even underwritten with government funds, the provision of the public good is better served or worse off by harnessing the tools of the market, namely private capital and the profit motive (see the feature on public choice theory on the following page).

‖‖‖‖‖‖‖‖‖‖‖‖‖‖‖‖‖‖‖‖‖‖‖‖‖‖‖‖‖‖‖‖‖‖‖‖‖‖‖‖‖‖‖‖‖‖‖‖‖‖‖‖‖‖‖‖‖

## Public Choice Theory 101

The academic literature on privatization is vast and beyond the scope of this book. Broadly speaking, theories of government failure fall into two categories: problems of information and problems of agency. Public choice theory helps explain why government bureaucrats and other legislators may pursue perfectly rationale objectives, even those that are in the interests of their constituents, but with outcomes that, collectively, may not serve the greater good. The informational problems related to government often have to do with feedback mechanisms and questions of efficiency. Here, the thinking goes that government bureaucracies, particularly in the absence of competition or market signals, are less attuned to consumer demand and fail to provide the right goods and services at a level of quality or efficiency that, given a market, consumers (citizens) would demand.

‖‖‖‖‖‖‖‖‖‖‖‖‖‖‖‖‖‖‖‖‖‖‖‖‖‖‖‖‖‖‖‖‖‖‖‖‖‖‖‖‖‖‖‖‖‖‖‖‖‖‖‖‖‖‖‖‖

Finally, it is worth noting that the current practitioners of social innovation in the public sector, in its myriad forms, are neither doctrinaire advocates for privatization nor for the abdication of government responsibility for public goods. While some have a robust enthusiasm for customer orientation and choice and for injecting some degree of competition into systems to induce innovation, the latest crop of social entrepreneurs in the public sector are not biased toward the belief that for-profit, commercial providers are necessarily superior to their nonprofit or public sector counterparts, but rather that a broad spectrum of providers is needed to improve the value and social impact of the goods and services they deliver.

# Chapter 21

||||||||||||||||||||||||||||||||||||||||||||||||||||||||||||||||||||||||||||||||

# SOCIAL ENTREPRENEURSHIP FOR THE TWENTY-FIRST CENTURY

I n this book we have described many of social entrepreneurship's innovations; however, the movement has also flourished because of the rich traditions it draws on. This is particularly true when it comes to our understanding and celebration of the promise and power of the individual entrepreneur. Still, social entrepreneurship for the twenty-first century must embrace a second feature of our history and political economy: the role that government can and must play in fostering private entrepreneurial activity, social and otherwise. This vision for change making moves away from the states–markets impasse and instead imagines public policy that can shape markets to common purpose.

## The Entrepreneurial Spirit

Without a doubt, the great social entrepreneurs of the last generation— Bill Drayton, Wendy Kopp, Alan Khazei, and many more unheralded innovators — identify with and embrace the spirit and practice of entrepreneurship that has deep historical and cultural roots in our nation's history. Likewise, many new funders, those social entrepreneur philanthropists who have also fueled the field's growth, have emphasized the agency of the individual in the change-making process.

This vision, what Pierre Omidyar describes as a corollary of *economic democracy*, is consistent with his technological worldview and with much of our historic conception of capitalism, in which markets are driven by the choices and preferences of individuals, and the individual entrepreneur is the primary proponent of industrial change.

Any number of theorists and historians have shown how this spirit of individual entrepreneurship undergirds the American experience, culture, and psyche, whether it is immigrants fleeing Europe for the United States, pioneers settling the American West, or Horatio Alger success stories of self-made business titans. According to Albert Hirschman, author of the 1970 classic *Exit, Voice and Loyalty*, "Success — or what amounts to the same thing, upward social mobility — has long been conceived in terms of evolutionary individualism."[1]

These notions of entrepreneurship also provide the ideological and political foundations of a distinctly American political economy. Carl J. Schramm, president of the Kauffman Foundation, writes in *The Entrepreneurial Imperative* that at our country's birth, "America presented a tabula rasa: our economy could be shaped in a way that reflected our democratic principles." Some of the nation's founders, such as Alexander Hamilton and Benjamin Franklin, believed that individual initiative was "key to exploiting emerging technologies" and that "discovery and innovation must be removed from aristocracy and democratized to create a new kind of economy and support for the American political creed." According to Schramm, "Our founding was thus a *joint* political and economic experiment that in time would provide the world a model of democratic capitalism."[2]

Although in recent years we observed the emergence of a more nuanced conception of social entrepreneurship, one that encompasses a collective or collaborative view of change making, the spirit and practice of individualistic entrepreneurship retain a powerful hold on the American imagination and its well-trod paths to prosperity.

## The Role of Government in Shaping Markets

The other gradual, though not universal, shift in social entrepreneurship we have noted is a more affirming view of the positive role government can play as a partner to private actors in fostering social change. Massive investments in advocacy work, for example, reveal that social entrepreneurs, both service providers and funders, recognize that philanthropy alone will not propel their work to scale. Rather, they must enlist government resources in the form of dollars and public policy to the task.

Curiously, discussion of the role of government as *catalyst* has been largely missing from the social impact capitalism conversation, whether it is a call for firms to think more broadly about shared or blended value or the ways in which the impact investing field can harness and harvest the potential of hundreds of billions of dollars in commercial capital. Some good analysis has been presented about the role of policy—most notably from Insight at Pacific Community Ventures and from the Initiative for Responsible Investment at Harvard[3]—but for the most part, a kind of new and improved capitalism has been envisioned as the primary responsibility of the private sector, with government in a supportive, secondary role. In *Capitalism at Risk*, Paine and her colleagues suggest that while government has work to do, "businesses should lead the way" in saving market capitalism. Porter, too, enjoins firms to "take the lead in bringing business and society back together."[4]

We posit here, instead, that this story is one of public policy. Catalyzing innovation and steering private capital productively and responsibly toward public purpose in the face of market failure are essential and cardinal purposes of government. From this perspective, *impact investing* and *social impact capitalism* should be considered more broadly in the context of national industrial policy and economic growth strategy, both with abundant precedent in this country.

## This Is Not New

This thesis is neither original nor, by any historical standard, describing a new or revolutionary view of government. Nearly three-quarters of a century ago, preeminent political economist Karl Polanyi forcefully argued that a thriving capitalist economy required a strong state, as markets were embedded in social and political relations.[5] Any number of historians and political scientists since then have demonstrated that this relationship holds, axiomatically, throughout the history of the United States. Recently, writers like E. J. Dionne and Michael Lind have traced the "partners, not adversaries" view of government and business back to the early *developmentalism* of Alexander Hamilton.[6] In this view—which has been endorsed by many political leaders since Hamilton, including Clay, Lincoln, FDR, and the progressives of the twentieth and now twenty-first centuries—government is an agent and promoter of technology, innovation, and economic development. "Industrial policy is not alien to the American tradition," Lind asserts. "It is the American tradition."[7] Dionne suggests that this decidedly American system, one in which "private initiative and public enterprise complement each other" has endured (until recently) because it respects and embraces our "twin longings" for individualism and community.[8]

The historical literature in this field is vast, and a thorough treatment beyond the scope of this book. However, a review of some of the examples of how government has incented the flow of private capital to bear on public purpose—from infrastructure development to innovation in science, technology, medicine, and other public goods like credit for housing or education—sheds important light on how this work can continue in the twenty-first century.

## Technological Advances

Perhaps the best-known achievements along these lines come from government-sponsored inventions during and after World War II, particularly through contracts to industrial firms and university researchers. As mentioned in the introduction to this book, wartime experimentation produced a number of breakthroughs for later civilian use, including nuclear power, jet engines, radar, early computers, and even a range of new drugs like penicillin, in the same way that later military-to-civilian research would create the Internet. Even earlier in the twentieth century, however, the government was involved in a significant way in the promotion of technological innovation. Lind shows that in agriculture, radio, and aviation, "the federal government acted as inventor, entrepreneur, and investor, in a return to the mixed-enterprise tradition of the early American republic."[9]

## Physical Infrastructure

When it comes to infrastructure and regional development, the government has also used a wide range of tools to steer private capital to large-scale public projects. Often this development was achieved through land grants, such as the Homestead Act of 1859 to settle the American West; Lincoln's massive land grants to the railroad companies; and the Morrill Land-Grant Act of 1862, which provided states with federal grants to pay for establishing state agriculture and mechanical colleges (A&Ms), which in turn, as Lind notes, paved the way for the promotion of scientific agricultural research with the establishment of a network of agriculture experiment stations under the direction of these land grant universities two decades later.[10]

The nineteenth-century American government used other market-shaping instruments as well to encourage infrastructure development, including modifications to commercial law. The first limited liability company, for example, was authorized to shield or limit the responsibility of partners who put money into companies pursuing public interest projects like building bridges. Investors in traditional general partnerships were less likely to expose themselves to risk (such as the possibility of the bridge collapsing), thus the limitation on liability encouraged the flow of private capital to these kinds of ventures. Different from today's LLCs, the originals had to demonstrate in their articles of incorporation that they were pursuing public interest projects.

# Credit and Other Public Policy Objectives

As notions of public goods have evolved, so, too, have public policies to encourage private investment for their provision. Take the case of housing. Under the New Deal, the National Housing Act of 1934 was designed not only to regulate interest and terms of mortgages (and protect home-buyers from the kinds of market crashes and foreclosures of the Depression) but also to promote a national policy of home ownership. By creating a federal program of mortgage default insurance and devising a number of other risk-mitigating features for conventional mortgage structures, the Act attracted more private lenders to the industry. Prior to the legislation, home ownership in the United States was about 40 percent. Today, even in the current crisis, it stands at closer to 70 percent.

Of course, home ownership was further enhanced by the creation of government-sponsored entities (GSEs) like Fannie Mae and Freddie Mac, which were also formed deliberately to serve as government-backed subsidies to private lenders to extend credit for housing purchases. In the 1960s and 1970s, GSEs became a regular feature of industry promotion. Sallie Mae, for example, was designed to subsidize private actors to lend to students in order to make higher education more affordable and therefore more universal, an explicit economic and social policy goal. Today, as in the case of mortgages, higher education lending has become a massive industry. The fate of these sectors, particularly once they were privatized and deregulated, is a larger discussion for a different book. It is worth noting, however, that those that have remained government corporations, such as Ginnie Mae, have continued to accomplish important public policy objectives while avoiding commercial meltdown.

Credit has become a, if not the, most important tool of government-sponsored economic and industrial development. The twentieth century is filled with examples of public investment banks or tax incentives for lenders, from home lenders and farm credit to import-export firms, and sometimes, in the case of community development, laws like the Community Reinvestment Act that mandate lending in underserved markets. Even the creation of the venture capital and private equity fields bears the imprint of intentional public policy, first by the passage of legislation in the 1950s that gave rise to privately funded investment firms that provided capital to early stage companies; then by changes to ERISA (the Employment Retirement Income Security Act), which allowed pension funds to invest in venture funds; and ultimately through changes to the tax code, particularly on capital gains. The point of these examples is not to be exhaustive but rather to show that private enterprise in this country doesn't exist sui generis; it thrives because of well-crafted public policy.

Of course, government-nurtured market capitalism is not an exclusively American phenomenon. Hamilton's vision for economic development was inspired by the early mercantilist models of (pre-laissez faire) Britain and France. And in modern times, the great economic success stories of the late twentieth and early twenty-first centuries are all a function of targeted government industrial policy, including the so-called East Asian Miracle of Japan, Taiwan, and South Korea;[11] China's extraordinary growth today; and India's rise in the global economy.

## What Does This Have to Do with Social Entrepreneurship?

This history reminds us of the role government can and must play, not only as regulator but as active promoter and catalyst of entrepreneurship, social and otherwise. It also gets to the heart of the innovation-in-the-public-sector discussion explored in the previous section of this book, particularly the efforts—whether it be the New York City Acquisition Fund or the social impact bond pilots at the local or federal level—to bring private capital to bear on economic development and social challenges.

# Public Policy to Shape Markets and Incent Private Capital to Public Purpose

Public policies to incent private investment for public purpose, and to promote innovation and social entrepreneurship more broadly, can take a number of forms including "sticks" (laws and regulations requiring investment), "carrots" (incentives like subsidies, matching grants, prizes, and tax breaks, all of which can change both the risk and reward structure for investors), infrastructure building (setting industry standards necessary for investor participation), and convening power.

## Mandate Laws About Public Goods

As we saw previously, so much of the U.S. domestic impact investing market is really an extension of the decades-old community development field, one that was substantially bolstered by the passage of the 1977 Community Reinvestment Act (CRA), which has steered hundreds of billions of dollars to communities across the country for a range of beneficial activities, from affordable housing to enterprise development.

This legislation continues to encourage innovation from today's social entrepreneurs. For example, the New York City social impact bond pilot to reduce recidivism relied on a $10 million investment from Goldman Sachs, which came not from the firm's charitable arm, but from its Urban Investment Group, which helps satisfy Goldman's CRA obligations. Reauthorization of the CRA Act, in addition to simplification and other modernizing elements of its reform, is probably the most important step the government can take to "crowd in" further private sector capital for the public good of credit in poor and underserved communities, and to incent further innovation in the emerging field of social finance.

Interesting counterfactuals also illustrate the power and promise of these kinds of legislative mandates. In anticipation of cap and trade regulation, for example, investors raised hundreds of millions (or by some estimates, billions) of dollars to develop green tech, alternative energy, and other environmental businesses. Cap and trade, a market-based mechanism to cost-effectively reduce emissions (proven with a number of pollutants like sulfur in the United States and carbon in European and regional markets), effectively puts a price on carbon and allows entrepreneurs and investors to mobilize resources toward environmental innovation. Congress's failure to pass this legislation in 2011 left huge sums fallow, stalling further environmental investment and innovation.

## Change Underlying Risk and Reward for Private Capital, Helping Build Markets

As we explored in earlier chapters, government can often entice private capital to public investment by changing the underlying risk and reward structure.

### Absorbing Risk

For example, by guaranteeing the purchase of massive quantities of the pneumococcal vaccine, the GAVI advanced market commitment (AMC) removed investment risk for pharmaceutical companies. Much of the funding for this AMC came from a coalition of government donors. Some also came from the Gates Foundation, although it is important to note that, because of the sheer size of its financial commitments, Gates essentially functions as a government in these kinds of collaborations. The AMC *pull* funding model of cash on delivery, pay-for-performance could be used by governments more broadly to create markets for other underfunded public goods.

Governments can remove investor risk with other kinds of guarantees, particularly for bonds or other debt instruments in both the domestic and international development fields. This approach is increasingly and deliberately being targeted to impact investments. For example, USAID, the U.S. international development agency historically responsible for humanitarian aid, has in recent years provided more in the way of financial assistance and has often done so by absorbing credit risk for private sector allies. In 1999, for example, USAID launched the Development Credit Authority, which provides loan guarantees to banks in poor countries to encourage them to lend to poor people. In the 13 years since, the DCA has made hundreds of loan guarantees to local private financial institutions in more than 60 countries, helping to foster approximately $2.5 billion in private sector lending.

Recently the DCA has focused even more explicitly on impact investors. Recall that USAID was one of the many actors in the $25 million blended capital deal for the African Agricultural Capital Fund, which included $17 million in equity from the Gates, Rockefeller, and Gatsby foundations and an $8 million commercial loan from J.P.Morgan Social Finance, for which DCA provided a 50 percent guarantee. The DCA also now uses loan guarantees to support microfinance institutions in Peru and local lending in Egypt, where the upheaval following the Arab spring has meant a credit freeze from local banks to small and medium-sized enterprises.[12]

OPIC, the traditional finance arm in the United States for international development, which pioneered many forms of risk insurance to encourage American companies to invest in developing countries, has also moved more formally into the impact space. In March 2011, OPIC issued a call for proposals from impact investing funds and committed $250 million in financing to investors targeting social and environmental impact in emerging markets while at the same time generating financial returns. The idea was to use OPIC's traditional range of debt, insurance, and guarantee products to attract new investors. In October 2011, the OPIC board approved $285 million to six funds, aiming to catalyze $875 million worth of impact investment in emerging markets, including mobile banking for the unbanked in Latin America, small business development in post-conflict Liberia, Sierra Leone, and Mexico, healthcare in Africa, and preservation of vulnerable forestland across the developing world. OPIC plans to announce another round of facility funds in 2012.[13]

In the domestic context, federal and local governments can deploy a similar guarantee or first loss position approach to encourage private investment. This tactic was the genius of the New York City Acquisition

Fund, which combined philanthropy and government guarantees to incent commercial investors to underwrite affordable housing development. Along these lines is a proposal in Congress for what might be, depending on one's definition, the greatest impact investment in recent memory: a national infrastructure bank.

The idea to create of this kind of bank was first introduced in the U.S. Senate in 2007. President Obama supported the plan in 2008 and 2010, and today proposals in both the House and Senate would use start-up funds from the federal government (initially about $10 billion) to identify "clear public benefit" transportation, water, or energy infrastructure projects that lack funding, and then use low-interest loan or loan guarantees to encourage private investors to finance the projects. This would represent an innovative model: although we have used public investment banks in other periods in our history, infrastructure today is mostly funded through direct federal spending or state or local municipal bonds. We have no equivalent to, say, the European Investment Bank, to encourage large private investment in public purpose construction.

In the spring of 2012, Rahm Emmanuel, the new mayor of Chicago, created an infrastructure bank for that city, which has attracted interest from J.P.Morgan and Citibank and is being closely watched by governments (and privatization critics) at all levels.

(Of course the 2009 stimulus bill, the American Recovery and Reinvestment Act, included loan guarantees for investments in designated sectors like green energy, as part of its much larger efforts to incent investment in infrastructure, education, health, and environmental technologies to revive the economy.)

## Improving Reward

### Prizes

Other market-shaping tools focus more on the reward side of the equation and can use handsome financial incentives to create markets that would not otherwise exist. Many of the prizes we saw in earlier chapters, particularly some of the larger ones, like the X prizes, offer prize money of at least $10 million and in the process can help build an industry (e.g., as in the case of personal spacecraft). As with Gates and GAVI, these philanthropic investments are so large they effectively function like and offer a model for government.

## Matching Funds or Leverage

Matching funds also help direct private capital to social purpose investment. The Small Business Administration (SBA), the government agency that has long supported the work of small enterprises and entrepreneurs through "capital, contracts, and counseling," often via loan guarantees and investment subsidies, created a kind of innovation fund in 2011. This $2 billion Startup America initiative includes a $1 billion impact investment fund designed to increase the economic impact of small business investment by providing leverage or matching funds to impact investors that specifically fund entrepreneurs located in underserved communities. This kind of directed financing toward intentionally impactful and financially sustainable business could create quality jobs and encourage economic growth in areas that most need it.

## Tax Breaks

We have seen how tax incentives have long been used to amplify the reward of investments that might not otherwise attract commercial capital. The New Market Tax Credits and the related New Market Venture Fund incentives are sterling examples, but there are also any number of other industry or geographical or company size targets (the SBA often uses tax levers) steering investment toward particular ends.

Although we have consistently skirted environmental policy in this book, we would be remiss not to note how critical government subsidies and incentives, often in the form of tax breaks, have been in shaping new environmental industries that did not previously exist. Take, for example, the case of green building and sustainable community development that relies, profitably, on instruments such as tax credits for LEED buildings and energy efficient construction. In this multibillion dollar market, firms like Jonathan Rose Companies, a "green real estate policy, planning, development, civic development, and investment firm" can collaborate with nonprofits and municipal governments to create affordable green urban solutions in areas of urban revitalization and renewable energy. A large number of tax incentive schemes exist at the state and local levels to encourage investment in the development of alternative and renewable energy and related technologies.

For that matter, the entire field of philanthropy, which is tax advantaged, is meant to direct more private dollars to nonprofits to be spent on public purpose activity. Even within philanthropy, tax policy can be used to shape more active impact investing. Encouraging this kind of low-interest lending to nonprofits out of a foundation's 5 percent payout requirement was the point of the initial 1969 PRI ruling by the IRS.

In May 2012, the Treasury Department and the IRS jointly proposed a clarification as to exactly when and how foundations could use PRIs to buy stock in or make loans to for-profit ventures (along the lines Gates and others have begun to use) if the company's activities promoted the foundation's charitable objectives. The proposal was not a change to the PRI regulations but nevertheless was meant to enhance greater use of PRIs for debt or equity purposes by clarifying some of the legal uncertainty surrounding them.

As we have seen, PRIs have allowed some public sector social entrepreneurs to be particularly innovative in how they work with philanthropic partners, enlisting them to participate in stacked capital deals to help attract commercial investors, as in the case of the New York City Acquisition Fund.

### Tariffs

If we pursue the industrial policy paradigm further, it is possible to imagine nascent industry protections for social enterprises or impact investments. Any number of countries today (China, South Africa, India) use tariff-like tools to direct foreign and domestic investment to preferred sectors where the government has decided to promote a particular kind of industry.

## Build Infrastructure for the Social Impact Market

In addition to laws and tools that alter investment risk and reward, government, often working with philanthropy, can help build the market infrastructure necessary to attract private investment. As we saw in the case of microcredit, for example, many governments and multilaterals worked alongside nonprofits to build the kind of ratings and due diligence information flows about microlending that helped establish the industry before commercial investors had the confidence to enter the market.

Similarly, the United States or other governments could play a role in helping to promote certification standards for domestic impact investments—if not rating systems along the lines of B Lab's GIIRS (something like the Energy Star program for energy efficiency), then perhaps some kind of national standard for accounting, definitions, or ratings akin to GAAP accounting rules. The same might hold for legal definition. Right now, the various L3C, B-Corps, and other new corporate forms, like most companies, are incorporated and regulated at the state level. Some have advocated for the national adoption of some of these kinds of corporate entities to help standardize and promote their use. The 6,000 CICs now registered in Britain, for example, provide one such national corporate form.

## Public Policy to Promote Social Entrepreneurship More Broadly

Government has the power to broadly shape a field, in this case the field of social entrepreneurship.

### Dedicated Office

Sometimes nurturing a field means having a dedicated office, like Britain's Office of the Third Sector or the U.S. Office of Social Innovation and Civic Participation, that can administer things like innovation funds, publish and promote best practices within an administration and within the community, or simply convene large numbers of actors and constituents from across the country who have a shared interest in developing the field further. This notion is gaining currency globally. In 2011, for example, the Korean government created a Social Enterprise Promotion Agency. In Europe, nations that have supported social enterprise and entrepreneurship within their own economies are increasingly using the EU to promote social enterprise more broadly.

### Convening Power

The White House Office of Social Innovation has hosted groundbreaking meetings on impact investing broadly and on more focused topics like pay for performance and social impact bonds. Similarly, when Todd Park was at the Department of Health and Human Services, he was able to bring together policy makers, entrepreneurs, innovators, and funders to participate in some of the first Datapaloozas to devise innovative and often commercial applications.

## Advance New Norms

The recent Treasury-IRS clarification of PRI use is instructive. It did not change the PRI regulations so much as convey to a number of philanthropic investors when and how they could use PRIs, which will lead to their greater use.

The same can be true when it comes to influencing norms. For example, while a number of public pension funds make what they call *economically targeted investments* (ETIs, investments in underserved regions or communities, often called *domestic emerging markets*), many others are concerned that such investments might not accord with their legal fiduciary responsibility to pensioners. ETIs are not uncommon; nearly 1.5 percent of Florida's retirement system pension fund is invested in in-state businesses in technology and other growth sectors, and the California Public Employees' Retirement System (CalPERs), the largest pension fund in the country, invests 2 percent, or approximately $2.7 billion, in ETIs. In both cases, state regulators concurred that these investments, which were benchmarked against other market rate options, conformed to "prudent" investment standards and to legal fiduciary responsibility. Making it more widely known that ETIs are legally permissible could go a long way toward unlocking huge sources of capital: It is estimated that state and local pension plans control approximately $2.2 trillion, and total institutional assets (owned and invested by pension funds, endowments, and insurers) comprise approximately $20 trillion in assets.[14]

## Promote Individual and Community Empowerment

We conclude with an obvious but important observation about the locus of energy and innovation when it comes to public sector promotion of social entrepreneurship. Despite the tired and often caricatured concerns about "big government" as lumbering bureaucracy and centralized planning, most government efforts to foster social entrepreneurship succeed when they empower individuals and communities. That is to say, federal programs like AmeriCorps, Promise Neighborhoods, and the i3 and SIF innovation fund competitions, among others, provide a kind of infrastructure of funds, guidance, and networks in which local organizations and entrepreneurs can thrive.

○

Over the course of this book we have explored the evolutions and achievements of social entrepreneurship on its own terms: how the movement has changed the way we think about and work toward social change across the nonprofit, private, and public sectors. This conversation has also situated social entrepreneurship within a larger political and ideological context.

Accordingly, we have probed our rich and deep attachments to entrepreneurship, the business and market orientation of those conceptions, and their utility in the context of the nonprofit sector. We also examined how, in recent years, social sector mores have come to inform the way some firms and investors think about value creation. Finally, in charting the arrival of social entrepreneurship in the public sector, we have observed a new kind of approach to governance, one that embraces, to varying degrees, measurement and evaluation, competition, and innovation in a number of forms.

The broader pursuit of this innovation agenda requires a reconception, or better said, a reclamation, of the role government as market shaper, steering private capital, profitably and responsibly, to public purpose. This view transcends the paralytic states-versus-markets ideological rift and affirms that collaboration between government and business is necessary for entrepreneurship, social and otherwise, for a more shared prosperity in the twenty-first century.

# NOTES

## Introduction

1. David Bornstein, *How to Change the World: Social Entrepreneurs and the Power of New Ideas* (New York: Oxford, 2004); David Bornstein, *The Price of a Dream: The Story of the Grameen Bank* (New York: Oxford, 1997); and David Bornstein and Susan David, *Social Entrepreneurship: What Everyone Needs to Know* (New York: Oxford, 2010). See also, for example, John Elkington and Pamela Hartigan, *The Power of Unreasonable People: How Social Entrepreneurs Create Markets That Change the World* (Boston: Harvard Business School, 2008); Christopher Gergen and Gregg Vanourek, *Life Entrepreneurs: Ordinary People Creating Extraordinary Lives* (San Francisco: Jossey-Bass, 2008); and Jacqueline Novogratz, *The Blue Sweater: Bridging the Gap Between Rich and Poor in an Interconnected World* (New York: Rodale, 2009). A literature of useful how-to guides for budding social entrepreneurs or prospective investors has grown up and includes books such as Leslie Crutchfield and Heather McLeod Grant, *Forces for Good* (San Francisco: Jossey-Bass, 2008); and Paul Brest and Hal Harvey, *Money Well Spent* (New York: Bloomberg Press, 2008).
2. Lester M. Salamon, "The Rise of the Nonprofit Sector," *Foreign Affairs* (July–August 1994).
3. Stephen Goldsmith and William D. Eggers, *Governing by Network: The New Shape of the Public Sector* (Washington, DC: Brookings, 2004), 10.
4. Lester M. Salamon and S. Wojciech Sokolowski, "Employment in America's Charities: A Profile," *Nonprofit Employment Bulletin* Number 26, Johns Hopkins Nonprofit Employment Data Project (2006), http://adm-cf.com/jhu/pdfs/NED_Bulletins/National/NED_Bulletin26_EmplyinAmericasCharities_2006.pdf. Wages in 2004 dollars. Lester M. Salamon, S. Wojciech Sokolowski, and Stephanie Geller, "Holding the Fort: Nonprofit Employment During a Decade of Turmoil," *Nonprofit Employment Bulletin* Number 39, Johns Hopkins Nonprofit Employment Data Project (2011).
5. "The Nonprofit Sector in Brief: Facts and Figures from the Nonprofit Almanac 2007," *Independent Sector* (2007).

6. Ronald Reagan, "Inaugural Address, January 20, 1981," in The American Presidency Project, by John T. Woolley and Gerhard Peters, http://www.presidency.ucsb.edu/ws/index.php?pid=43130#axzz1t9ifHsYb.
7. Michael Sandel, "What Isn't for Sale" *The Atlantic* (April 2012). See also, Michael Sandel, *What Money Can't Buy: The Moral Limits of Markets* (New York: Farrar, Straus and Giroux, 2012).
8. See, for example, Michael Lind, *The Land of Promise: An Economic History of the United States* (New York: Harper, 2012).

## Chapter 1

1. In the 1964 ruling on pornography, Justice Potter Stewart famously wrote, "I shall not today attempt further to define the kinds of material I understand to be embraced within that shorthand description ["hard-core pornography"]; and perhaps I could never succeed in intelligibly doing so. But I know it when I see it, and the motion picture involved in this case is not that."
2. David Bornstein's *How to Change the World: Social Entrepreneurs and the Power of New Ideas* provides both a fascinating biographical account of Drayton's formative years as well as the history of the Ashoka organization and some of its first Fellows.
3. The Fellow selection process is explored in more detail in Georgia Levenson Keohane, "Ashoka: Innovators for the Public," Stanford Graduate School of Business Case No. SM203 (February 2012).
4. J. Gregory Dees, "The Meaning of 'Social Entrepreneurship,'" Stanford School of Business (October 31, 1998, rev. May 30, 2001), 1.
5. Roger L. Martin and Sally Osberg, "Social Entrepreneurship: The Case for Definition," *Stanford Social Innovation Review* Spring 2007, 31; uses citation Joseph A. Schumpeter, *Capitalism, Socialism and Democracy* (New York: Harper, 1975 [orig. pub. 1942]), 82–85.
6. *How to Change the World*, 119.
7. Martin and Osberg, "Social Entrepreneurship: The Case for Definition," *Stanford Social Innovation Review* (Spring 2007), 31; uses citation Peter Drucker, *Innovation and Entrepreneurship* (New York: Harper Business, 1995), 28.
8. As quoted in Jane Wei-Skillern, James E. Austin, Herman Leonard and Howard Stevenson, *Entrepreneurship in the Social Sector* (London: Sage, 2007), 3.
9. In *Innovation and Entrepreneurship*, for example, Drucker includes a number of examples for entrepreneurial activity in entities he classifies as nonbusiness entities—many major universities, service organizations like CARE and the Girl Scouts, hospitals, research labs, and even a number of labor unions. See Peter Drucker, *Innovation and Entrepreneurship* (New York: Harper and Row), 1985.
10. J. Gregory Dees, Jed Emerson, and Peter Economy, *Enterprising Nonprofits: A Toolkit for Social Entrepreneurs* (New York: John Wiley and Sons, 2001), 161.

11. Dees, et al.
12. Dees, et al.
13. Dees, et al.
14. Martin and Osberg, 35; citing Dees, 2.
15. Dees, "The Meaning of 'Social Entrepreneurship.'"
16. Wei-Skillern, et al., 1.
17. Research by the Aspen Institute estimates that 20 percent of nonprofits' resources come from private giving, including individuals, foundations, and businesses; 30 percent comes from the state and federal government; and 40 percent to 50 percent is earned from service fees.
18. J. Gregory Dees, "Social Entrepreneurship is About Innovation and Impact, Not Income," *Social Edge* (September 2003). Reprinted, http://www.caseatduke.org/articles/1004/corner.htm.

## Chapter 2

1. "City Year: National Expansion Strategy (A)," Harvard Business School Case Study 496001 (December 21, 1995); and "City Year Enterprise," Harvard Business School Case Study 396196 (April 19, 1996).
2. These revenue-generating experiments are documented in "City Year Enterprise," Harvard Business School Case Study 396196 (April 19, 1996), and in Crutchfield and McLeod Grant, *Forces for Good*.
3. Nicole Wallace, "A Narrower Focus Helps City Year Win Grants and Increase Its Impact," *The Chronicle of Philanthropy* (December 4, 2011), http://philanthropy.com/article/A-Narrow-Focus-Helps-a-Charity/129962/.
4. "Jumpstart: a Culture of Performance Measurement and Management," Harvard Business School Case Study 301037 (May 7, 2010).
5. Michael Anteby and Erin McFee, "Freelancers Union," Harvard Business School Case Study 412056 (rev. January 25, 2012), 2.
6. Anteby and McFee, 2.

## Chapter 3

1. See, for example, Gertrude Himmelfarb, *Poverty and Compassion: The Moral Imagination of the Late Victorians* (New York: Knopf, 1991).
2. Christine W. Letts, William Ryan, and Allen Grossman. "Virtuous Capital: What Foundations Can Learn from Venture Capitalists," *Harvard Business Review* (March–April 1997), 3–7.
3. "Tiger Foundation: Profile in Engaged Philanthropy," The Bridgespan Group (March 2007).
4. See, for example, Laura Arrillaga-Andreessen "Giving 2.0: Getting Together to Give," *Stanford Social Innovation Review* (Winter 2012); and *Giving 2.0* (San Francisco: Jossey-Bass, 2012).
5. Jessica E. Bearman, *More Giving Together: The Growth and Impact of Giving Circles and Shared Giving* (Washington, DC: New Ventures in Philanthropy initiative of the Forum of the Regional Associations of Grantmakers, 2007).

6. Michael Balin, Annual Report letter (1997), as quoted in "EMCF: A New Approach at an Old Foundation" Harvard Business School Case Study 302090 (rev. June 21, 2002).

7. "Edna McConnell Clark Foundation—Enabling a Performance Driven Philanthropic Capital Market" Harvard Business School Case Study 312006 (rev. July 28, 2011).

8. Craig C. Reigel, "Philanthropic Equity: Promising Early Returns," *The Nonprofit Quarterly* (Fall/Winter 2011); David Bornstein, "For Ambitious Nonprofits, Capital to Grow," *New York Times* (June 27, 2012), http://opinionator.blogs.nytimes.com/2012/06/27/fixes/.

9. "Rockefeller Revolutionary: Judith Rodin is shaking up one of the world's most venerable charitable foundations," *The Economist* (December 13, 2006).

10. Paul Brest and Hal Harvey, *Money Well Spent: A Strategic Plan for Smart Philanthropy* (New York: Bloomberg, 2008).

11. Diane Ravitch, *The Death and Life of the Great American School System* (New York: Basic Books, 2010), ch. 10. In addition, see Steven Brill, *Class Warfare* (New York: Simon and Schuster, 2011).

12. William F. Meehan, Derek Kilmer, and Maisie O'Flanagan, "Investing in Society: Why we need a more efficient social capital market—and how we can get there," *Stanford Social Innovation Review* (Spring 2004).

13. Robert S. Kaplan and Allen S. Grossman, "The Emerging Capital Market for Nonprofits," *Harvard Business Review* (October 2010).

14. William Meehan and Kim Jonker, "The Rise of Social Capital Market Intermediaries," *Stanford Social Innovation Review* (Winter 2012).

## Chapter 4

1. "The Robin Hood Foundation," Harvard Business School Case Study 310-031 (rev. May 19, 2010), 7.

2. As quoted in "Edna McConnell Clark Foundation—Enabling a Performance Driven Philanthropic Capital Market" Harvard Business School Case Study 312-006 (July 28, 2011), 4.

3. Abhijit V. Banerjee and Esther Duflo, *Poor Economics* (New York: Public Affairs, 2011).

4. For example, see Dean Karlan and Jacob Appel, *More Than Good Intentions* (New York: Dutton, 2011).

5. "Is Grantmaking Getting Smarter? A National Study of Philanthropic Practice," Grantmakers for Effective Organizations December (2008).

6. Matthew Bishop and Michael Green, *Philanthrocapitalism* (New York: Bloomsbury, 2008).

## Chapter 5

1. James Surowiecki, *The Wisdom of Crowds* (New York: Anchor, 2004).

2. Georgia Levenson Keohane, "The Facebook Philanthropos," *Slate* (February 11, 2008).

3. Karim R. Lakhani, Lars Bo Jeppesen, Peter A. Lohse, and Jill A. Panetta, "The Value of Openness in Scientific Problem Solving," Harvard Business School Working Paper 07-050 (October 2006).
4. Jon Gertner, "From 0 to 60 to World Domination," *New York Times* (February 18, 2007); "Genchi genbutsu: More a frame of mind than a plan of action," *The Economist* (October 13, 2009), http://www.economist.com /node/14299017.
5. Cliff Kuang, "Six Bite-Sized Innovation Lessons from Ebay's New Design Think Tank," *Fast Company* July 6, 2011), http://www.fastcodesign.com /1664404/six-bite-sized-innovation-lessons-from-ebays-new-design-think-tank.
6. Tim Brown, "Why Social Innovators Need Design Thinking," *Stanford Social Innovation Review* (November 15, 2011).

## Chapter 6

1. The vast economics literature on prizes supports this belief.
2. Jonathan Bays, "And the Winner Is . . . Capturing the Promise of Philanthropic Prizes," McKinsey & Company (2010), www.mckinsey .com/App_Media/Reports/SSO/And_the_winner_is.pdf; Jonathan Bays and Paul Jansen, "Prizes: A winning strategy for innovation," McKinsey: What Matters (July 7, 2009), http://innovbfa.viabloga.com/files /McKinseyQuarterly_Prizes_a_winning_strategy_for_innovation_july_2009 .pdf. See also Liam Brunt, Josh Lerner, and Tom Nicholas, "Inducement Prizes and Innovation," CEPR Discussion Paper (2008), http://people.hbs .edu/tnicholas/CEPR-DP6917.pdf.
3. Alpheus Bingham and Dwayne Spradlin, *The Open Innovation Marketplace: Creating Value in the Challenge Driven Enterprise* (New York: Financial Times Press), 2011, p. 17.
4. Ruth Levine, Michael Kremer, and Alice Albright, "Making Markets for Vaccines: Ideas to Action" (Washington, DC: Center for Global Development, 2005), http://www.cgdev.org/doc/books/vaccine /MakingMarkets-complete.pdf.
5. Stephen Maurer, "The right tool(s): Designing cost-effective strategies for neglected disease research," Report to World Health Organization Commission on Intellectual Property Rights, Innovation, and Public Health (March 29, 2005).

## Chapter 7

1. Nathan Cummings Foundation, "Changing Corporate Behavior through Shareholder Activism: The Nathan Cummings Foundation's Experience" (September 2010), http://www.nathancummings.net/shareholders /Changing%20Corporate%20Behavior%20thru%20Shareholder%20 Activism.pdff (accessed June 10, 2012).
2. http://www.fbheron.org/documents/ar.2007.mri_gatefold.pdf.
3. Anne Stetson and Mark Kramer, "Risk, Return and Social Impact: Demystifying the Law of Mission Investing by U.S. Foundations," FSG

Social Impact Advisors (October 2008), http://www.fsg.org/Portals/0/Uploads /Documents/PDF/The_Law_and_Mission_Related_Investing_Full .pdf?cpgn=WP%20DL%20-%20The%20Law%20and%20Mission%20 Related%20Investing%20FULL (accessed June 10, 2012).

4. http://www.livingcities.org/catalytic-capital/catalyst/faqs/.
5. http://www.nycif.org/about.html.
6. "Buying Property in a Hot Market: NYC Creates a Fund to Keep Affordable Housing Developers in Play," Kennedy School of Government Case C16-09 -1907.0 (2009).

## Chapter 8

1. William F. Meehan, Derek Kilmer, and Maisie O'Flanagan, "Investing in Society: Why we need a more efficient social capital market—and how we can get there," *Stanford Social Innovation Review* (Spring 2004).
2. Pierre Omidyar, "Ebay's Founder on Innovating the Business Model of Social Change," *Harvard Business Review* September 2011.
3. http://www.omidyar.com/about_us.
4. "Google's Way—Don't Be Evil," Richard Ivey School of Business, The University of Western Ontario, Case No. 907M67 (2008), 6.
5. Georgia Levenson Keohane, "The Rise and (Potential) Fall of Philanthro-capitalism," *Slate* (November 13, 2008).
6. Lincoln Caplan, "Premium Blend: Is Google.org the future of philanthropy," *Slate* (September 21, 2006).
7. Larry Brilliant, "Gandhi's Talisman: How Google decided what to give to," *Slate* (February 11, 2008).
8. Ibid.
9. http://www.acumenfund.org/knowledge-center.html?document=56.
10. http://www.acumenfund.org/about-us.html.
11. "Acumen Fund: Measurement in Impact Investing," Harvard Business School Case Study 9-310-011 (rev. May 11, 2011), 2.
12. C. K. Prahalad, *The Fortune at the Bottom of the Pyramid: Eradicating Poverty through Profits* (University of Pennsylvania: Wharton School Publishing, 2004).
13. In 2008, the distribution was two-thirds equity, one-third debt.
14. Antony Bugg-Levine and Jed Emerson, *Impact Investing* (San Francisco: Jossey-Bass, 2011), 10–11.
15. http://www.rootcapital.org/our-impact.
16. http://www.acumenfund.org/about-us/what-is-patient-capital.html (accessed February 14, 2012).

## Chapter 9

1. "Investing for Social and Environmental Impact," Monitor Institute (January 2009), 1, 14.
2. Antony Bugg-Levine and Jed Emerson, *Impact Investing* (San Francisco: Jossey-Bass, 2011), 9.

3. See, for example, how Parthenon and Bridge Ventures apply this framework to specific case studies and different asset classes. http://www.parthenon.com /GetFile.aspx?u=%2fLists%2fThoughtLeadership%2fAttachments%2f15%2fI nvesting%2520for%2520Impact.pdf

4. Yakemin Saltuk, "Insight into the Impact Investment Market," J.P.Morgan (December 2011), 9; J.P.Morgan, "Impact Investments: An Emerging Asset Class," J.P.Morgan Global Research (November 29, 2010), 5.

5. "Investing for Social and Environmental Impact," Monitor Institute (January 2009), 9. Extrapolated from 2008 data of assets under management.

6. J.P.Morgan, "Impact Investments: An Emerging Asset Class," J.P. Morgan Global Research (November 29, 2010), 12.

7. Ibid.

8. "Investing for Social and Environmental Impact," 14.

9. "Investing for Social and Environmental Impact," 14. Emphasis added.

10. See, for example, "IBM v. Carnegie Corporation: The Centenarians Square Up," *The Economist* (June 9, 2011), http://www.economist.com/node /18802844.

11. Bugg-Levine and Emerson, 31 32.

## Chapter 10

1. http://www.morganstanley.com/about/press/articles/8d25155d-790c-4926 -be23-dd559696b3b7.html.

2. http://www.asiaiix.com/.

3. Yasemin Saltuk, "Insight into the Impact Investment Market," J.P.Morgan (December 14, 2011), 6.

4. Ashish Karamchandani, Michael Kubzansky, and Paul Frandano, "Emerging Markets, Emerging Models: Market-Based Solutions to the Problems of Global Poverty," Monitor Group (March 2009); Michael Kubzansky, Ansulie Cooper, and Victoria Barbary, "Promise and Progress: Market-Based Solutions to Poverty in Africa," Monitor Group (May 2011), http://www .monitor.com/Portals/0/MonitorContent/imported/MonitorUnitedStates /Articles/PDFs/Monitor_Promise_and_Progress_Exec_Summary_ May_24_2011.pdf and http://www.monitor.com/Portals/0/MonitorContent /imported/MonitorUnitedStates/Articles/PDFs/Monitor_Emerging_Markets _NEDS_03_25_09.pdf.

5. Michael Kubzansky, Ansulie Cooper, and Victoria Barbary, "Promise and Progress: Market-Based Solutions to Poverty in Africa," Monitor Group (May 2011), 14–15.

6. Kubzansky, Cooper, and Barbary, 19.

## Chapter 11

1. Adapted from Georgia Levenson Keohane, "Subprime on the Subcontinent: What Can We Learn from the Microcredit Crisis?" *New Deal 2.0* (July 6, 2011), http://www.newdeal20.org/2011/06/06/subprime-on-the-subcontinent -what-can-we-learn-from-the-microcredit-crisis-47122/.

2. Georgia Levenson Keohane, "Subprime on the Subcontinent: Commercialization and its Discontents," *New Deal 2.0*, (July 7, 2011), http://www.newdeal20.org/2011/06/07/subprime-on-the-subcontinent -commercialization-and-its-discontents-47132/. See also Ruth David, "Threat of Microfinance Defaults Rise in India as SKS Prepares IPO," Bloomberg (June 14, 2010), http://www.bloomberg.com/news/2010-06-14 /india-microfinance-evokes-risk-of-subprime-in-the-east-as-sks-prepares-ipo .html.
3. Muhammad Yunus, "Sacrificing Microcredit for Mega Profits," *The New York Times* (January 14, 2011).
4. Georgia Levenson Keohane, "The Bold Vision of Grameen Bank's Muhammad Yunus," *Harvard Business Review* (May 10, 2010), http://blogs .hbr.org/cs/2010/05/the_bold_vision_of_grameen_banks_muhammad_yunus .html.
5. Neha Thirani, "'Yunus was Right' SKS Microfinance Founder Says," *New York Times* (February 27, 2012).

## Chapter 12

1. "History of New Communities Program," *HUD News*, U.S. Department of Housing and Urban Development (January 18, 1978).
2. Community Development Venture Capital Alliance, http://www.cdvca.org/. Some put the estimates at closer to $20 billion, but this amount includes venture capital funds administered at the state level (for all small businesses, not necessarily those in poor communities) and funds directed toward minority entrepreneurs, again, not necessarily targeted at poverty fighting.
3. Julia Sass Rubin, "Developmental Venture Capital: Conceptualizing the Field," *Venture Capital: An International Journal of Entrepreneurial Finance* 11, no. 4 (October 2009), 335–360.
4. "Reinventing Prosperity," Pacific Community Ventures Annual Report 2010.
5. Matthew Bishop and Michael Green, *Philanthrocapitalism* (New York: Bloomsbury, 2008).
6. "IBM v. Carnegie Corporation: The Centenarians Square Up," *The Economist* (June 9, 2011), http://www.economist.com/node/18802844.
7. Ibid.
8. Yvon Chouinard and Vincent Stanley, *The Responsible Company*, Patagonia Inc. (May 2012).
9. Stephanie Strom, "To Advance Their Cause, Foundations Buy Stocks," *New York Times* (November 24, 2011).
10. Georgia Levenson Keohane, "Mission Driven Companies Seek Beneficial Label," *City Limits* (April 20, 2008).
11. See, for example, Generation Investment Management, "Sustainable Capitalism" (February 15, 2012), or Insight at Pacific Community Ventures and the Initiative for Responsible Investment at Harvard University, "Impact at Scale: Policy Innovation for Institutional Investment with Social and Environmental Benefit" (February 2012), 32.

12. "B Corps: Firms with Benefits" *The Economist* (January 7, 2012); Seth Stevenson, "Patagonia's Founder Is America's Most Unlikely Business Guru," *Wall Street Journal* (April 26, 2012), http://online.wsj.com/article/SB1000142 4052702303513404577352221465986612.html; Angus Loten, "With a New Law, Profits Take a Backseat," *Wall Street Journal* (January 19, 2012), http://online.wsj.com/article/SB10001424052970203735304577168591470161630 .html.

## Chapter 13

1. Michael E. Porter and Mark R. Kramer, "Creating Shared Value," *Harvard Business Review* (January–February 2011), 4.
2. Robert Reich, "Why Creative Capitalism Gets in the Way of Democracy," in Michael Kinsley, ed., *Creative Capitalism: A Conversation with Bill Gates, Warren Buffett and Other Economic Leaders* (New York: Simon and Schuster, 2008), 99. See also, David Vogel, *The Market for Virtue: The Potential and Limits of Corporate Social Responsibility* (Washington, DC: Brookings: 2005).
3. Milton Friedman, *Capitalism and Freedom* (Chicago: University of Chicago, 1962), 133. See also Milton Friedman, "The Social Responsibility of Business to Increase Profits," *New York Times Magazine* (September 13, 1970).
4. Bill Gates, "A New Approach to Capitalism," remarks delivered to the World Economic Forum (January 24, 2008), Davos, Switzerland. Reprinted in *Creative Capitalism: A Conversation with Bill Gates, Warren Buffett and Other Economic Leaders*, Michael Kinsley, ed. (New York: Simon and Schuster, 2008), 10.
5. Antony Bugg-Levine and Jed Emerson, *Impact Investing* (San Francisco: John Wiley, 2011), 10–11.
6. See, for example, Generation Investment Management, "Sustainable Capitalism" (February 15, 2012).
7. Rosabeth Moss Kanter, *SuperCorp: How Vanguard Companies Create Innovation, Profits, Growth and Social Good* (New York: Crown Business, 2009).
8. Joseph L. Bower, Herman B. Leonard, and Lynn S. Paine, *Capitalism at Risk* (Boston: Harvard Business Review Press, 2011), 3–4.
9. Bower, Leonard, and Paine, ch. 4.
10. Generation Investment Management, "Sustainable Capitalism" (February 15, 2012).
11. Ibid.
12. See, for example, Rob Bauer and Daniel Hann, *Corporate Environmental Management and Credit Risk* (Maastricht University, European Centre for Corporate Engagement, 2010); Beiting Cheng, Ioannis Ioannou, and George Serafeim, "Corporate Social Responsibility and Access to Finance," Harvard Business School Research Paper No. 1847085 (May 19, 2011); Robert G. Eccles, Ioannis Ioannou, and George Serafeim, "The Impact of a Corporate

Culture of Sustainability on Corporate Behavior and Performance," Harvard Business School Working Paper No. 12-035 (November 14, 2011).

13. See John Kanie and Mark Kramer, "Roundtable on Shared Value," *Stanford Social Innovation Review* (Summer 2011).

14. Bill Drayton and Valeria Budinich, "A New Alliance for Global Change," *Harvard Business Review* (September 2010).

15. Georgia Levenson Keohane, "Ashoka: Innovators for the Public," Stanford Graduate School of Business SM203 (February 2, 2012).

16. Muhammad Yunus, *Creating a World Without Poverty: Social Business and the Future of Capitalism* (New York: Public Affairs, 2007).

## III

1. See, for example, Stephen Goldsmith, *The Power of Social Innovation* (San Francisco: Jossey-Bass, 2010).

2. This is a kind of application of theories of private sector entrepreneurship and innovation. See for example William J. Baumol, *The Free-Market Innovation Machine: Analyzing the Growth Miracle of Capitalism* (New Jersey: Princeton University, 2002).

3. See, for example, David Osborne and Ted Gaebler, *Reinventing Government* (Boston: Addison-Wesley, 1992).

4. Kim Smith and Julie Petersen, "Steering Capital: Optimizing Financial Support for Innovation in Public Education," Bellwether Education Partners (April 2011), 2.

5. See, for example, Clay Christensen, *The Innovator's Solution* (Boston: Harvard Business School, 2003).

## Chapter 14

1. Michael Bloomberg, State of the City Speech (January 2003), http://www .nyc.gov/portal/site/nycgov/menuitem.b270a4a1d51bb3017bce0ed101c 789a0/index.jsp?pageID=nyc_blue_room&catID=1194&doc_name=http percent3A percent2F percent2Fwww.nyc.gov percent2Fhtml percent2Fom percent2Fhtml percent2F2003a percent2Fstate_city_2003.html&cc=unused 1978&rc=1194&ndi=1.

2. Dennis C. Smith and William J. Grinkler, "The Transformation of Social Services Management in New York City: 'CompStating' Welfare" *Seedco* (March 2005).

3. "Linda Gibbs and the Department of Homeless Services: Overhauling New York City's Approach to Shelter" Harvard Kennedy School of Government Case Study, C16-07-183 (August 2007), 3.

4. "The Second Decade of Reform: A Strategic Plan for New York City's Homeless Services" Department of Homeless Services (June 2002).

5. Helen Zelon, "The Education Business: Teachers Missing at the Top," *City Limits* (June 1, 2009).

6. Joel Klein, "The Failure of American Schools," *The Atlantic* (June 2011).

7. Jonathan Mahler, "The Fragile Success of School Reform in the Bronx," *New York Times Magazine* (April 6, 2011).

8. Klein, "The Failure of American Schools."

9. Helen Zelon, "The Education Business: Teachers Missing at the Top," *City Limits* (June 1, 2009).

10. Mahler, "The Fragile Success of School Reform in the Bronx."

11. Ibid.

12. Mayor Michael Bloomberg Discusses Center for Economic Opportunity's "Innovations in American Government Award" from Harvard Kennedy School of Government, Bloomberg Weekly Radio Address (February 12, 2012).

13. Interview with Kristin Morse (October 17, 2011). See also, Veronica White and Kristin Morse, "Innovate, Research, Repeat: New York City's Center for Economic Opportunity," *Pathways* (Summer 2011).

14. Interview with Veronica White (October 17, 2011).

15. Veronica White and Kristin Morse, "Innovate, Research, Repeat: New York City's Center for Economic Opportunity," *Pathways* (Summer 2011), 16.

16. As quoted in Janny Scott, "A National Housing Innovator Leads City's Effort for the Poor," *New York Times* (September 26, 2006).

17. Ibid.

18. Ibid.

19. "Buying Property in a Hot Market: NYC Creates a Fund to Keep Affordable Housing Developers in Play," Harvard Kennedy School of Government Case C16-09-1907.0 (2009).

20. See, for example, Julian Brash, *Governing with "Class": Politics the Bloomberg Way* (University of Georgia, 2011).

21. In 2012, New York City's Department of Investigation discovered that Seedco, the nonprofit organization that was working with the Bloomberg administration to find jobs for unemployed New Yorkers, had falsely claimed to have helped 1,400 (of 6,500) to find jobs. According to the *New York Times*, Seedco employees "described a culture of unrelenting pressure from the Bloomberg administration to produce data showing that the job placement effort was working." Agencies that produced high numbers of placements—particularly challenging given the weak economy—were awarded performance-based bonuses. At the time of the fraudulent job placements, Seedco was competing for a new contract from the city. See Michael Powell "Fraud Found in Jobs Effort; Blow to Bloomberg," *New York Times* (March 9, 2012).

## Chapter 15

1. Dan Eggen and Michael A. Fletcher, "Obama Promotes an Array of Financial Proposals," *Washington Post* (November 26, 2008), http://www.washingtonpost.com/wp-dyn/content/article/2008/11/25/AR2008112500948.html?hpid=topnews.

2. http://www.ebpdn.org/resource/resource.php?lang=en&id=1175.
3. Peter Orszag, "Memorandum for the Heads of Executive Departments and Agencies: Increased Emphasis on Program Evaluations," Executive Office of the President, Office of Management and Budget (October 7, 2009).
4. Executive Office of the President, National Economic Council, Office of Science and Technology Policy: "A Strategy for American Innovation: Driving Towards Sustainable Growth and Quality Jobs" (September 2009), 17.
5. "Congress Grants Broad Prize Authority to All Federal Agencies," White House Open Government Initiative Blog (December 21, 2010), http://www.whitehouse.gov/blog/2010/12/21/congress-grants-broad-prize-authority-all-federal-agencies.
6. See also Thomas Kalil, "Prizes for Technological Innovation," The Hamilton Project, Brookings Institution (December 2006), http://www.brookings.edu/views/papers/200612kalil.pdf; and David Bornstein, "Innovation for the People, by the People," New York Times (February 22, 2012), http://opinionator.blogs.nytimes.com/2012/02/22/from-the-white-house-incentives-to-innovate/ (accessed March 5, 2012).
7. "Promoting Innovation: Prizes, Challenges, and Open Grantmaking" (April 30, 2010), http://www.casefoundation.org/case-studies/promoting-innovation.
8. "Congress Grants Broad Prize Authority to All Federal Agencies," White House Open Government Initiative Blog (December 21, 2010), http://www.whitehouse.gov/blog/2010/12/21/congress-grants-broad-prize-authority-all-federal-agencies.

## Chapter 16

1. Interview with Suzanne Immerman, Special Assistant to the Secretary, Director of Philanthropic Engagement, U.S. Department of Education (December 2011).
2. Simon Owens, "Can Todd Park Revolutionize the Health Care Industry?" The Atlantic (June 2, 2011), http://www.theatlantic.com/technology/archive/2011/06/can-todd-park-revolutionize-the-health-care-industry/239708/.
3. "Big Data: the Next Frontier for Innovation, Competition and Productivity," McKinsey Global Institute (June 2011); and Steve Lohr, "New Ways to Exploit Raw Data May Bring Surge of Innovation, a Study Says," New York Times (May 13, 2011).
4. Owens, "Can Todd Park Revolutionize the Health Care Industry?"
5. Eric Braverman and Michael Chui, "Unleashing Government's 'Innovation Mojo': An Interview with the U.S. Chief Technology Officer," McKinsey Quarterly (June 2012).
6. Owens, "Can Todd Park Revolutionize the Health Care Industry?"
7. David Bornstein, "Innovation for the People, by the People," New York Times (February 22, 2010), http://opinionator.blogs.nytimes.com/2012/02/22/from-the-white-house-incentives-to-innovate/ (accessed March 5, 2012).

8. Ibid.
9. "Safety Data Jam Connects Tech Innovators with Public Safety Officers," OSTP Blog (June 8, 2012), http://www.whitehouse.gov/blog/2012/06/08/safety-data-jam-connects-tech-innovators-public-safety-officers (accessed June 14, 2012).
10. Braverman and Chui, "Unleashing Government's 'Innovation Mojo': An Interview with the U.S. Chief Technology Officer."
11. Lydia Polgreen, "Scanning 2.4 Billion Eyes, India Tries to Connect Poor to Growth," *New York Times* (September 1, 2011).
12. Michele Jolin, "Investing in Social Entrepreneurship and Fostering Social Innovation" Center for American Progress (December 2007); and Michele Jolin, "Innovating the White House: How the Next President of the United States Can Spur Social Entrepreneurship," *Stanford Social Innovation Review* (Spring 2008). Jolin was also coauthor with Mark Green of the New Democracy Project of a book entitled *Change for America: A Progressive Blueprint for the 44th President* (Fall 2008), which covered much more broad proposals for the organization and policy agenda of the White House in areas of domestic policy, economic policy, and national security policy, with contributors ranging from Tom Friedman and Sandy Berger to Elena Kagan, Mitch Kapor, Van Jones, and Gene Sperling.
13. Dana Goldstein, "The Innovation Administration," *The American Prospect* (November 16, 2009).
14. Interview with Sonal Shah (October 4, 2011).
15. Michele Jolin, "Social Innovation in Washington, D.C.," *Stanford Social Innovation Review* (Summer 2011).
16. Since 2009, AmeriCorps has fallen victim to the budget crisis. While the 2012 budget still expands AmeriCorps, it does so much less significantly than the Serve America Act called for. The original legislation looked to triple the number of AmeriCorps members from 75,000 to 250,000 by 2017. Instead of 140,000 AmeriCorps members envisioned for 2012, Congress only approved funds to expand to 82,000. See, for example, Suzanne Perry, "National Service's Fight for the Future," *Chronicle of Philanthropy* (March 22, 2012).
17. http://www.kauffman.org/Section.aspx?id=About_The_Foundation.
18. As quoted in "Edna McConnell Clark Foundation—Enabling a Performance Driven Philanthropic Capital Market," Harvard Business School Case Study 9-312-006 (July 28, 2011), 9.

## Chapter 17

1. "HBR's List of Audacious Ideas to Solve the World's Problems," *Harvard Business Review* (January 1, 2012).
2. "From Potential to Action: Bringing Social Impact Bonds to the U.S." McKinsey & Company (May 2012).
3. "Pay for Success: Investing in What Works," Nonprofit Finance Fund and the White House (January 2012).
4. Dan Adams, "Mass. Program Ties Nonprofits' Pay to Success," *The Boston Globe* (August 1, 2012).

5. Michael Belinsky, "Social Impact Bonds: Lessons from the Field," *Stanford Social Innovation Review* (January 23, 2012), http://www.ssireview.org/blog /entry/social_impact_bonds_lessons_from_the_field.

6. David Chen, "Goldman to Invest in City Jail Program, Profiting If Recidivism Falls Sharply," *New York Times* (August 2, 2012).

7. Kim Smith and Julie Peterson, "Supporting and Scaling Change: Lessons from the First Round of the Investing in Innovation (i3) Program" Bellwether Education Partners (July 2011). See also Michele McNeil, "49 Applicants Win i3 Grants," *Education Week* (August 4, 2010).

8. One of the SIF reviewers, Paul Light, noted that process should have been more transparent, given how enmeshed the world of social entrepreneurship funders had been in the creation of the OSCIP and the SIF itself. See Paul Light, "Stonewalling at the Social Innovation Fund," *Washington Post* (August 18, 2010), http://views.washingtonpost.com/leadership/light/2010/08 /stonewalling-at-the-social-innovation-fund.html.

9. Geoff Mulgan, "Cultivating the Other Invisible Hand of Social Entrepreneurship: Comparative Advantage, Public Policy, and Future Research Priorities," in Alex Nicholls (Ed.), *Social Entrepreneurship: New Models of Sustainable Social Change* (New York: Oxford, 2006).

10. This was the original mandate of the OTS, from the agency's original website, as quoted in Goldsmith, 77. Today, the mission of the office, which has been renamed the Office for Civil Society, is stated slightly differently. See http://www.cabinetoffice.gov.uk/big-society (accessed April 13, 2012).

## Chapter 18

1. Matthew Bishop and Michael Green, *Philanthrocapitalism: How the Rich Can Save the World* (Bloomsbury Press, 2008).

2. Bishop, 119.

3. Georgia Levenson Keohane, "The Rise and Potential Fall of Philanthrocapitalism" *Slate* (November 13, 2008).

4. Phil Buchanan, "Seven 'New' Concepts That Are Not So New After All: Reflections on a History of Philanthropy," The CEP Blog (January 10 2012), http://www.effectivephilanthropy.org/blog/2012/01/seven -%E2%80%9Cnew%E2%80%9D-concepts-that-are-not-so-new-after-all -reflections-on-a-history-of-philanthropy/ (accessed June 12, 2012).

5. Lauren Foster, "Gut Instincts and Good Ideas," *Financial Times* (September 4, 2007) http://www.ft.com/intl/cms/s/2/5ad579da-5a43-11dc-9bcd -0000779fd2ac.html#axzz1nUuIF7Qa (accessed February 26, 2012).

6. Michael Edwards, *Just Another Emperor: The Myths and Realities of Philanthrocapitalism* (New York: Demos, 2008), 14.

7. Edwards, 81.

8. Edwards, 64–65.
9. Mario Marino, "Business Entrepreneurs & Philanthropy: Potential and Pitfalls," Keynote Speech to the National Philanthropic Trust (September 28, 2007).
10. Jim Collins, *Good to Great and the Social Sectors*, HarperCollins (2005).
11. Stephanie Strom and Miguel Helft, "Google Finds it Hard to Reinvent Philanthropy," *New York Times* (January 29, 2011).
12. Jeffrey Bradach and William Foster, "Should Nonprofits Seek Profits?" *Harvard Business Review* (February 2005), http://hbr.org/2005/02/should -nonprofits-seek-profits/ar/1.
13. "The Limits of Social Enterprise: A Field Study and Case Analysis," Seedco (June 2007).
14. Steven LeFrance and Nancy Latham, "Taking Stock of Venture Philanthropy," *Stanford Social Innovation Review* (Summer 2008).
15. James A. Phills, Jr., Kriss Deiglmeier, and Dale T. Miller, "Rediscovering Social Innovation" *Stanford Social Innovation Review* (Fall 2008).
16. See, for example, Paul Bloom and Edward Skloot (eds.), *Scaling Social Impact: New Thinking* (New York: Palgrave MacMillan, 2010).
17. Jeffrey Bradach, "Foreword: From Scaling Organizations to Scaling Impact," in Paul Bloom and Edward Skloot (eds.), *Scaling Social Impact: New Thinking* (New York: Palgrave MacMillan, 2010).
18. See, for example, "What Do We Mean by Scale? Reframing the Conversation" Grantmakers for Effective Philanthropy Briefing Paper Series on Growing Social Impact, Topic 1 (February 2011), http://www.geofunders .org/storage/documents/GEO_SWW_WhatDoWeMeanbyScale_Redesign _vFinal.pdf.
19. Jeffrey Bradach, "Scaling Impact," *Stanford Social Innovation Review* (Summer 2010), 27.
20. William A. Schambra, "The *Real* Social Entrepreneurs," 2010 William E. Simon Lecture, the Manhattan Institute for Policy Research, New York City (December 9, 2010).
21. Georgia Levenson Keohane, "Ashoka: Innovators for the Public" Stanford Graduate School of Business Case Study No SM-203 (February 2, 2010).
22. From http://www.skollfoundation.org/approach/. See also Paul Bloom and Greg Dees, "Cultivate Your Ecosystem," *Stanford Social Innovation* Review (Winter 2008), https://www.self-help.org/about-us/about-us-files/SH_SSIR _Ecosystems.pdf.
23. John Kania and Mark Kramer, "Collective Impact," *Stanford Social Innovation Review* (Winter 2011), http://www.ssireview.org/articles/entry /collective_impact (accessed February 24, 2012).
24. Ibid.
25. Jane Wales, "Metrics That Matter: Venture Philanthropy Pioneer and Aspen Philanthropy Group Draw Similar Conclusions," Aspen Philanthropy Blog (September 10, 2010), http://www.aspeninstitute.org/policy-work/nonprofit

-philanthropy/blog/metrics-matter-venture-philanthropy-pioneer-aspen
-philanthro (accessed February 24, 2012).

26. Alana Conner Snibble, "Drowning in Data," *Stanford Social Innovation Review* (Fall 2006), http://www.ssireview.org/articles/entry/drowning_in_data (accessed February 24, 2012).

27. Edwards, 66.

28. Collins, 7.

29. Giving USA Foundation (June 2011); Hope Consulting, "Money for Good" (May 2010).

30. See, for example, Mario Marino, *Leap of Reason: Managing to Outcomes in an Era of Scarcity* (Washington, DC, Venture Philanthropy Partners, 2011); "Learning for Social Impact: What Foundations Can Do," McKinsey & Company (April 2010), http://lsi.mckinsey.com/ (accessed February 25, 2012).

31. "Evaluation in Philanthropy: Perspectives from the Field," Grantmakers for Effective Organizations and Council on Foundations (2009), 7, http://www .organizationalresearch.com/publicationsandresources/evaluation_in _philanthropy_GEO_COF1.pdf (accessed February 25, 2012).

32. Joel Fleishman, *The Foundation: A Great American Secret* (New York: PublicAffairs, 2007), 212.

33. Gary Walker, "Midcourse Corrections to a Major Initiative: A Report on the James Irvine Foundation's CORAL Experience," James Irvine Foundation (May 2007); Prudence Brown and Leila Fiester, "Hard Lessons About Philanthropy & Community Change from the Neighborhood Improvement Initiative," William and Flora Hewlett Foundation (March 2007), http:// hewlett_prod.acesfconsulting.com/uploads/files/HewlettNIIReport.pdf (accessed February 25, 2012). See also Paul Brest and Hal Harvey, *Money Well Spent* (New York: Bloomberg, 2008), 96–99.

34. *To Improve Health and Healthcare*, Volume XIII, Robert Wood Johnson Foundation (2010).

35. Stephen L. Isaacs and David Colby, "Good Ideas at the Time: Learning from Programs That Did Not Work Out as Expected," in *To Improve Health and Healthcare*, Volume XIII, Robert Wood Johnson Foundation (2010).

36. Jean Case, "The Painful Acknowledgement of Coming up Short," Case Foundation Blog (May 4, 2010), http://www.casefoundation.org/blog/painful -acknowledgement-coming-short (accessed February 27, 2011).

37. www.admittingfailure.com.

38. Suzie Boss, "What's Next: Thriving on Failure," *Stanford Social Innovation Review* (Summer 2010), http://www.ssireview.org/articles/entry/whats_next _thriving_on_failure (accessed March 4, 2012).

39. As quoted in "Interview with Jodi Nelson," *Alliance Magazine* (May 1, 2011), http://www.alliancemagazine.org/node/3699.

## Chapter 19

1. Steven Tells and Mark Schmitt, "The Elusive Craft of Evaluating Advocacy," *Stanford Social Innovation Review* (Summer 2011).

2. Ibid.
3. Lisa Ranghelli, "Leveraging Limited Dollars: How Grantmakers Achieve Tangible Results by Funding Policy and Community Engagement," National Committee for Responsive Philanthropy (January 2012), http://www.ncrp .org/files/publications/LeveragingLimitedDollars.pdf (accessed February 28, 2012).
4. Leslie R. Crutchfield and Heather McLeod Grant, "Creating High Impact Nonprofits," *Stanford Social Innovation Review* (Fall 2007).
5. Alan Khazei, *Big Citizenship: How Pragmatic Idealism Can Bring out the Best in America* (New York: Public Affairs, 2010), 165–166.
6. David H. Herszenhorn, "Billionaires Start $60 Million Schools Effort," *New York Times* (April 25, 2007), http://query.nytimes.com/gst/fullpage.html?res=9 C03E2DA143EF936A15757C0A9619C8B63&pagewanted=1.
7. Aaron Dorfman, "Bloomberg Makes Largest Advocacy Grant Ever," *Huffington Post* (July 21, 2011).
8. Megan Tomkins, "Private Actors in the Public Arena," *Alliance* 16, no. 3 (September 2011).
9. Joan Spero, "The Global Role of U.S. Foundations" *The Foundation Center* (2010), 9.
10. Edward Skloot, "The Gated Community," *Alliance* Volume 16, no. 3 (September 2011).
11. Todd Moss, Center for Global Development.
12. Skloot, "The Gated Community."
13. Donald G. McNeil, Jr. "Gates Calls for a Final Push to Eradicate Polio," *New York Times* (January 31, 2011).
14. Timothy Ogden, "How Much Difference Is It Making?" *Alliance* Volume 16, no. 3 (September 2011).
15. Interview with Richard Horton, *Alliance* 16, no. 3 (September 2011), 38–39.
16. Laura Freschi and Alanna Shaikh, "Gates: A Benevolent Dictator for Public Health?" *Alliance* 16, no. 3 (September 2011).
17. Diane Ravitch, *The Death and Life of the Great American School System* (New York: Basic Books, 2010), ch. 10.
18. Megan Tomkins, "Private Actors in the Public Arena."
19. Jonathan Mahler, "The Fragile Success of School Reform in the Bronx," *New York Times* ( April 6, 2011), http://www.nytimes.com/2011/04/10 /magazine/mag-10School-t.html?pagewanted=all.
20. John Miller, *A Gift of Freedom* (San Francisco: Encounter Books, 2005).
21. See, for example, Andrew Rich, "War of Ideas," *Stanford Social Innovation Review* (Spring 2005.), http://www.ssireview.org/articles/entry/war_of_ideas.
22. See, for example, Jane Mayer, "Covert Operations" *The New Yorker* (August 30, 2011).
23. Michael Porter and Mark Kramer, "Philanthropy's New Agenda: Creating Value," *Harvard Business Review* (November–December 1999), 122–123.
24. See, for example, Evelyn Brody and John Tyler, "How Public Is Private Philanthropy?" *The Philanthropy Roundtable* (2009).

## Chapter 20

1. Abhijit V. Banerjee and Esther Duflo, *Poor Economics* (New York: PublicAffairs, 2011).
2. Daryl Collins, Jonathan Morduch, Stuart Rutherford, and Orlanda Ruthven, *Portfolios of the Poor* (New Jersey: Princeton University, 2009).
3. Over 35 years, an estimated $15 billion in direct grants and subsidized loans flowed from government development agencies and foundations to microfinance businesses and non-profits.
4. Michael J. Sandel, *What Money Can't Buy: The Moral Limits of Markets* (New York: Farrar, Straus and Giroux, 2012).
5. Michael Sandel, "What Isn't for Sale," *The Atlantic* (April 2012).
6. "Louisiana Incarcerated: How We Built the World's Prison Capital," *New Orleans Times-Picayune* (May 2012), http://www.nola.com/prisons/ (accessed June 5, 2012). See also Charles Blow, "Plantations, Prisons and Profits," *New York Times* (May 25, 2012).
7. Richard A. Oppel, Jr., "Private Prisons Found to Offer Little in Savings," *New York Times* (May 18, 2011).

## Chapter 21

1. Albert O. Hirschman, *Exit, Voice and Loyalty* (Cambridge: Harvard University, 1970), 108. See also Richard Hofstadter, *Social Darwinism in American Thought* (Philadelphia: University of Philadelphia Press, 1945).
2. Carl J. Schramm, *The Entrepreneurial Imperative* (New York: Harper Collins, 2006), 17–18.
3. Insight at Pacific Community Ventures and the Initiative for Responsible Investment at Harvard University, "Impact Investing: A Framework for Policy Design and Analysis" (January 2011); and Insight at Pacific Community Ventures and the Initiative for Responsible Investment at Harvard University, "Impact at Scale: Policy Innovation for Institutional Investment with Social and Environmental Benefit" (February 2012). See also, "Counter(Imp)acting Austerity: The Global Trend of Government Support for Impact Investment," J.P.Morgan Social Finance Research (November 28, 2011).
4. Michael Porter and Michael Kramer, "Creating Shared Value," *Harvard Business Review* (January 2011).
5. Karl Polyani, *The Great Transformation* (New York: Farrar and Rinehart, 1944).
6. Michael Lind, *The Land of Promise* (New York: HarperCollins, 2012); and E. J. Dionne, Jr., *Our Divided Political Heart* (New York: Bloomsbury USA, 2012).
7. Lind, 465.
8. Dionne, 7, 69.
9. Lind, 203.
10. Lind, 149.

11. Robert Wade, *Governing the Market: Economic Theory and the Role of Government in East Asian Industrialization* (New Jersey: Princeton, 1990). See also Joseph Stiglitz and Shahid Yusuf (eds.), *Rethinking the East Asian Miracle* (New York: Oxford University, 2001).
12. "Development Credit Authority: Putting Local Wealth to Work" USAID Impact Brief 2011, http://www.usaid.gov/our_work/economic_growth_and _trade/development_credit/dca_usaid_impact_brief2011.pdf.
13. "In Historic Commitment to Impact Investing, OPIC Board Approves $285 Million for Six Funds Catalyzing $875 Million in Investments," OPIC press release (October 27, 2011).
14. Insight at Pacific Community Ventures and the Initiative for Responsible Investment at Harvard University, "Impact at Scale: Policy Innovation for Institutional Investment with Social and Environmental Benefit" (February 2012).

# INDEX